AF249121

Coming Home to Wisconsin

Stanton & Lee Publishers, Inc.

Coming Home to Wisconsin

Robert E. Gard

First Edition
Copyright 1982 by Robert E. Gard
All rights reserved.
Direct all inquiries to:
Stanton & Lee Publishers, Inc.
44 East Mifflin Street On the Square
Madison, Wisconsin 53703

Library of Congress Cataloging in Publication Data
Gard, Robert Edward.
  Coming home to Wisconsin.
  1. Gard, Robert Edward — Biography. 2. Authors, American — 20th
century — Biography. 3. Wisconsin — Biography. 4. Wisconsin — Social
life and customs.
I. Title.
PS3513.A612C6   808'.0092'4 [B]   81-16563
ISBN 0-88361-084-1 (pbk.)   AACR2

Edited by Doug Bradley
Designed by Marian Lefebvre
Printed in the United States of America
by the George Banta Company

Dedicated to my friend and editor
Mark E. Lefebvre

Contents

Author's Note

This is a book filled with the present and the past, with achievement and failure, with love for a state which I have made my own; it is about land and wind and people who came seeking the meaning of their lives; and it is about me who also came seeking the meaning of mine. I hope that the book is filled with the spirit of mission, and of the enrichment of human life. I hope that within it broods something of the fascination I feel when I contemplate the word "Wisconsin." I hope that within this book a person (myself) and the land (Wisconsin) are portrayed as inseparable. . . . The book is not intended to be an autobiography in the strict sense; memory alone has been relied upon. In certain instances names have been changed and incidents altered, times condensed to make a more cohesive story. For the most part the incidents really happened, liberties taken with fact have been taken in interest of drama, or to protect innocent persons who may still be living.

The River—the Source

From time to time I inhabit a kind of cave in Madison, Wisconsin, where I often retire to think, and to wonder. There are so many things nowadays to think and to wonder about. Science, astronomy, religion, have opened so many immense speculations; a simple faith has become most difficult to accept in view of the now-proven complexity of the universe; yet a simple faith might likely be the only stability I have against the grandeur of limitless space, of particles which somehow drifted through something like time toward intelligence ... I find all that sort of speculation fascinating; but I suppose my thoughts are most ordinarily concerned with my adopted state, Wisconsin, where I have lived happily for nearly forty years. When I originally arrived in the early 1940's, folks often asked whether I was a native Wisconsinite, and when I said, "no," they shook their heads sadly and said that I had really missed out, and that not being a Wisconsin native was something from which I could not expect to recover. But I did recover and adopted Wisconsin as my spiritual and physical home, and I have done my best through the writing of many books and through the conception of innumerable literary and cultural programs to recall and to preserve what I could of the history, heritage, and cultural image of this great Upper Middle Western state, so rich in lore and tradition, and human sensitivity. I believe this book has the central purpose of telling how and why I "came home to Wisconsin."

Perhaps this story of a search and a mission that ended in Wisconsin must start in my boyhood, and at my boyhood home in Kansas; for the germinal sign of the search lies in the spirit of the prairie and all that the prairie has symbolized in a quest for meanings in my own life, and in the life of my state, Wisconsin.

There are two rivers involved here: the river of my youth and its flood of memory pouring out of my family whose roots were deep in the sod that lured them west so long ago; and the river of my hope to unfold and make plain, at least to myself, the soul and spirit of a State which has become dear to me and to which I was swept by the youthful river. Always, it seems, I am upon one river or the other; they meet at times, then they separate. They branch and merge eternally with past and present. There are rushes of memory and observation and savor.

I regard my cherishing of this flow of memory with awe and curiosity for everything that has happened is now observable by me through the spiritual window of a tiny office I occupy from time to time in Madison: a room at the Wisconsin Academy of Sciences, Arts and Letters which I temporarily adopted as my private place of seeing and telling. This sanctuary, which is apart from that more busy and sometimes frantic setting at the University of Wisconsin where I have labored for so many years, is a sort of cave, private, mine for one year, to discover through its window, source and meaning.

Today, for example, because Dr. John Thomson, a noted botanist, has been at the Academy and we have been talking about prairie plants on which he and his wife, Olive, are authorities, I find that I am more and more intrigued and moved by the vestiges of the Wisconsin prairie and all that it meant in Wisconsin: primitive wildlife and new hope for settlers. I trace my emotion thereof to my boyhood where the prairie was a major theme of my young life. It grew more so as I further understood what the prairie represented. My father journeyed west from his boyhood home in Illinois because of the prairie and its indefinable call that moved so many young people. Perhaps it was the grass, and the images of the grass and the movement and freedom and openness which the grass and the fall time migration of birds, that motivated him.

I well know that the existing Wisconsin prairies are no longer worthy of an epic imagining. I realize that only relic prairies exist now of all the wide expanse that was once the southern Wisconsin prairie. Some prairie plants remain along old roads, at the edges of a wood; beside fields cultivated now for a hundred years there are some prairie plants; and along old railroads and, of course, where the prairie is being restored in a few places as preservation of something that once was very precious.

One of the great prairies of Wisconsin was the beautiful Empire Prairie of Fond du Lac County. How tragic that the reality of that prairie has vanished; all one can do is try with eyes closed to picture the land the way it was when the pioneers arrived. Into the wild, tall grass they came, and their tales of the fertile land, the swales, the hills with the rolling grass, give some idea of the way it was, and the way their spirits responded to the sense of bigness, the roll, the wildness.

There is little sense today of the joy of the arriving people. The older cemeteries throughout southern Wisconsin tell part of the story. Nathaniel Tallmadge was the best known of all the early Empire farmers. He was a York State man, as many were in that part of the state, and the name of Empire they brought with them from New York. Tallmadge had served fourteen years as United States Senator from New York. When William Henry Harrison was nominated for President, Senator Tallmadge was offered the Vice Presidency. He declined. Perhaps he knew that more than political fame he wished to move to the great new West. Had he accepted the nomination he would have been President of the United States as Harrison died in office. At any rate, Tallmadge became interested in lands in Wisconsin, resigned from the Senate and was appointed governor of the Territory. He located a farm in the town of Empire; he spent the remainder of his life there and died in 1864. He was buried in the Reinze Cemetery, donated by him from his farm lands. The old Tallmadge farm is located in section nineteen; on the land today stands the St. Mary's High School.

I am very much moved by the whole prairie experience. I can imagine, almost as though I were there myself, the elation of the pioneers when they encountered the tall prairie grass. The whole experience has a special meaning for me, too, because I, in a way, am a product of the prairie encounter. I was raised in Kansas, of course, not in Wisconsin, but I think the experience of the prairie was very much the same. It is a temptation to relive, and my mood today is one of retrospect. I value the Academy experience because it affords me an opportunity to think back.

Retrospect can go anywhere your mind has ever been. My mind ranges often, and often far backward to all that I ever heard about my family, their roots, the countries from which they came. And beyond all frontiers, to a weak grasp of human history . . . all of man's comprehension can be confined, made real, for him, how ineptly he may speak or write of it, and meaning that seems pertinent, is another matter. I comprehend my own span, that's all I can safely say. From the moment of my birth, as I have heard of it, through the remembered days of my childhood, to now, through a devious way, forwards and backwards in the shadows of time always along my two rivers . . . this is what I do often, searching the kernels of events that happened, that shaped my thought, that made me what I became eventually.

My regrets now, if I may speak of regrets, are those relating to the recollections of members of my family who might have revealed secrets that I have not been able to uncover. Who, really, was great, great, great, grandfather? An absurd question, but not to me, not after twenty years spent in futile genealogical searches, trying to find out what happened in those years after the American Revolution when my ancestor migrated from New Jersey to Pennsylvania, then to western Ohio. Who was he? Often I have almost had his identity, then it eludes me.

But what pleasure in genealogical research! What fascinating hours looking among old papers, obscure books, in written accounts in old Bibles . . . the clue, looked for in courthouses among ancient deeds, land records, the pale ink that recorded old births and deaths. The hours of excitement of the search for family, for identity, for knowing who and of what you are!

Perhaps my father might have told me. But then, when I was young and careless of such things, I didn't ask. He never said. How can we be so blind? Now, for forty years he is dead. I could have asked him how it was when he was a boy in eastern Illinois, and about his father, whom I never knew. Grandfather Jacob Gard died in 1906, before my birth. I might have asked him about things which I have since discovered, that grandfather lived in a part of eastern Illinois where there were many Southern sympathizers; how he was fired upon by Copperheads in the woods because he expressed deep sentiments in favor of the Union, and how he joined the Illinois infantry . . . perhaps to escape being slaughtered from ambush . . . Ah yes, and I remember grandfather's medals which grandmother Mary Gard prized in her room at our house in Kansas; the medals I, a little boy interested only in the shape of the metal, in faded ribbon ... not until I was nearly fifty, in a library at Madison, did I come to know what grandfather did in the Civil War. There I found the record of his regiment in the muster rolls of Illinois soldiers. And my letter to the National Archives in Washington brought me documents of his enlistment, his discharge, his pension. But I never asked my father about these things, and between us the book remained closed forever and forever.

The strange ways of a father and a son. Mysterious, obscure. How do they find their way to each other through time? Through time when the barrier of youth and age exists immutable between them? Family relationships are the things that make the most difference in our lives, no doubt, but when are we ready to comprehend?

I understand, somehow, that my Wisconsin experience is not complete, and my view of the place I live and love now is not complete without exploring how and why I am here. And the Prairie is very real to me. I recognize the Latin names of some Wisconsin prairie plants and I have learned how to look for the vestiges of the prairie when it lay virgin among clumps of oaks. And I wonder why I bother? Why is it all so dear? And then, as a novelist, or a playwright, I know why, of course, for all character is sourced in the past.

The prairie indeed has a dark and hidden vision. When I seek to rediscover the Wisconsin prairie I seek to rediscover my own soul. Suddenly as my fingers lie idle on typewriter keys, my mind plunges into the depths of my own span. I was a lad of eighteen, and in a certain darkness after midnight on a June night in the 1930s I was asleep in my room in our tall, narrow, Kansas farmhouse, and I was awakened by my mother who placed her hand nervously upon my shoulder and propelled me awake. I felt her hand very hard, desperate, shaking me and she was saying, "Bobby, wake up. Dad hasn't been here all night. I'm sick with worrying."

It took me awhile to get enough awake to figure out where I was and who it was shaking me; and then I heard what she was saying, and I began to feel scared. She kept shaking and talking, "He's been gone since suppertime. Get up, please Bobby, go out and look for him."

"Now? What time is it?"

"It's about two."

"My gosh, he'll come back, won't he?"

"I don't know. Please."

"He shouldn't go off alone like that."

"I guess he's sick. Hurry, Bobby."

"You got any idea where he went?"

"Well, probably over toward the Neosho River. That's where he usually goes. You know that."

"Yeah, I know. Well, I'll try to find him."

"He might be hurt."

"I doubt it. He's always messing around over there. I'll go, though."

I got up, not hurrying, but feeling uneasy. I knew there wasn't any reason for it, but I began to get images of him lying out somewhere in a field, hurt or dead, maybe, and how I would feel and what I'd do if I did find him. I saw the whole picture all the way through; stumbling over the body, seeing that he was dead, maybe, if I could really tell; then running as fast as I could back to the house to tell my mother. Then the calls for help, the lanterns lighted and carried by hurrying neighbors, and all of us running and muttering to each other while my mother stayed at home with a neighbor woman or two looking out after us from the back porch, crying for us to hurry. . . .

I pulled on my overalls and blue shirt, fumbling for the buttons. The upstairs hallway light was on, but my mother hadn't turned on any light in my room, and I had to search for my heavy shoes back under the bed. I laced them up, and stood, ready to go, but not feeling much like it, except that the urgency of my mother now standing in the doorway made me hurry a little.

"Do you want to carry a lantern, Bobby?"

"No. It'd just be in the way."

"Be careful, don't *you* get hurt."

"Nothing to hurt me, and don't worry about him, either."

The old house was so tall and narrow that the stairs seemed to go straight up. As I stumbled down them, feeling for the wall on one side and the rail on the other as I'd done ever since I was big enough to go up and down by myself, I was reminded of the game I played when I was little—seeing how many steps I could jump down from the top. But tonight my mother followed me anxiously. I went through the downstairs hall, through the dining room and the kitchen and out onto the back porch. It was screened in and the screen door always squeaked when it was pushed open as I did it now, and I went down the three steps, the bottom one loose, and stepped onto the flagstone walk that was laid to the barn.

The night sky was clear, there wasn't any moon, but in the early morning, before dawn in Kansas, there is a night light in the open sky that illuminates the fields. Eastern Kansas is a land of wind and rolls of small hills, and creeks and slow rivers. It was open prairie land once, but no longer, and on about every side around our part, there were cornfields running right up close to many farmhouses. And there was a cornfield behind our barn.

I went through the gate and across the barnyard, smelling the manure, and saw that the work team, Jack and Pet, were over in a corner of the yard. I could hardly see them; they were there, faint against the starlight, but it was comforting to know that the horses were near. Friendly horses are comforting in the night, especially if you know them as well as I knew those two. I thought for a moment of putting a bridle on Pet and riding her bareback out to look for him, but then I decided I wouldn't, because there were fence gates to open and it'd take more time and she'd be a trouble, actually, in getting through the corn.

I cut across the edge of the cornfield, trying to not step on the new corn too much. It was coming up good, and would be indeed knee-high or better by the Fourth. It was due to be cultivated soon.

Beyond the cornfield there was the railroad track with tight barbed wire fences on both sides of the right-of-way. I knew where to get through the fence, where we'd worn a place under it, and I slid down this little hollow under the fence and down the embankment. I crossed the Santa Fe track, the rails glistening and going away, away, north toward the town of Iola and south through Humbolt to Chanute and Independence, and on down to Tulsa. I'd never been down that far and someday I thought I would set out to walk down the track, maybe catching onto a freight train as it came past, and riding some and walking some, clear down to Tulsa, and maybe clear on down to Texas. I had never been away from home for any time and felt the urge to go, to leave, and had a funny kind of thrilling feeling in my guts when I thought of myself all alone, walking on the railroad, or maybe out on the high road, just ambling from place to place, not caring, free and easy, just me to worry about. Not like now, with a worry on me and the uneasiness of my mother driving me, and I not knowing what to expect.

It isn't easy to find somebody in the real early morning hours; not out in a country of cornfields and pastures and small ravines and woods and rocks. It isn't easy to know where a person will go alone in those hours; but I knew something about how a certain person would go and where, especially if the person is your father and if you like him real well, and if you are worried about him, too, no matter what you have told your mother. Your father hasn't been acting just normal lately, maybe, and he has done some strange things like sit at the dining table and not say anything at all during a whole meal, and this is strange because he has been very talkative the times you sat with him at the table. He has sat there staring at nothing special, eating a few mouthfuls and then he cries out, "Damn it, God damn it," and this isn't like him, because he has always been very considerate of Mom. He wouldn't ever let a hired man swear in front of her. She was so particular about the name of God, the way all of the Baptists were in that part of the country about swearing. But here he was shouting the name of God right out and looking as if God had done a bad thing to him. It was shocking and I couldn't forget it, really, though it was buried down inside me somewhere. But here I was in the night walking out across the fields looking for him, and I was really scared. I know my mother was thinking that he had lost his mind or something, though she had said so often that there had never been a breath of insanity on either side of the family.

By the time I had crossed the little creek that never had much water except in flood time, and had crossed the pasture where our cows were still resting . . . I almost stumbled onto them in the dark and one rose, I guess it was Anabell, as Dad called her, big, red-spotted, and she gave out a loud grunt when she got up. I circled around the herd and went through a grove of trees that was near our south line fence and went off across the big alfalfa field. There was heavy dew on the alfalfa, and I felt the wetness sopping my overalls and seeping through my shoes. It wasn't cold at all, just wet, and I never had paid any attention to wetness really. I just took wetness and dryness and temperature as they came, and the way I felt about feeling things like that, was part of the way I felt about everything . . . not caring, just going along. But now I did hurry, because it was as if something was driving me beyond my mother's fear and my own uneasiness.

I started to trot, keeping close to the line fence, and I guessed I would follow it along until it got close to the river, and then I would turn north, because that was one way that he did like to walk sometimes. There was an old burying ground over that way near the river, and the grass in there was pretty high. I never did understand why he liked to go over that way, but it was a favorite hike of his, and one on which he hardly ever took anybody else along. It might be where he was now, I didn't know, and if he was dead or something, then I figured that he might be in there in the tall grass among the old graves that had been there ever since the country was settled back in the 1850s and 60s. One thing that Dad liked to do was talk about that old graveyard, and he could sure interest me in it when he told how it seemed to him. Dad had something special in him, that was sure. When he got to talking it was really something, and neighbors of ours who heard him talk about earlier times and about some of his ideas said they'd never heard anything like it.

Dad was self-educated. Maybe, all added up, he had the equivalent of a high school education, and he was a member of the Kansas Bar and practiced law as well as farming. He used to say that he didn't get much schooling in Illinois after the Civil War. But he had all the words he needed to say whatever he wanted to say, and he read anything that was good: he had a set of the *Encyclopedia Americana* that he had read from Volume One on and just kept reading and studying it, and there was something else he had, that my mother said was like he was gifted with poetry or something. She said he was like a wind-harp that could play any kind of music that the wind decided. But you know it's not easy to live with somebody like that.

Every now and then as I moved along through the wet grass I yelled out for him, but I didn't get any answer, and my voice sounded loud and strange in the silent early morning. The birds weren't even awake, and there just wasn't any sound at all as I stood every once in a while and listened. I thought I might hear him coming, or walking, through the grass, the way shoes sound in grass when it is wet, a soft shushh-shushh, but I didn't hear that sound at all.

I turned north and went across a plowed field that had some hickory trees and oaks growing around the edge. It was over at the far edge of this plot that the old burying ground and the long grass was, and I headed for there. I hadn't been that way for a long while—the place was kind of eerie, actually. It sat all alone at the far edge of the plowed ground, a little island there, just something left over; but I had to go now, that was sure. I kept calling and getting no answer; but as I got closer to the tall grass I thought I saw a little flicker of light and I hurried up a little, running now, breathing hard, stumbling along over the rough earth. What I saw might have been just my imagination, because I wanted so much to see a sign of Dad. It could even have been a flicker of a will-o-the-wisp that I had heard him tell about so often.

But when I got near to the grass and came up to the edge, I could see that there was indeed light shining out from the middle of the plot. My heart started to beat really fast, because I was sure, then, that I would find Dad in there and that he would be dead or something. So I called "Hey, Dad, Dad," and pushed into the grass.

He was there all right. He was lying back, his head on a piece of old log, and he was sprawled out, his legs and feet stretched wide, lying back with the lantern beside him. And he didn't say anything when I came up beside him. I did, though. "Hey, you got Mom really worried. Why'd you stay out here all night?"

"I was told to come out here."

"Who told you? Who *could* tell you?"

"All of them."

He was getting old, you could see that. In the yellow light of the kerosene lantern his face looked thin and his body seemed very small and tired. He lay there with his hat back from his forehead. I was really worried now, because I thought sure that he was sick, or had lost his mind, and I didn't know what to do or say. It would be bad enough if this was somebody you didn't know at all, but to be confronted with such behavior suddenly, in your own father, who had always seemed so interesting and ahead of other people ... that is hard.

"I heard you yelling." He whispered.

"Why didn't you answer?"

"I didn't want to spoil it."

"Spoil what?"

"Why, all this. And it's a good thing you came to find me. Because, boy, you are the last of the wandering Gards. It has to be up to you, boy."

"What has to be up to me?" I asked nervously.

"You'll find out."

"Come on back home with me."

"Sit down. I've got to talk. Your mother thinks I'm running out of time; or that I'm crazy, maybe. Do you think I'm crazy?"

"Nope. But you've been acting awful funny."

"Is it funny, boy, to see the way things are?"

"I don't follow you, Dad."

"Sit over here. Here, sit down on this log. You and I always been pretty good friends, haven't we?"

"I guess."

"And we've reached a time when things have to be evened out . . . when the Gards have run out of time. Not just me. All of us. All of us Gards. We moved west joint by joint, we just kept pressin' on and on, and all of us had something we saw that we had to have. And now we've come to the end."

"To the end of what?"

"To this land here. To this grass. This tall grass here. So tall you couldn't see me, or hardly see my lantern. Look how this grass sets here in the middle of the land ready for growing. Everything's gone. All that I saw here is gone. Do you know what I'm talking about, boy?"

"Not really."

"I'm seventy-two years old. You're young. Nobody else had the vision. But you got to have it. You are all the chance I got left."

I unhinged myself down beside him on an end of the log. I knew we ought to be getting back to the house; that Mom would be worrying sick, that she would think that both of us had got into trouble, or hurt. I felt nervous, and the wind had come up a little bit and I heard the wind in the trees that weren't far away.

"Let's go home."

"Nope. Not yet. What I've got to say might be the most important thing I ever said. Because you are my blood, boy. You are my chosen messenger, the one who can save my dreams for me."

He reached over and took hold of my ankle. I felt his hand, very strong, an old man's strong hand shaped by years of labor. It was the first time he had ever really touched me that I could recall. We Gards were never folks who touched and showed our affection for each other that way. But he held onto my ankle, like the claws of an eagle I thought. He pulled on my ankle and my leg, and sat up, scraping his heels into the grass in front of the log. He kept hold of my ankle, squeezing harder, and I let him do it; it was a strange sensation being held so hard by my father, and he used my leg to pull himself over so he could get his feet under him. He rose, very stiffly, letting me go as he stood. The grass in there was about shoulder high, very coarse prairie grass, and we couldn't see much in the dark, though by that time the sky was just beginning to lighten. He looked like a dark shadow in the wavering grass and in the dim lantern glow, for he left the lantern sitting on the ground. He took hold of my arm when he got straightened up, and I stood up too. He pulled me beside him and started to move out through the grass.

"Come here. I want to show you."

"Mom'll be excited. We ought to be going."

"She's waited and waited for me. She'll wait some more. She isn't like me, boy. Her family isn't like mine. Hers is religious. They put a lot of store by God and how he tells them what to do. The Gards ain't that way. We go by God, but we go the way we got the strength to go. The way the wind goes; the way the clouds go. Come over here."

He pulled me along with him to the edge of the prairie. At the edge of the grass he stopped. The edge of the unbroken grass was higher than the plowed ground. We couldn't see very far out into the field, just a little way, but you could feel and tell that there were two different things: the prairie and the plowed ground, and I began to get a feeling that we were really all alone out there, and that maybe we wouldn't be able to get away. He kept holding my arm, harder now, and I thought of his hands, the way a man's hands get as he grows old, when you feel the hard bones and the muscles. My arm ached, but he didn't let up.

And strangely, he began to put into words what I was feeling before about being alone, unable to leave.

"We been cast up here," he said. "Cast up on this shore. This is an island in the whole ocean, and we are castaways, you and me, boy. No ship brought us here, but our wandering selves brought us here. This is the island of the Gards. And the Gards made the ocean, too."

I kind of knew what he meant. He'd told me many times when we were sitting out in the yard on a Sunday afternoon, and Mom had made a big pitcher of lemonade and Dad was sitting in his old wicker rocker that Mom had bought at the 1893 World's Fair at Chicago . . . I'd heard him tell plenty of times how the land was when he came out to Kansas in the 1880s . . . all prairie grass, hardly any plow broken, and the prairie flowers and plants all growing. Mom said Dad should have been a poet or a writer or something, and she couldn't see how he had got the talent to talk like he did; because there had never been a poet or a writer in the Gards as far as she knew. But now he just kept holding me, and he began to talk like he did out in the yard; but this time I seemed to be a real part of it.

"You know, boy, we saved this prairie grass here in the old burying ground, because we never wanted to disturb these graves. I don't know who these people are who're buried here. They were buried long before I came. But when the plow was turning the new sod, and the roots were breaking, when they drove the teams up to this part here they always stopped. Never broke this. Broke all the rest, and year after year we grew crops. Now this is all there is left, and the dream of the Gards is ended. You see why I come out here in the night and stay all night while your mother stays up at the house and worries about me? You see why I do it?"

"Not really. You ought to go home; you might get sick out here."

"Boy, it ain't sickness that is worrying me. Your mother wouldn't know. But I am worried about the death of dreams and the death of a country. I'm out here in the night because this is all there is left."

He stood for a moment, and with his left hand he grabbed at some of the prairie grass and jerked it loose. He held the grass over against me, so I could feel it and smell it. It had a dew-grass-acid smell, sort of pleasant.

"Here, take the grass. Ball it up, roll it around, tear it apart. Put it in your mouth, taste it. Chew on it."

I tried to do what he said, getting more nervous all the time because what I wanted him to do was go home with me across the fields over to the house. I wanted to get him inside, into bed so Mom could watch out for him; and what I really wanted, I guess, was to get rid of the responsibility of him. But he wasn't going. I put a blade of the grass into my mouth and chewed on it. The juice was a taste I knew because I often grabbed spears of grass when I was walking along a fence or railroad and put them in my mouth. The taste always made me think of spring, somewhere about May, when everything is blooming in the fields in Kansas, and the new grasses are well up. There's a taste and spirit about fields and woods, and tastes of greens you can cook, and dandelions out in the yard, and meadow flowers and wild onions . . . all that came to me as I chewed on the prairie grass that night with Dad holding onto my arm.

"Now you look," he said, "this grass here, this old burying ground that I have kept for you, boy, nobody else; this piece, this acre or so . . . this is not of our time, neither yours nor mine. It belongs to itself: the wild, the grasses, the roots, the fermenting soils; the wild things, the bugs, the people who used to live here . . . they all own this grass. I don't own it, and you don't own it. And look, how these grasses have browned and brittled in the fall, and laid rotting under the snows. Look how the new shoots of the grasses push up in the spring out of the rot, and their roots are down in the rot, but the grasses taste sweet. You got to know how to listen. How to listen, boy."

He stopped talking and I was afraid to answer him right then, for fear I would start him going again, and we had to get home.

"Listen to the wind," he said. "Listen to how she breathes out, over the long grass; listen to how it is in August when she swirls out the corn leaves all over and acrost the field and rasps them together and roughens up acrost you as you walk in the tall corn at night. Feel the wind file the corn leaves against your cheek, boy, you felt *that*, and so have I, and listen to the sound of the wind in the August corn. Listen to the wind the way she whirls up the dust along the road and settles it down over the hedge rows, and how she sways the sunflowers in the fallow field and lightens up their yellow with white dust. You got to know how to listen to the wind in these tall grasses, and how it stirs up the grasses outside you and inside, too, and breathes the day, and the sunup and the evening. You got to know how to listen to the shadow of the past, and to the way this prairie grass was left here . . . all alone, a little prairie strip of all that was, and all that was hoped for; for there isn't anything in what a man can remember that can't be listened to."

He was talking about the same way he talked on Sundays to Mom and me out in the yard; or to neighbors if they happened to come by. I was kind of cold now, I hadn't worn any jacket, just my work shirt with sleeves rolled up, and I shivered a little in his grasp. I guess he felt me shiver; he pulled me around to face him. He wasn't near as tall as I was, but he was a little bit heavier, sturdier built than I. I was a lot taller all right but I wasn't near as strong as he. Even now when he was old, I could feel the strength of him coming down into his hand. He came around a little now and looked me more directly in the face. I saw his face dimly, but it was sharp, like a hawk's bill, I thought, because he seemed so tense and eager, like a bird coming down out of the sky. It was when he was talking about the prairie and the way things were that he got tight and kind of desperate.

"I was there in the night, and the tall grasses were everywhere, weaving the wind, and I walked out into it, just me, alone, feeling something I never felt before, like this was the beginning of the world. The Creation. The Genesis. And like I was God himself, mastering over all, calling on all. My voice heard above the wind and up to the clouds. And I was young. Young. And I had come out seeking, searching, like my father and his father, never stopping, ever searching on and on. And I found the tall grasses—the roots of man and the roots of grass are all the same, and both of them require freedom to live and to be."

I felt like I was in some kind of a crazy play, and that I was playing one of the parts whether I wanted to or not. I tried to get away, but Dad was awfully strong, and I couldn't break his hold. He kept saying, "Don't spoil it, boy. Let it be. I want to show you how it was."

"We haven't got time. We got to go home."

"We'll go soon. I got to show you this, then I have something to ask you."

"What?"

As he spoke the words came out like little poems, and I remembered the time when my older sister was in high school and had to give a little talk about how the southeastern Kansas country looked in the days when the settlers came into it. She told her English teacher what Dad said and the teacher made her ask him to come to the school and give a little talk to the students about the early days. My sister didn't much want him to come, because she was afraid that he wouldn't change his clothes, and might shame her, I guess, but he did clean up real good after the morning chores were finished and went up to school and came right into the classroom and sat down in a back seat until the teacher asked him to come up to the front and talk. Mom heard all about it from the teacher, because my sister never did get it so she could tell what happened. But the teacher called up Mom on the telephone and said that Dad was the greatest poet she ever heard, and that Walt Whitman never made any better poems than Dad did as he was talking to the students. Mom tried to get him to tell what he said but he never would and the students, like my sister, never could describe it either. But I guess he was pretty wild when he was talking.

"God, boy," he suddenly continued, "you never held the handles of a sodbreaker. You never had the experience, as I did, of hearing the roots of the sod cutting and breaking; then it was a happy sound to me, like a million fiddle strings snapping; the cut of the blade of the plow, and the slow strength of the horses. Look, boy, get hold of the plow handles!"

He made me lean and take hold of imaginary plow handles, and he yelled, "Hey! Gitup!" to imaginary horses, and I swear I felt something in my hands and arms, the power of a plow cutting through sod, the grasses bending over and breaking down; the turning under, the fall of the heavy strips of cut roots and grass. I felt it, and as he yelled at the horses, I was there in the old days with him, walking along behind the plow. I felt unreal and foolish, too, and I couldn't get completely into the game he was playing with himself and with me. I knew it was a game and I think he knew it was a game, too, but someway he was living over his life.

We came to the edge of the grass and he stopped, and forgot the game and the imaginary horses all at once. He took hold of my hand.

"Boy, you've got to help me. I raised you up to understand. It's the time for you to go seeking as I did. You never yet met the Stranger, and you never felt the roots and the body of the grass as I did. And I broke all the sod that I could get that was mine. It's gone. The tall grass is gone, and you ain't going to find that. But you got to find something. There's something out there that is like the grass was to me. I come searching for it. And you got to find out what they left in place of the grass, because I am an old man and I have to know before I die. I can't go, because I have no youth left in me. But you go. You go and find and tell me what it is that you are searching for. I got this feeling so deep and bitter. You go, boy. You go searching and find a Stranger in the grass like I did; unless you do, boy, my life is over and all that I found in the middle of the grass is nothing. All the Gards will be dead. You go. Go, boy go."

"Where do you want me to go?"

He grabbed me hard by the arm. "Say you'll go."

I wanted to humor him, and I didn't have any idea what he wanted me to do. He said he wanted me to go somewhere, nowhere, where there was a stranger, whoever *that* was, standing in the middle of a big field of prairie grass. He had never mentioned a stranger before. I guessed that in his mind he could go anywhere or do anything. There wasn't any limit. But I was different. I couldn't talk like he could, and make everything seem like a story or a play. I couldn't do any of that and hadn't. And I didn't want to go wandering away without knowing where I was headed. The Depression was a tough time to go anywhere, anyhow. All the tramps and hobos that were drifting through the country, and you could see them anytime as you stood along the Santa Fe track, riding in the coal cars, or maybe on top of the box cars. Dad just expected me to start going, looking for some more prairie grass that wasn't out there anymore. Well, I wasn't going to do it. But I said, "Oh, sure I'll go. I'll go if you'll come home with me. Mom'll be crazy with worry."

"When will you leave?"

"Oh, I don't know, soon."

"Tomorrow."

"I can't tomorrow. But soon, I promise if you'll come home."

"Go tomorrow if you can," Dad said. "Go tomorrow if you can, boy. You got a long ways to go."

He let go of my arm and walked into the grass to get his lantern. The light wavered and dimmed and then got strong again as he lifted the lantern above the grass and turned up the wick. The light was growing in the sky, and the morning Kansas wind was rising. The grass lay bent over, combed out by the wind, and I shivered in the early morning coolness. I couldn't make a thing out of what had happened. I just had the feeling that something tremendous had happened to me, and I wanted to get home. And as far as going away was concerned, I would forget about that, because I was sure that he would forget it . . . after he'd had a good rest, and we'd let him sleep in the morning. I would do all the chores myself, and maybe Mom would help some. But I wasn't going anyplace, no matter what. He was an old man and talked a lot, and needed to calm down, from what, I didn't know. I knew that he was excited and that he figured something had gone sour with his world, and that there wasn't any more wild prairie . . . that much I understood; but I was awfully tired.

He took hold of my arm as we started across the plowed field. "You got an awful lot to do to get ready to go," he said.

Pioneer Spirit

I suppose that I have always wanted to float through the writing of a book; just to let things happen as they will; to relax and enjoy it. Writing is very hard work for me. Words sometimes flow easily, but mostly they don't. I really must labor to produce the daily quotas one tends to set for himself ... one thousand words, two thousand, even four thousand or more if the day is exceptional. But a poor day of writing can lead me to a sleepless night, and sleepless nights to other kinds of frustrations; I wasn't seeking new stress, so this one time, just this once, I decided to adopt a very easy attitude, to fool myself into thinking that the self-punishment of writing a book was nothing but pleasure.

I set up an elaborate mechanism to accomplish this. I was elected President of the Wisconsin Academy of Sciences, Arts and Letters for a year, and I imagined during that period that I might just sit in the isolated small office the Academy provided for me and be productive and free of complication. But I soon grew to understand the Academy as something very special and very precious to the Wisconsin people and rather than passively sit back, I tried to decide why this was so.

Sometimes I call the Academy a fortress, other times an island, but within the nation as it is today there is a great need for institutions and agencies that possess symbolism. I believe such symbolism is the last hope for the sensitive, the curious, the searcher who has been cast adrift by confusions arising from so many unsolvable problems. Within the Academy there is hope for such souls, since its purpose is and remains clear: that we, a collection of diverse persons with varying backgrounds, are essentially striving for the same goal: that man may better realize his potential and that he may become more magnified in purpose, as around him traditional values and landmarks seem to crumble.

I am keenly aware of this: that the old security I used to find in old established principles of aesthetics and ethics has now gone astray. For a time I was bereft and sought solace in the company of other bereft persons who were likewise without much bearing. Then I began to discern that islands, beacons, did still exist. I found in the Academy one of these wherein I could again believe in the glory, not the degradation, of man. I found that I was not alone in the hope that it was still possible to believe that there were verities, that there was truth in human aspiration . . . that life itself was more than a chain of happenstance, or circumstance. That a humanism for our time was essential and that it included a definite possibility of aspiration, of hope, of striving and search with purpose.

Light; illumination. What is it that illuminates the world of man? It is knowledge, and a reverence for knowledge is what has really motivated the Academy through the years. It was what inspired our earliest Wisconsin scientists, our earliest Wisconsin writers, our enduring Wisconsin pioneers. It was curiosity combined with zeal that drew the explorers to the Wisconsin country. Religious zeal might have been flat without great curiosity about the new country and the new people. Who were they? How did they get to the wild inland country of lakes and forests?

Samuel Champlain sent Jean Nicolet to find the mysterious "People of the Sea." No doubt Marquette and Joliet on their 1673 journey of discovery to the Mississippi saw old copper knives and implements in the hands of the Winnebago, and they may well have had curiosity about where such implements came from. Or else it was the curiosity and drive to bring those early travelers' accounts to life and into the service of scholars that inspired 19th century Reuben Gold Thwaites, historian, writer, Academy member, honored Wisconsin author, to edit from the French the 93-volume set of the *Jesuit Relations*, accounts of and by curious adventurers who explored to learn. The volumes have become our source of knowledge of exploration times in Wisconsin.

And two centuries after the explorers' accounts of their adventures, began the collecting mania of that strangely motivated man from Burlington, Wisconsin, Frederick Perkins, 1833-1899. Perkins was an artist of the "Hudson River School" those landscapists from New York State, some of whom emigrated to Wisconsin. As an artist, Perkins was good. He did portraits more than landscapes, and traveled to New York and to other places to paint famous or affluent persons. Then one day, near Burlington, a change came over his life. He was watching a farmer plow, and suddenly the farmer reached down into the furrow and lifted a piece of strange metal. It was, as Perkins examined it, copper, obviously ancient, which had lain in the earth a long while. But it was identified as a spearpoint. Up to about this time, 1850, it had been supposed by many authorities that copper had not been much used by the prehistoric Indians as weapons or utility instruments. In the entire state, until about that time or a little earlier, there were perhaps only a few hundred casually preserved specimens and these were thought to be mere happenings, curiosities. Perkins didn't think so. He set out, at great personal expense, to collect every specimen of old copper he could find. He haunted the farms in the Burlington area, advertised in the newspapers. He spent almost all of his own money, and virtually all of his wife's, in payment to farmers for their copper discoveries. To pay his wife back some of the money expended from her estate, he willed her the front yard of their Burlington home. His efforts were rewarding. He started a wondrous collection of copper pieces, spearpoints, knives, hammers which proved beyond any doubt that there were ancient peoples—sometimes known only as "the copper people" who had mined copper and had scattered it through the Middle West.

In 1876 Perkins sold to the state of Wisconsin a portion of his collection, and it was these copper pieces, carefully watched over by Wisconsin historian Lyman Copeland Draper and University Professor James D. Butler, and shipped to the Legislature in many boxes, which became the central Archeological exhibit from Wisconsin at the Philadelphia Exposition celebrating the Centennial of the United States. The exhibits attracted attention from famous archeologists in England, Ireland, and Scandinavia, many of whom believed the copper showed a connection, somehow, between ancient civilizations in Europe and America.

By 1876, of course, the source of the copper had been long discovered. It was recognized that the glacial drift had brought into the Mississippi and Ohio valleys much copper in small pieces and "floats". But it had been known for long that there was a much greater supply and that this supply lay in the Lake Superior region. Early geologists had found hundreds of ancient "diggings" and pits in the Keweenaw Peninsula, and later on, when more ambitious explorations of old, old, Indian mining pits were conducted, great mines, such as the Calumet-Hecula mine (largest and deepest copper mine in the world) resulted. Ancient Indian miners, however, broke off such pieces of the copper as they could carry and shaped it into ornaments and weapons. These were spread very widely. But just who these earliest miners were has never been really decided. At first they were thought to be Indians of Sioux stock, as Radisson, the earliest observer of the Lake Superior peoples, noted that Sioux visitors wore ornaments of polished copper. Yet there have been very few copper ornaments found on Sioux sites and even the Winnebago (originally a Sioux people) acquired their copper by inter-tribal trade, not manufacture. More likely, thought Louise Phelps Kellogg, Wisconsin historian, the copper makers were of Algonquin origin. Ohio and Georgia mounds where copper was discovered were thought to be burial places of Algonquin Indians.

Academy members have been curious about nearly everything. The files of the Academy *Transactions* show the track of their search for illumination, for truth. Here is Increase A. Lapham, 1811–1876, Academy member to whom every leaf, every piece of bark, every cloud, every stone, every Indian mound was an invitation to research. He established science in Wisconsin and spread his curiosity to nearly every person. In *My Land, My Home, My Wisconsin*, a book written by my wife Maryo and me, we heard a farm woman say: "Yes, my great grandfather. He knew Increase Lapham. Lapham stayed at grandfather's house one night in 1850 when he was mapping the Indian mounds. He talked and talked, and grandfather said that the family was never the same. Lapham brought in a kind of wonderful intellectual light and made their whole part of the country come alive." Lapham did that for so many.

A young man employed in canal building in Ohio, Lapham drifted in 1836 to Milwaukee and to a Wisconsin he never left. He had small formal education, but he used the wondrous textbook of nature to be his ever-expanding school. Certainly Lapham was one of the reasons I myself made Wisconsin a permanent home, after years of wandering. for there was in Lapham's time an air of adventure, of taking a chance, of providing excitement through discovery of the better ways of living an American life on a frontier which was at its boom when Lapham arrived. Although it was definitely gone when I arrived, I am sure that Wisconsin was still feeling the frontier tempers and hangovers in Lapham's day. He came because his friend Byron Kilbourn was hoping to build a great canal called the Milwaukee and Rock River Canal. Kilbourn, who was one of the greatest dreamers Wisconsin ever had, hoped the canal would go a long way toward Milwaukee's realizing its dreams of metropolitan greatness.

Lapham didn't stick long to building canals. One of the first things he did was plunge into the furious speculation in lands then going on in the Wisconsin of 1836, purchasing two lots with no money whatever to pay for them (at a time when there were only fifty houses in Milwaukee). But he wasted no further time in business enterprises, and began an activity that was to result in the first scientific study ever conducted in Wisconsin: A CATALOGUE OF PLANTS AND SHELLS FOUND IN THE VICINITY OF MILWAUKEE AND THE WEST SIDE OF LAKE MICHIGAN, by I. A. Lapham.

From then on his curiosity was boundless. By 1838 he had started what was to be the first history of Wisconsin, and this book, printed in hard cover, was the first real book published in the new Territory. It was entitled, "A Geographical and Topographical Description of Wisconsin: With Brief Sketches of the History, Geology, Minerology, Natural History and Population." The book was published by P. C. Hale, Milwaukee, and was a major influence in attracting Europeans and settlers from other parts of the United States to Wisconsin. Perhaps Lapham's most ambitious writing project was the mapping and description of the Indian Effigy Mounds in southern Wisconsin, a major work which the Smithsonian published in 1855.

But all of Lapham's life was the same. Curious about everything, he recorded his observations. Late in life, after doing most of the scientific study of the state for nothing, he was given the unimpressive job of "state geologist." He held this position for a short time, was on the point of publishing the first great report on the geology of the state, and then suddenly had his job whisked away in one of the crassest and most political moves ever made by a Wisconsin governor. Gov. William R. Taylor took Lapham's job and gave it to a "Doctor Wight," a spoils seeker of the governor's own party, who had never read a book on geology and who, when he was appointed, borrowed a geological text book from Increase Lapham! Still, Lapham's spirit was not broken.

His contemporary, Doctor Philo Hoy of Racine, said of him, "To know Lapham we must go with him to his work-shop—the great out-of-doors. We stroll out on the prairies. He pulls up the grass and speaks familiarly of the spikes and spikelets, the rachis and the glume, inspects the roots, digs down and examines the soils from which they spring. We go into the forest and he talks of the various species of trees, the vines that clamber up their trunks and nestle in their branches. He inspects the lichens that grow on the rough bark, examines the moss that adheres to the roots, and unearths a tiny helix that he has found there. We go to the rapids and he immediately interests himself in the rare ferns that festoon the rocks; or he clambers among the quarries, marks the stratification of the Silurian rocks, and chips out rare forms of Crinoids and Trilobites—those wonderful representations of the fauna of the dim past. We seek the mounds; those records of a pre-historic race, dig beneath their foundations and wrest from them their secrets. The position of the bones is carefully noted, their rude pottery restored, the curious stone implements treasured up, and 128 mounds are surveyed and mapped. We stand upon our lake shore and he discourses on the force of the waves and describes the ingenious contrivance by which he discovered the lake's miniature lunar waves. He talks of the force of the winds and the velocity and direction, then looks up the clouds and tells their indications and speaks of the annual rainfall and of the average temperatures of the past thirty years, during which time he has kept a careful record."

He died alone, in his row boat on Oconomowoc Lake engaged in lake research. Lapham was the soul of understanding the Wisconsin of his day. The strange thing was that early Wisconsin was full of such characters as Lapham . . . possibly not with his magnificent abilities, but with equal curiosity and energy.

Lying back of another motive that brought me to Wisconsin was the fabled story of Lyman Copeland Draper. Undersized . . . about five feet tall, Draper had only one mission in mind, called "pioneer's mission" by his biographer William B. Hesseltine. The mission, very ineptly put, was to gather the reminiscences and stories of the American pioneers before they finally left the scene. In his young manhood Draper personally knew survivors of the Revolutionary War: he was in constant contact with the brother of Daniel Boone; he knew men and women in the South and East who remembered the Battle of King's Mountain . . . he was fraught with tension to act, to collect, to visit and record all they had to say about the very origins of this nation. He was too late for George Washington; but President James Madison reluctantly responded to him . . . Draper's notebooks grew and grew . . . he traveled on foot largely, going into the back country where old veterans had made farms. He wrote everything down in a tiny script that eventually amounted to more than 80,000 handwritten pages . . . the rarest collection of first-hand American history ever made. And eventually he came to Wisconsin where he established the State Historical Library, using the collections of rare materials which he had begged and borrowed (never really stolen) from the relatives of pioneers.

Draper's life was a hard one. He had little support; finally the Legislature recognized what he had done and established a job for him, but he was nearly always a poor man. His dream (like mine, in my minor way) was to write a series of great books "Sketches Of The Pioneers" which he never did. Writing was a terrible burden for him. He had collaborators but they didn't work out. One book, eventually published, was about the giant dream history he had collected for so long, entitled *The History Of The Battle Of King's Mountain.*

But the spirit of Draper, his devotion to the sources, his work to found one of the greatest regional history libraries in America . . . all these things, plus his suffering of soul, appealed to me. The great library of the Wisconsin State Historical Society he formed with fifty books. Before I came to Wisconsin I had heard of Draper's mission. I myself had engaged in one of much less magnitude, also before the day of tape recorders, in Alberta, where I wrote down in longhand the memories of the founders of that part of Canada. Could I somehow do the same in Wisconsin? Of course the founders were long gone; but their descendants had great materials unrecorded.

And not nearly so early, but also haunting my memory in the Academy is a big-framed man, moving lightly, filled with nervous energy . . . a book protrudes from his shirt pocket, a sack hangs from his back, for he is collecting morels . . . perhaps he is the greatest mushroom collector the state has ever known. He likes them prepared in many, many ways, best, perhaps, piled high on a tender porterhouse. He listens to birds, to wind, sees the way the branches sway; the track of wild animals he observes and notes, for he keeps a copious journal of everything, every day. In the town, the people admire him, fear him a little, for he seems to hear all, tell all. He is August Derleth of Sauk City, 1909–1971, who has made his home environment the course and scene of his literature. He, too, is noted for his curiosity; some local residents think that he has nosed too deeply into their personal affairs, but, after all, August Derleth has written a mammoth series of novels and books: more than 150. The *Sac Prairie Saga*, among them, one of the notable regional literary efforts in American history, numbering more than twenty books.

And what a crowding host of memories are in my mind today about August Derleth. I relied on him to an extent for literary advice, and he was unfailing in providing it. He was never too busy to see me. He provided me with the title for one of my books (*This is Wisconsin*), and when he was in the University Hospital in Madison, sick almost unto death after an operation, and I brought the published book for him to see, his pleasure was genuine. He cried "Good, good!" and fell back on his pillow too ill to say more. From time to time I was perhaps able to repay his literary kindnesses. I employed him for years to teach at the Rhinelander School of the Arts, was able to bring him together with Cap Pearce (of Duell, Sloan and Pearce, New York) when Augie was searching for a new publisher to handle his books in New York; at my suggestion he wrote *The Moon Tenders*, the enchanting boy's story of adventure on the Wisconsin River, perhaps the best boys' book ever written in Wisconsin.

But Augie was his own man, always, very jealous of his standing and prerogative as Wisconsin's foremost author. We were proud of him, and his place will not soon be filled. Before his death, a strange thing happened, which I have recounted many times. The last photograph of August Derleth was taken by Spring Green photographer Dale O'Brien at the farm of regional poet Edna Meudt, west of Dodgeville. Augie and Edna were closest friends, and Edna was staging a writers picnic there that day. Augie's photograph was taken against

an open field   n standing rugged and alone; and
strangely, on   there appeared in a corner a human
skull. The ph   s published in a book of mine (photo-
graphs by O   *Down in the Valleys*, and I make the
observation   ion to Augie's death which occurred
on July 4, 19   on after the photo was taken.

Derleth was a singer of the Wisconsin land. Of all
that was living of the land he loved, he sang; and also of the
people who were dead: the people of his creative memory. Lines
from his "Ode to the Sac Prairie Dead" remain in my mind:

> Gone those twilights,
> gone those wildernesses of winter nights;
> gone, gone those first paths, those days,
> the reaches of new land in farther haze;
> gone, gone the pioneers,
> the wild hugeness of frontiers—
> alas, alas! we shall not know their
> kind again,
> those singing unsung heroes and the plain
> women who bore them—alas!
> even their age could pass!

And there was still another pioneer, my friend whose
office I now occupy. You might have called her the spirit of the
Wisconsin Academy, for she gave it a large share of her affection and her life. Dr. Elizabeth McCoy, 1901–1977, was a scientist and farmer, living on the McCoy farm where she died on
the south outskirts of Madison. The house, still standing, is a
large square one, and on the farm was grown the first tobacco
in Wisconsin in 1853. Elizabeth experimented constantly with
her soils, her crops of hybrid seed corn and soybeans. She was
a noted micro-biologist, and herself trained more than fifty
Ph.D.'s at the University. She was always a source of much
curious information. For instance, she knew where the carcass
of a steer had been buried near Picnic Point on the Madison
University Campus in 1912. Dean Harry Russell of the Agricultural College, himself a noted scientist, was demonstrating
on the carcass the presence of the dreaded cattle disease, Anthrax. The infected steer, buried, spread the disease into the
earth. Seventy-five years later Elizabeth told me that the
microbes of Anthrax are still there in that spot. The place must
still be protected, and could still infect innocent diggers in that
locality.

What an opportunity, I thought, with a background of giant people, missions and ideas, for me to perform, during my year as president, the role of a kind of receiving station for all sorts of thoughts about my State; a receiver of strange bits of information, of curious characters who float through the past; views of life relating to the Arts, which are my own field. And what an opportunity to sum-up my own attitudes, my viewpoints about the State and its lore, to estimate where I had come from and where I was going . . . all within the fascinating welter of detail and story that would surely surround me. I thought it likely that no other Academy President had ever tried to do just that . . . to narrate and relate a personal view of the State as well as the form of the State's romantic being as it came to him during his tenure. I decided to try it, and to be exceptionally free-wheeling, barring nothing, accepting thoughts, and memories, as they came . . . to present myself, and my State in any way they appeared . . . preferably together, but if not, then so be it. That was when the idea of two rivers forming within me began.

I got a lift the very first day I came as President to the structure on University Avenue. The building was formerly a monument works, but had been remodeled to become one of the charming, small cultural gathering-places of Madison. It is called the Steenbock Center after the noted biochemist Dr. Harry Steenbock, who left a residual amount of his fortune gained from patents on his discovery of Vitamin D to the Wisconsin Academy. The residual amount turned out to be much more than anybody dreamed, and the endowment placed the Academy, for the first time, in comfortable operating circumstances. Dr. Steenbock left the Academy a million dollars.

On that morning in January, 1977, I was told by Jim Batt, the Academy's executive director, that he had discovered, by chance, the typewriter that Dr. Steenbock had used for years and years in his office at the Biochemistry Building. Jim said that he had rescued the typewriter from among belongings that Steenbock had left, and that if I wanted, I could keep the ancient machine in *my* office and use it during my tenure as President! While I was a little startled because, of course, I have my own typewriter, a battered and cherished old Olympia which has served me well, I nevertheless told Jim that I'd be delighted to place the Steenbock machine on my desk, and some miracle might occur, even if I didn't use it much. Actually, I *have* used the old typewriter a lot. I enjoy old clattering machines, cannot, or will not, use an electric, and I have discovered that the battered typewriter has a fascination for me. It is old enough to make me think of Christopher Lathem Sholes of Milwaukee who invented the typewriter, but that's another story. When I sit before the Steenbock typewriter, I do transfer myself into a receptive mood to look forward and backward and inward. One does condition himself in that way, and objects do attain a symbolism of purpose. And somehow all the pioneers, and all of the present and the past, become one.

WILD BLUE

I sat back and stared out the window of my tiny office at the Wisconsin Academy, gazing not so much at the out-of-doors as I was looking backward into my own past. I reached for the sheet in the old Steenbock typewriter to see what I had written about Dad and his behavior that night in the prairie. Of course, I realize now what I also knew then—that I had to leave my Kansas home. Still, I tried every which way to get out of leaving, but I was blocked by Dad every time.

Soon, I also came to understand how the idea of a Stranger that one meets by chance, coincidence, or predestination became more and more a part of the search I was making. And so began one of the great landmarks that ever happened to me. That's the way it almost always goes . . . you get, for the first time, a feeling that you have an indication of your own span of time, and that all along it are things that happen . . . things that influence you for the whole rest of your existence. That's the way it was with me when I left home that time. The world opened up. I guess I didn't find exactly what Dad wanted me to find . . . a great, vast sense of the nation in development, always on the edge of an ever-changing frontier; of tall, waving grasses, where a man could carve out his own life, but I found something. I have to tell it, because my Wisconsin life and the way I feel about Wisconsin, wouldn't have much meaning unless I did tell it. What I mean is, everything in my life has been interconnected. One happening doesn't mean much without the whole tissue.

It seemed as though in one summer I covered the whole world. I thought my experiences were unique, and they were, for me, the way everyone's experiences are different . . .

even though millions of others have done pretty much the same things. I thought my Dad, and the way he arranged for me to go was unconventional, too, but I've since realized that others have had similar fates. Why just the other day I was talking to Joe Bradley, a colleague who is a son of Dr. Harold Bradley, the famed medical scientist who was at the University of Wisconsin in the early twentieth century, and who was wealthy by marriage to an heiress to the Crane plumbing fortune. Yet Dr. Bradley sent each of his sons out into the world, just as Dad did me, and gave each one a hundred dollars when he left. Those who departed were supposed to return in a year and bring back with them a hundred dollars!

I didn't have any hundred dollars, but I did make a great attempt to find what Dad sent me to discover. I went west and north, survived many new adventures, became terribly conscious of the Depression and the turmoil and movement of humanity in those days. I had no sense that my odyssey was going to lead to anything, to adventures that would someday carry me to Wisconsin, and that I would meet persons who would make all the difference. I sure didn't know what had happened, if anything had. But the way I left home in Kansas, was something I dwelt on for years and years ... and in a curious backwards and forwards in time, had made my Wisconsin experience both possible and real.

Maybe you have had thoughts about going away from home the first time on your own, and you get to thinking that you might not ever come back again, or that you might not ever come back again in the same way when you left. A lot of people have had those thoughts, and I sure had them the night before I left. I really loved our part of Kansas. I guess I didn't feel deeply about it like Dad did, but I had wandered all over and knew every fence corner, almost, in our whole part of the country. Our river, the Neosho, would sometimes be very shallow and muddy, with little rills here and there and a few deep holes that were fine for swimming; but it wasn't a big, always-flowing river. In drought times the catfish came up to the surface in the holes and gasped for oxygen, and sometimes we went over and scooped out some fish and put them into tubs of clear water to wash the mud out. They always tasted kind of muddy, even so.

But in flood times the river really got savage and spread out over all the flatlands, and looked like one big lake from our upper windows. That was the way the country was;

we had too much water, or we didn't have enough. And the people always seemed like that too ... they were really happy when things were going well, and there was a good corn year, and the price for pigs was good. But in the 1930s, prices were just terrible, and folks were sad. And when there would be a flood they'd watch the waters rise and cover the bottom-land cornfields and they wouldn't say much, just stand and watch. The smells, the feelings, about everything I knew, were right there at home. Well, I went to sleep the night before I left home, thinking about things like that, and I really felt homesick and nervous.

Mom came into my room about half-past four in the morning. I was lying with my head away from the door to the room and didn't hear her come in. She must have stood for a while at the head of the bed, not saying anything, and I must have sensed her there or something because I woke up and turned over and got straight in the bed.

It was going to be hard, leaving Mom. She and I had always been close. She didn't want me to go either; yet someway I suppose she knew I had to go. I sure didn't want my parting from Mom to be too abrupt or matter-of-fact. I felt deeply about her and she did about me, too. Only we just weren't all that demonstrative. Coming and going had to pretend to seem ordinary and matter-of-fact.

"You better get up. Dad's got the car ready to go."

"Up awful early."

"I put some underwear and clean overalls and a blue shirt in the old alligator valise. It's not too big to carry. I put some sandwiches in too."

"Thanks, Mom."

"You'll let us hear from you I reckon."

"Sure."

"Well, I put some postcards in the valise too. Let me know where you are."

"All right."

"I still don't understand what's going on. More of your father's impractical nonsense. We'll have to hire somebody to help with the corn. Maybe we ought to just give the farm up."

"I won't be gone so long."

"I hope not. But not to know where you're going or anything. It's crazy."

"Don't worry. I'm big enough to take care of myself. Dad wants me to find a great thing. A stranger or the wild prairie or something."

"Sometimes your Dad's a stranger to me!" she said.

I got up and put on the clean overalls she had laid out for me the night before. Mom had baked pancakes and fixed sausage, and when I went down to the kitchen Dad was sitting at the table, finishing up. He was real cheerful, said good morning and asked how I felt, and I said I was feeling kind of sleepy but otherwise okay. Dad got up from the table and took my valise and started for the door.

"I'll put this in the car. Better hurry along. The boys probably won't wait, and we got to be in town pretty soon."

The "boys" were a couple of local characters named Zill and Harry. There was always local talk about their doings.

Mom kind of turned away. "Those awful fellows. Does he have to ride with them?"

"It'll be fine," came the response from the door. Mom said something that sounded like "Huh!" and didn't say anything more.

"I'll be coming right away."

"I'll turn the cows into the barnlot while you're finishing. Got hay down for them so they're all ready to come into the barn."

There wasn't much more for Mom and me to say. I got up from the table and she said, "Well, son, we'll be thinking about you. You'll be fine. You've got good blood in you. I guess you got to go sometime, somewhere."

"I'm going to miss being home," I said, and there was a strange feeling across my stomach, an excited feeling that I'd never had before. It was like something great or big was going to happen, and I didn't know what it was and could hardly wait for it to happen. I gave her a hug and went out into the yard. Dad had come back from the barnyard and was standing beside the car, an Overland touring model that we had had ever since Dad got rid of our old Overland a few years before. This Overland wasn't much of a car, and it was getting pretty old now too, but it ran okay. I walked to the door on the driver's side because I wanted to drive into town for the last time, and we didn't much like to have Dad drive anyway. He was an okay driver but getting unsure of himself every now and then, or maybe he just got to thinking about how things used to be and forgot where he was.

"You feeling excited?" Dad asked. "I sure remember how excited I felt the morning I left Illinois ... fifty-four years ago, boy. There's nothing like going away, first time."

I got in to drive and he got in beside me. Mom came over to my side of the car just before I started the engine, and slipped some money into my hand. She really didn't want Dad to see her do it, and he hadn't said a thing to me about any money. Maybe he knew she would give me some. I didn't know how much she'd given me, but I couldn't see how it could be very much. She just didn't have it to give. She leaned into the car and gave me a kiss on the cheek, and I sort of gave her one back. It wasn't that I didn't want to give her a lot more affectionate goodbye. It was just that our family didn't do it, or couldn't do it. We just took it for granted that we felt deeply about each other.

"Well, here we go," Dad shouted. I rammed the car into reverse and backed around the kind of circular drive we had. There was a silver maple tree growing right in the middle of the place where the drive circled in front of the house; I missed the tree all right and shifted into first gear as we started grinding out toward the road. I waved back to Mom and she waved at me, and that was the last I saw of her, because we struck the road then and turned north toward Iola and the courthouse square where we were supposed to meet Zill and Harry.

It never occurred to me to wonder why Mom hadn't come to town with us, but it wouldn't have seemed right if she had, because it was Dad's operation all the way, and she knew it. She wouldn't break in on it for anything. One thing there was no doubt about, though, she didn't care for Zill and Harry. She considered them outlaws and criminals and wasn't wrong in her estimate.

There was a thing I felt about my mother, quite different from Dad. It was connected with blue blossoms rooted in small memories so far back I could hardly draw them out of the murk. When I was a little kid there were blue flowers growing along the Santa Fe railroad track back of our house, and Mom had often taken me for walks along the track in the summer. The sun melted the tars on the cross ties and the rails shimmered off the great summer heat; the flowers, creeping almost to the tracks themselves, swayed faintly and hung down a bit in the shimmer. When I broke one off, reaching and pulling, a whitish stickiness came out of the broken stem and when Mom took my hand again the milk welded my hand into hers. The blue flowers clutched at my legs when Mom and I crossed the right-of-way, climbed through a fence strung with taut, barbed wires, and went into the woods. And as we walked Mom said something about the flowers that sounded like a poem—she said, "The blue, the blue, the wild blue," and a peaceful sense, a tiny, remembered sense of the blue came over me, and when I sought her in pain or trouble the blue feeling of the railroad flowers moving so breathlessly in the waves of summer heat was always there. I went into the remembered sensation of the blue flowers with a security of unspoken peace. I took that with me as the Overland rumbled its way to the Iola Courthouse.

The Cave and The Mounds

Again, the cave I inhabit, and where I cogitate about dreams and departures, is the Wisconsin Academy of Sciences, Arts and Letters, founded 1870, a symbol and a building, located at 1922 University Avenue in Madison. I had been using a small office there that was, until recently, occupied by the great Wisconsin bacteriologist, Elizabeth McCoy. I knew her best in her later years, when she was in her seventies, and she was often my confidant. What an evening of grief for her friends in 1977 when she lay alone in her 1850 house built of Tennessee brick which had been shipped down the Ohio River and up the Mississippi to Prairie du Chien, then transhipped overland to Madison by wagon. On that evening she was quite alone.

The McCoy farmhouse is set well back from the Syene Road on Madison's south side; and when her tenant farmer came, in that February dark, to visit her, to see whether she was all right, he found her incapable of speech; he placed her in his car and she expired on the way to the hospital. She hadn't known how sick she was, and had she not been so tragically independent and proud, and had asked earlier for the help hundreds of her friends were eager to give, I am sure she would be living today.

But I now inhabit Elizabeth's old office, and it is still filled with her memorabilia. I have tried not to touch things very much. Her desk clutter is about the same; her notes spread out for articles she was writing. A curious wooden clock that some country carpenter had whittled for her still waits to tick in a corner, and her favorite Boston rocker seems to give gently back and forth sometimes, impelled by zephyr forces which I do not try to explain. I do not sit in that chair. It remains Elizabeth's by right. But in her office the atmosphere is suitable for a dreamer who loves to think about the past. It is easy for me to understand how the Academy becomes a take-off pad for many, many things. Of what I hear at the Academy I maintain, of course, my favorite stories of Wisconsin. There are quite a few.

Yet many times I am newly puzzled and intrigued. I hear of strange monsters in lakes; of spirits that inhabit caves; of hills that speak in dark tones of distant mystery.

I hear of natural bridges near Leland, Wisconsin, created by wind and water, say the old Indians because a rainbow had become attached to the earth at both ends. One morning it disappeared and left only the colorless arch of the natural bridge. Again at Rockbridge in Richland County—the natural bridge there was also caused by a rainbow that carried away an Indian maid and left a stone arch in its place; and near Mount Vernon, the retreat of Wakanda, the Earthmaker. And of Indian treasure caves, one in La Crosse County now lost, where an inner chamber was discovered in early days covered with the skeletons of many Indians all lying in one direction toward a sort of altar of stone at one end. And of lovers' leaps, of which there are dozens in Wisconsin: at Maiden Rock where Wenona, beautiful daughter of Red Wing, leapt to her death to avoid marriage to an old man; near Viroqua, named after a lovely Indian maid who sacrificed herself for love of a young Yankee; of Point Jude named after Judith McCloud who jumped off to avoid capture by the Sioux, near Lone Rock; or Roche a Cris in Adams County, or in Peninsula State Park in Door County, or off a bluff near Lynxville . . . all sites where young women made the big leap for love or fear.

I am avid at the Academy, in listening to these and all other strange accounts. The great "elephant" mound that once existed about eight miles south of the mouth of the Wisconsin River, in lowlands near the Eastern bank of the Mississippi, was somewhat obliterated even in 1872 when Reverend S. D. Peet, another curiosity seeker, attempted to measure the mound and to conjecture about its meaning. Was it, indeed, meant to resemble an "elephant" or at least a mastodon? For the figure sketched upon the earth was vast, more than a hundred and thirty feet long, with what the good Reverend was sure was a depending "trunk" or "proboscis". Unfortunately, farmers of the region, eager to produce crops of corn and clover, had worn and scrapped the mound down, and the great effigy bird that spread mighty wings at an unusual angle above the "elephant" was also damaged.

The "elephant" mound was first noted in 1852 by a Dr. Jared Warner of Patch Grove, Wisconsin, and his account was published in the Smithsonian report of 1872. Later, Moses Strong, member of the 1870's Geological Survey of Wisconsin, took measurements in 1876 and confirmed Jared Warner's observations. Strong described the "elephant" mound and its extended trunk as easily visible. Later researchers weren't so sure that the figure had a trunk. They thought the effigy more likely resembled a buffalo; but I have always gone along with Moses Strong who was a wise man. If the effigy was indeed a mammoth or a mastodon, or even an "elephant," then there were very ancient peoples in that part of Wisconsin a long, long while ago.

But such tales and conjectures about an obliterated past are not so unusual if one recalls the tons of copper artifacts created by a people so ancient that we have no real knowledge of them. We know only that their skulls show that they were indeed Indians. Likewise, when one reads the tale in the *Lake Mills Leader* of how a petrified man with the ledge of limestone running through his body was discovered in a quarry near Aztalan in 1903—the stone man broken apart by ignorant workmen swinging stone hammers ... well, something did go on here a long while before the birth of Jesus.

Before the time of Jesus? Well, maybe. The early files of the Academy *Transactions* are filled with conjectures by learned members as to who did actually make the effigy mounds. At first it was widely thought that a special race of human beings made them in the dim ages. But that viewpoint changed. Eventually it became accepted that the builders of the mounds were indeed Indians and that some of the mounds were much older than others. In some mounds, early explorers digging into them found glass beads of European manufacture and remnants of white man's tools. One curious fact, in none of the mound excavations did the early diggers find any of the old copper implements. There were stone tools and weapons but no copper. Dr. Philo Hoy, early Racine physician and amateur bird and artifact collector, said that the copper, then, must have been made after the mounds! This certainly turned around the theory that the copper was the work of a very ancient people. Also Dr. Hoy wrote that he and Increase A.

Lapham, both devoted to expanding knowledge about the new Wisconsin land, found, on a mound near Racine, a great tree growing which, when it blew down and was sawed, was seen to have a blaze near the center, as though an early axeman had made it to mark a trail. Counting the rings backward from the tree's edge, the scientists discovered that that portion of the inner trunk which contained the blaze corresponded in years of growth to the trip through that locality made by Father Hennepin, early French explorer. The tree was about a hundred years old, they thought, when the blaze was cut.

Interesting conjecture, but not very definitive about the age of the mounds, since many of the mounds, when the first settlers arrived, had huge trees growing upon them. Obviously, the mounds were there when the trees started to grow. Joan Freeman, an archeologist for the State Historical Society, told me one morning when I called her after reading Dr. Hoy's account, that now archeologists think the earliest mounds go back only to about 300 A.D., but that the ancient copper could go back to at least 3,000 B.C. Dr. Ed Bruder, Milwaukee dentist, in the 1930s spent night after night taking sightings on the stars to try to show that the effigy mounds in the Horicon Marsh area were the work of a Druid-like people who worshipped the sun and moon, and placed the mounds accordingly. His researches were never adequately published.

The greatest value to me in thinking about the old Indians and the effigy mounds is certainly the sense of mystery I feel in their presence. I never seem to get tired of tracing out the spread of effigy wings, of the body of an animal, or a man. I only know that I am, when I am doing that, part of something that is very old, very mysterious, and very precious.

Regardless of the age of the mounds, copper was mighty important as a commodity used by the ancient Indians, that much is also certain. My folklore-minded friends tell me that very likely Winneboujou, culture hero of the Chippewa tribe, had something to do with the production of copper tools. For Winneboujou, the blacksmith, was an all-powerful manitou. His forge was near the Eau Claire Lakes, in northern Wisconsin. He used the highest flat-topped granite peak for his anvil. Here he shaped the "mis-wa-bik," or native copper of the Brule River region, into various useful weapons and implements. He was especially skillful at shaping the strong copper spear points and fishhooks required for the catching of the giant "sen-e-sug-ge-go," or speckled trout, which abounded in the clear spring waters at the Lake Superior mouth of the Brule.

Much of Winneboujou's forging was done by moonlight and the ringing blows of his "pe-wabik" (iron) hammer were heard by the Indians even as far down the shore of Lake Superior as the Sault Rapids. These booming noises yet echo down the Brule Valley and the lake region, especially on clear, moonlight nights. The glow of his forge fire often lights up the entire sky.

The sound of the smith-manitou's great hammer was considered "good medicine" by the Chippewa, and was held in great awe by the visiting Sioux. An Indian hearing the noise became possessed with industry and strength.

Winneboujou's summer home was on the Brule near its source because it was necessary for him to keep an eye on Ah-mik, the Beaver, a rival manitou, who might, if not watched, slip across the "o-ne-gum" (portage) to the St. Croix River, and then, by the way of the Mississippi River, reach the Gulf.

A great interest I have now in hanging around the Academy is that there, yarns like these can be enjoyed. Glancing once more through the index of the mighty files of the Academy *Transactions,* volumes published each year since 1870, I note even more fascinating subjects all pertinent to Wisconsin: the existence of tides on the Great Lakes, for example, apparently first discovered and proved by an Academy founder, Increase A. Lapham; conjectures by amateur archeologists as to whether there were Indian villages always attached to the locations of the effigy mounds; much writing about the birds of southern and eastern Wisconsin observed and collected by Dr. Philo Hoy between 1855 and 1900; surveys of lakes, fishes, trees, plants; studies of the prairies; of fossils; of geological curiosities; of animal life. So many, many subjects were covered or written about, discussed by these eager and earlier Academy members. Their names boom down the years like the realities of the early state of which they were the founders: Nelson Dewey, first governor; Hercules Dousman, merchant, trader, millionaire; Alexander Mitchell, railroad builder; Morgan Lewis Morgan, lawyer, developer of waterways; Increase A. Lapham, first scientist; Lyman Copeland Draper, historian . . . and on and on. The whole aspect of Wisconsin life was immensely important to them; yet scarcely any of them were "natives." They all arrived from elsewhere. Their personal motives appeared always strong; they were aware of their roots, they transported their heritages to Wisconsin: the songs they sang, the tales they told originated in other regions or nations. And so I feel no hesitation whatever, in trying to explain my own feelings about Wisconsin and to connect them to emotions about other places I have lived, or other motives which sent me forth on missions comparable in spiritual scope at least, to the missions of the Wisconsin pioneers who left us the legacy of what they saw and did.

Since my own advent in Wisconsin was definitely of a "mission" nature, that of a young man inspired to search for an ineffable mystery of the meaning of his life, and of his relationship to American places, of the exploration of his creative urges, conversations about personal motivation and purposes come naturally into my Academy office. Yesterday, Emily Osborn, a talented young woman from Richland County, former publisher of the *Ocooch Mountain News*, herself eager to understand something of the mysterious unfolding of her life, sat with me for an hour and we discussed why we were there, that morning . . . her early roots were in 1940s Indiana; mine in Kansas. I told her briefly of the drive of my father which had sent him forth from Illinois in 1882, searching for the adventure, the lure, the poetic call that the frontier of his day still offered to the young. For the hunger of his questing spirit, he discovered the wild prairie, the untouched western lands which the imaginative historian from Portage, Frederick Jackson Turner, later characterized in his famous "Frontier Thesis," at the Chicago World's Fair in 1893, as the reason for the unique character of America and of American history. As Turner phrased it, the simple availability of land, cheap and for the taking by any person of strength, courage, persistence and perhaps of mission, was the motivating force.

Since the reality of our frontier as a calling and driving force was mostly over by 1890, it then became a chief part of our national folklore to be relived over and over again in many kinds of media. The reality has become the main part and reason for our fantasy with which we have embellished the frontier, and have substituted now for the real drive that opened our western lands, making it necessary for such young spirits as I to search for the meaning of the illusion, which came as aftermath of that drive.

But before I had my "cave" at the Academy I never acquired much time to analyze how I felt about Wisconsin or how and why I was here. As I see it, Wisconsin is country that, in winter, seems etched rather than painted. There are the clear, black lines like wood engravings; the skeletal shapes of trees; hard-to-distinguish beginnings of the shores of lakes under the heavy snows; rivers frozen, with here and there a spell of free water in a channel; the figures of people against the snow at a distance moving slowly and darkly in heavy clothing; children huddled in a small shelter at the crossroads waiting for the school bus . . . and I have followed the busses themselves often, with the children gaping at me out the back windows. . . .

I have wanted to see, to feel the pulse and the tempo; to run with the tides that drive people, to seek through their presents and their pasts. I think I have felt and seen these things but always they have been against the outlines of the land itself; for the call of the earth, whatever season, is mighty. People respond in season to the need to break open the earth, and I have watched the beginnings of spring plowing, and have imagined a farmer's exultation as the first earth spews upward over the moldboard.

I have tried to keep a kind of record of the impressions I received from the Wisconsin land as I have journeyed through it. Wisconsin takes on a light springtime red quite early, as the willow and the low undergrowth begins to quicken, and intimations of the wild itself are there to feel and see. My friend Mark and I drove lately to Sac Prairie to see the bald eagles that winter there, fishing in the Wisconsin River below the dam. The river was open, though it had been very cold, but swinging in the blue sky was one of the great birds, and dangling from its leg was some object, we couldn't tell what, until a woman standing near us at the rail above the river near the Firehouse Restaurant, said it was a steel trap. We could recognize it then, knew what it was, and thought we could see the chain. Mark said, "The chain will surely snarl." And I thought, with horror, of that magnificent bird, dying, held by the leg, the chain caught in the fork of a branch, jawed by an animal trap. I couldn't abide the thought and said to Mark, "Let's go."

We drove down Water Street to the Wisconsin bridge in Sauk City, and Mark said we'd ease on down the river, on west. And there we saw near the railroad trestle that

Augie Derleth wrote about so often, another eagle in an oak tree on the further bank. We walked across on the trestle and came softly up on the bird. He let us get quite near, perhaps only fifty yards away before he went in flight, upwards in a mighty thrust, and I marveled at his size and strength. He seemed indeed the spirit of the whole state. I said this to Mark and he replied, "Except when we trap them."

Man in Wisconsin is nature's child. I dwell in memory on those who came here when the land was unbroken and had an awed sense of the primitive which we will never now possess. But our activities upon the land are still a celebration of God and man, for it is nature that man celebrates best. His celebrations are in honor of the forgotten primitiveness, and of his own muted feelings of land, of sky, of water, birds and plants. He approaches the small lake with reverence; he watches the goose flight in the sky; sees insects gathering and air dancing in evening places. He regards small flowers with amazement, and in celebrations he signals the seasons. He draws to himself the symbols of reverence: country roads and bright weeds in ditches; morning glories at the end of cornrows; mysterious circles in backwaters; woods' trails that animals have furrowed; chipped stone, drawn by rain out of dark earth; blue glaciers fantastically recalled. Man must revere. The protector must revere, watch over waterways, hold court with conscience. Man in Wisconsin is nature's child. In memory of those who came here when the land was new: preserve, protect. Protect, preserve.

I constantly live in a multitude of sensations as I drive through the state . . . and always these sensitive reactions are placed against a background of earth and people. I conversed once in a dust-odorous library of rare books at Mineral Point. The library was the second floor of a sandstone Cornish miner's dwelling. Robert Neal had collected the books from the area, as through the years he and Edgar Hellum rebuilt several old stone houses. An impression of the books, of old maps, an odor faintly exuded from the root cellar dug into the stone hillside, has stayed with me. A complex atmosphere. I carried the setting and the odors away in my memory, and they are with me now, as are the moments I have spent in Neal's and Hellum's garden behind the Pendarvis House, with a thread of clear summer water seeping down ancient stone walls and into a collecting pool where there were many bright-colored fish.

When you lay it all on, the hues of the landscape in winter, in spring and summer, and in fall. When you lay it all on with sights more intimately connected with habitation, with animals, with cowbarns and the slow shifting of heavy bodies in half-night; with jingling chains and clanking irons; with rustling dry hay; with odor of silage; and you mingle these smells and sounds with those of a farm kitchen when the work outside is done and there is a little space of warmth and of set clothing removed . . . a trickle of moisture from boots standing at the door; a woman, children, voices, food: an open book here and there. A pipe. Or perhaps it is of a church basement on a Sunday morning; I, listening from above, in a stairwell, to child voices murmuring, and then a sudden far bell, and a clashing of metal chairs and steps on cement, running. . . . It is memory, memory. . . . Yes, it is memory, and memory is transportable. How easy to go from a sensitivity to a rural Wisconsin . . . across fifty years to a rural Kansas morning. The years are as nothing. The woven fabric is everything.

The Leaving

From our farmhouse in eastern Kansas it was about three miles into Iola, the County seat, and the road was all country. Off the road, on both sides, were hundreds of places where I had rambled so many, many times. For instance, back up Elm Creek about a mile was a cave in the limestone ledge where old John Brown was supposed to have hidden out in the days just before the Civil War, and sometimes a gang of kids from town played John Brown and the Missourians, because the ruffians from Missouri were after him for killing some of their folks; and there was another place still further up the hill from the cave where Jesse James was supposed to have had a hideout. I reflected on the good times I'd had playing around there when I was younger, and I supposed I'd never think of John Brown or Jesse James again.

One thing I knew I would sure miss, though, were the wild roses which were just beginning to bloom. There absolutely isn't any flower that I have ever seen that I like as much as wild roses. I guess I got my liking for flowers from Mom, because she always told me how her father had made the very first flowerbed in their part of eastern Kansas (Bourbon County), because he thought his neighbors ought to be able to see some beautiful flowers, set out like they did it in the East.

Along the way, Dad and I didn't say anything to each other; though I could tell that he was about bursting to talk. I didn't want him telling me what to do and how to act. Now that I was going, I wanted to do it the way I saw it. And I guess he understood how I felt, because he kept still. The road winded up to the top of a little hill, and we could see the clock steeple of the Allen County courthouse. A shaft of early sunlight was striking it, and it looked awfully big and impressive, rising up in the middle of a collection of low buildings and small houses. The courthouse had always seemed to me like the biggest building in the world, and once when Dad and I climbed up to the windows where the clock was, I felt as if I could look out over the whole country. In fact, it seemed like I was looking at the whole world.

The courthouse was a red brick building, square, with a tall steeple and big clock. All around the courthouse square was four-inch pipe railing. In older days, quite a while before I was born, they had struck a big field of natural gas all around Iola, and there was a kind of boom-time which Dad told us how as a young lawyer he helped to start. They eventually piped the gas into this railing around the park, boring holes every six feet or so. Every night, all night long, the lighted gas flared from the holes. Dad said it was a symbol of the vast wealth of the earth which Allen County folks figured would last forever. They wanted people everywhere to know how rich Allen County was, and how they were going to stay that way; but when the gas suddenly petered out the railing became just a hitching place for horses.

As we rolled up to the courthouse square the big clock began to strike six. I tooled the Overland around the south side of the square, and noticed there wasn't a single person in sight. The birds were beginning to sing in the great old Elms planted in the park, and that was the only sound. We came around the east side and saw a Model T Ford coupe parked near the old horse water trough. Though not many horses drank there these days, the trough was kept full of water. The town board wanted to remove the trough, but the folks in Iola still felt sentimental about the old days and wouldn't let them.

The Model T was an old one, about a '23 or '24 model I thought, and it was as dirty as it could have been. There was even chicken manure on the hood and top, because Zill had probably parked it under a tree where the chickens roosted by his shack. The body of those old model T's was very high, as if they had sat a high box on a little raft and then had put on a low turtle in the back and a small, low hood in the front. One of the windows on the driver's side was busted, too.

Zill and Harry were waiting on a bench beside the water trough. They looked about like the car, sort of unwashed and partly hooked-up. Zill, the biggest, had only one suspender of his overalls hooked, and Harry looked bashed-up some with a scar over his right eye. They were clean *enough*, I guess, but just sort of casual. They wore straw hats, the working kind, with big brims. The first thing that Zill said was, "Hey, kid, where's your hat at?"

I never knew how to take Zill. He had a reputation for being mean. I'd seen him hanging around town a lot, and everybody knew he was a bootlegger, but there were plenty of them then on the square on a Saturday. He was smiling now in a funny, snotty way, as he and Harry got up and came over to our car.

"I ain't met this kid," Harry said. He stuck his hand into the Overland and we shook. "He's a right big guy, ain't he?"

"Going to jam us up in the Ford," Zill said. "Well, hell, we been cramped up before. Well, get your stuff, kid. We got to be moving." I got out and removed my valise from the Overland's backseat. Dad moved over into the driver's seat. So far he hadn't said anything. But now he did.

"Where you headed, Zill?"

"Damned if I know, Sam."

"Well," Dad said, "this boy is a hard worker. But he don't know a damned thing."

I got hot in the face and wanted to answer Dad back and to tell him that I knew a hell of a lot more than he thought I did, but I didn't say anything because it would have been embarrassing. Anyhow, I didn't know what it was he thought I didn't know anything about. I knew our farm about as well as he did, and could do about everything he could do, and some things, like taking care of machinery, I did a lot better than he did.

"Bob don't know a damn thing about being alone," Dad said.

"Well I be dang," Harry said.

"You don't know a damn thing, kid," Zill said. I just didn't like the way he said it, like he was trying to imitate or mock Dad, but I didn't reply to him. I did begin to get mad, though, down inside.

"We'll try to teach him something about that, Sam," Zill said.

"You teach him what to do when he's alone. Nobody to help him," Dad said.

"Sure. We'll do that. We'll teach him a lot of tricks."

Zill sure knew tricks. The year before, when he was about to get arrested for bootlegging, the sheriff came to his place to find the still he was using. Only that same night Zill hauled the still into town and put it on the front lawn of the judge's house, so they never did get the evidence on him. Anyway, what Zill did caused the judge to take a lot of joshing, and everybody knew Zill was the one who left the still, but they were never able to catch him. Dad seemed to think it was quite humorous.

"The kid know anything about gals," Harry said.

"I don't suppose so," Dad said. "But it's probably time he learned something." He took his hand outof his pocket and held out a bill to Zill. "Here's ten dollars. When you figure you've run out about that much, kick Bob out. I want him to know what it is to be on his own."

"Ten bucks, ten miles," Harry said.

"Here's two bucks for you boy," Dad said, and shoved the bills into my hand. "That's a dollar more than I had when I started out. A dollar was hard for my mother to get then, and it isn't much easier today. Damn, I wish I was going with you."

Dad opened the car door and got out and stood there with the car door open, and by the look that was coming on his face I knew that he was about to say something that'd sound pretty strange to Zill and Harry. To me he seemed like he was in the grass a couple of nights before; but to strangers Dad would probably sound kinda crazy. I shifted around and started for the Ford's door, but Dad had started to talk and it was too late.

"I want to go myself. Look at me, boys. I came to the tall grass and went into it . . . yes, in those days you could grab a big armfull around you. It was that tall. Ride a horse into it you couldn't hardly see the horse at all. And then we tore it open, boys. We tore it open for the heavens to wet down our corn. And we raised some crops, I tell you. And you should have seen the prairies when I come here. You never seen anything like the prairie flowers. Prairie violets, alumroot, them shooting stars, and that tall blue stuff, that indigo, and the roses, the little wild ones, they were everywhere. Oh it was a sight. And it was mine. I came into it and made it mine, boys."

I looked at Zill and Harry to see how they were taking Dad and what he was saying, and they were sure paying close attention, I will say that. Zill had his mouth about half open, and Harry's eyes were wide and big. I guess they'd never in their life heard anybody talking about how pretty wild flowers were . . . at least not right out loud. Folks in our part of Kansas didn't say much about pretty things, and one farmer we all knew, who lived away south of us in the river bottoms, had his wife put in the insane asylum at Osawatomie because she tried to write some poems. That's the way it was, mostly. Women folks were supposed to do whatever fixing up there was done, but the men didn't mess into that kind of thing — flowers and all that. It wasn't supposed to be manly. Dad was that way, too. I mean, the men were supposed to have all the big ideas, and do all the adventuring. Dad wondered why Mom didn't sew more, and do women stuff, but he sure didn't object to her coming out to the barn to help with the milking. But whatever he thought he sure loved to rant away about the way things looked . . . always through his eyes, of course.

"You own all this country once?" Zill asked Dad, mocking.

"No. I didn't have to own it. It was mine because I understood what kind of country it was. And I got my plow into it. That was when I made it belong to me." Zill tried to act kind of unconcerned, but he was interested, I could see that. He kept looking at Dad, and the two guys edged over toward the Ford, and Zill said he guessed we'd better be going. The far-away look disappeared from Dad's eyes, and he came and actually shook my hand.

"There ain't much left for you here, boy. Better you go, and I'll be here when you come back home. Guess you'll know where to look for me. And find the Stranger for me, boy!" And when he said "Stranger" he gave me a special look, as if he and I had a secret.

I knew where Dad would be all right, and that was where I sure *would* look when I came home. Just then I could still feel the tall grass out there in the prairie when I went looking for him, and the sound of the wind combing through it. I knew, though, I wouldn't find any Stranger, whoever that was. And probably no grass, either.

"You set in the center, kid," Harry said. "If you was to see a gal along the road you might jump right out the winder. Then you wouldn't likely see Bob again," he said to Dad. "This kid will give the women hell."

I edged in, sliding over on the torn seat.

"You come looking for me," Dad said to me, "I'll be here waitin' for your voice."

Well, you know how it is. Sometimes you get a kind of flash all at once, and I got one right then. I knew Dad cared a lot about me. He looked like he was going to cry. As I got settled in the car and turned away, Dad just stood there with his hand on the Overland's door. Anyway, that was all we said to each other.

Zill had taken my valise and put it into the turtle at the Ford's back. I heard the turtle door slam down, and Zill came around and cranked the Ford, yelling at me to pull on the wire that goosed her, and she caught, finally. Zill got under the Ford's wheel while Harry squeezed in beside me. It was a tight fit, too. I took up quite a bit of the seat and Zill was about as big as I was. Harry was smaller, and we had him smashed into the side. It was a good thing the weather was warm and the windows could be wide open, because we would never have made it in that Ford Coupe. Harry groaned and swore and Zill and I squirmed around until we got fairly comfortable. We were like sardines in a can.

Zill pressed down on the reverse foot pedal and the old coupe rolled slowly backwards, popping and snorting a cloud of blue smoke. I didn't really think we would make it to the corner of the square, but the Ford took ahold in a moment and we were off. I twisted around a little so I could get a last look at the square, and maybe of Dad. I saw him standing there, still with his hand on the Overland door, and he never waved or anything, but I didn't expect him to. That wasn't the way he did things. I had a kind of funny feeling leaving Iola, and the square, and I thought of the many times I'd walked around on a Saturday night when almost everybody was in town. There was usually a band concert on Saturday night, but I didn't hear the music much. The old folks had their cars parked up close to the railing, and when the band finished a number they would honk their horns. The young ones, though, walked around, looking for girls or boys who might make a date or go for a ride if there was a car. I had our Overland sometimes, and I occasionally hauled a load of kids around the square, yelling and honking. I looked back one more time, and I saw that Dad had come out into the middle of the street and was gazing after us. I pretty near made Zill stop so I could get out of the Ford and go back. Seeing Dad there affected me that much. Little did I know then that as I left home and started my odyssey, that one day it would lead me to Wisconsin.

Innocence or Guilt?

Who were they who came early to the Wisconsin land as they did to Kansas; heroes in their imaginations, crusaders against a primitive innocence of grass and trees?

They broke open the wild prairie with oxen and an iron plow. They were the iron-ringers shouting: "Iron on iron! Rock on rock! Iron on iron! Rock on rock!" They cried: "Here it is! This land, this valley, this hill, this link of woods is ours!" And they named the prairies for far places: Empire and Arlington; for star and sun; for Indian legends; for women; for joyous heart, or a human dream.

There was innocence in their joy. They thrust deeply into the warm, virgin womb of earth, planting, planting more and more. And with joy and with fury they tore open the primitive sod with oxen and an iron plow; they, the Iron-ringers. Their shares laid over the ribbons of severed roots, and turned under the yellow sunflower, buttercup, lobelia, the blue lead plant. Laid under the ribbons were the aster, the indigo and the star grasses.

And they chanted their dual hymns of religion and of work; work was often their religion, a glorious effort of despoilation and innocence. Above the severed prairie grew the grains; the trees uprooted burned through the nights; the wild land became transformed and wild waterbirds nested no longer on prairie wetlands. The pigeon flocks that once obscured the sun were there no longer, and a victory over an innocence had been won, an elemental conflict resolved.

They had no sense of violation, for home and family are concepts of the innocent. They had joy in the clear waters flowing through time; in valley springs and hillside brooks.

They discovered the crystal flood rushing from old springs, through white sand basins and amid crisp watercress. Pure water was violated only by the bend and thirst of those who revered pure, cold water; yet the waters stopped their innocent flow.

We who now look backward see clearly the beginning of the violation; when the grand passage of the ducks was no longer; when the Whooping Crane was not seen; when the Bald Eagles flew less and less, and the rivers grew dark with slime, and a cruel darkness emerged in the brain of man. We see an irony that the innocent violated the innocence.

For those who came to the land desired only freedom and work. Simple desires—to create, to build and to have a home. They were innocent of malice. See how many of the innocent lie in old cemeteries; their names on worn stones tell of an early passing. How it was when an epidemic of typhoid swept the new country, creeping into and through the cabins where a child lay gasping, and a woman bent above a pallet; and in the dooryard a man hidden in the night tensely waited listening for the sound of a physician's horse on a valley trail. Far, far too often it came too late, and the innocent one passed from typhoid or diphtheria. And at times the smallpox swept the land and there was no stopping it. The cemeteries tell little but the names are on fragmented stone and we must guess how the innocent died.

The names of many young mothers are there; they who died of overwork, and of disease, and in childbirth. The innocent labored to violate the land, yet they had no knowledge of evil. Of love they knew much and followed into danger and grief and left a spell of their innocence which lies still as a quality over the Wisconsin land. There is love in an atmosphere of old farmhouses, of ancient lilacs, and of small, rotting cabins at the edge of a wood. It was near such places that young mothers in the innocence of their young lives laughed and played with young children in the wild grass; who heard the birds, felt the wind, and played in grasses soft as cotton.

Once in early days a beautiful young woman arrived with her young husband on the Wisconsin frontier. They had few objects of their own, and their home was a primitive cabin. There was endless labor, little food, but worst for her was the loneliness. There were no other people, no neighbors, no other women. Day by day she grew more desolate. Then she became bitter and told him that she was leaving; she'd return to her

Eastern home. She wanted gentle things; music, poetry, but most of all a sense that he understood her loneliness and her hungers. He worked only in the woods and fields. What could he ever give her? What priceless gift that would feed her soul? Sadly he watched her preparations to go. He went finally, desperately, to the nearby clear spring and brought a pail of fresh water. As he placed the pail on the earth, the moon glimmered in the pail and he said, "But look, Lucy, I brung you the moon."

But though there was a quality of innocence in the experience of the pioneers, I think of those things that are no more. Sadly, the passenger pigeon is gone. The sound of their wings will never again mutter across the Wisconsin skies; the cloud of their passage will never again shade field or forest. One senior Academy member, Otis Bersing, stopped by my office one day and showed me how the settlers and hunters of the early days trapped passenger pigeons. Otis sketched out how a large net might be fastened to two springy, bent-down, young saplings. The net was also fastened to the earth at the other side, then flung loose by a trigger, and, sailing forward, would then trap hundreds and hundreds of the beautiful birds feeding on mast on the ground. Trapped under the net the pigeon's cruel slaughter began. Thumb and forefinger crushed the skulls of bird after bird.

Passenger pigeons did not perish from want of food, nor from the disasters of nature. The pigeon perished by the hand of man. Man alone is responsible for their extinction. An army of the greedy and the wasteful extinguished them; they shot, netted, destroyed, and the bird was finally gone. The last Wisconsin passenger pigeon was said to be shot near Babcock in September, 1899. Not long ago I was visiting the Hoard Museum at Fort Atkinson. There, I stood before one of the very few remaining mounted specimens of the passenger pigeon. As I contemplated the beautiful birds, Hannah Swart, curator of the Museum, said to me ... "this mounted specimen, one of a very few, is now worth more than $4,000." And I thought; how sad, how terribly sad, that our pioneers were themselves, in their striving, and their non-understanding of conservation, responsible for what happened. And I remember what Aldo Leopold said when the monument to the passenger pigeon was unveiled at Wyalusing State Park on the Mississippi River.

"We meet here," said Leopold, "to commemorate the death of a species. This monument symbolizes our sorrow. We grieve because no living man will see again the onrushing phalanx of victorious birds, sweeping a path for spring across the March skies, chasing the defeated winter from all the woods and prairies of Wisconsin.

"Men still live who, in their youth, remember pigeons; trees still live that, in their youth, were shaken by a living wind. But a few decades hence only the oldest oaks will remember, and at long last only the hills will know.

"There will always be pigeons in books and in museums, but these are effigies and images, dead to all hardships and to all delights. Book-pigeons cannot dive out of a cloud to make the deer run for cover, nor clap their wings in thunderous applause of mast-laden woods. They know no urge of seasons; they feel no kiss of sun, no lash of wind and weather; they live forever by not living at all.

"Our grandfathers, who saw the glory of the fluttering hosts, were less well-housed, well-fed, well-clothed than we are. The strivings by which they bettered our lot are also those which deprived us of pigeons. Perhaps we now grieve because we are not sure, in our hearts, that we have gained by the exchange.

"It is a century now since Darwin gave us the first glimpse of the origin of species. We know now what was unknown to all the preceding caravan of generations: that man is only a fellow-voyager with other creatures in the odyssey of evolution, and that his captaincy of the adventuring ship conveys the power, but not necessarily the right, to discard at will among the crew. We should, in the century since Darwin, have achieved a sense of community with living things, and of wonder over the magnitude and duration of the biotic enterprise.

"For one species to mourn the death of another is a new thing under the sun. The Cro-Magnon who slew the last mammoth thought only of steaks. The sportsman who shot the last pigeon thought only of his prowess. The sailor who clubbed the last auk thought of nothing at all. But we, who have lost our pigeons, mourn the loss. Had the funeral been ours, the pigeons would hardly have mourned us. In this fact, rather than in Mr. Vandevar Bush's bombs, or Mr. DuPont's nylons, lies objective evidence of our superiority over the beasts.

"We who erect this monument are performing a dangerous act. Because our sorrow is genuine, we are tempted to believe that we had no part in the demise of the pigeon. The truth is that our grandfathers, who did the actual killing, were our agents. They were our agents in the sense that they shared the conviction, which we have only now begun to doubt, that it is more important to multiply people and comforts than to cherish the beauty of the land in which they live. What we are doing here today is publicly to confess a doubt whether this is true.

"This, then, is a monument to a bird we have lost, and to a doubt we have gained. Perched like a duck hawk on this cliff, it will scan this wide valley, watching through the days and years. For many a March it will watch the geese go by, telling the river about clearer, colder, lonelier waters on the tundra. For many an April it will see the redbuds come and go, and for many a May the flush of oak-blooms on a thousand hills. Questing wood ducks will search these basswoods for hollow limbs; golden prothonotaries will shake the golden pollen from the river-willows. Egrets will pose on these sloughs in August, plovers will whistle from September skies, hickory nuts will plop into October leaves, and hail will rattle in November woods. But no pigeons will pass, for there are no pigeons, save only this flightless one, graven in bronze on this rock. Tourists will read this inscription, but their thoughts, like the bronze pigeon, will have no wings.

"We are told by economic moralists that to mourn the pigeon is mere nostalgia; that if the pigeoneers had not done away with him, the farmers would ultimately have been obliged, in self-defense, to do so. Perhaps this is true, but perhaps it is also true that we did away with an idea, as well as a bird. It is one of the ironies of science that it discovers, *ex post facto*, a philosophical significance in what it has previously tossed into the dust-bin.

"The pigeon was no mere bird, he was a biological storm. He was the lightning that played between two biotic poles of intolerable intensity: the fat of the land and his own zest for living. Yearly the feathered tempest roared up, down, and across the continent, sucking up the laden fruits of forest and prairie, burning them in a travelling blast of life. Like any other chain-reaction, the pigeon could survive no diminution of his own furious intensity. Once the pigeoneers had subtracted from his numbers, and once the settlers had chopped gaps in the continuity of his fuel, his flame guttered out with hardly a sputter or even a wisp of smoke.

"Today the laden oaks still flaunt their burden at the

sky, but the feathered lightning is no more. Worm and weevil must now perform slowly and silently the biological task which once drew thunder from the firmament. The wonder is not that the pigeon passed out, but that he ever survived through all the millennia of pre-Babbitian time.

"The pigeon lived by his desire for clustered grape and bursting beechnut, and by his contempt of miles and seasons. Things that Wisconsin did not offer him today he sought and found tomorrow in Michigan, or Labrador, or Tennessee; to find them required only the free sky, and the will to ply his wings.

"But there are fruits in this land unknown to pigeons, and as yet to most men. Perhaps we too can live by our desires to find them, and by a contempt for miles and seasons, a love of free sky, and a will to ply our wings. . . ."

It was our innocent ancestors who slew the pigeons and raped this virgin land in their effort to provide a "better life" for those of us who followed. But now as I listen to the wind across the prairie or grasp the soil between my fingers, I believe that I can almost hear the old pioneers recanting their actions, whispering softly, but audibly, "Preserve the land, conserve all species—do *not* blindly follow our questionable ways."

THE LESSON

Cramped into the old Ford Coupe, Zill, Harry and I crossed the Neosho River bridge on that Kansas June 1930's morning and headed west, the old car bumping and rocking on the gravel road. Along the way there weren't any sizable towns to speak of, in fact no towns of any kind except a "crossroads" which Dad said had at one time been a lot larger. Nearby was a hill that we thought was awfully high and hard to get up, especially since the Ford almost didn't make the Picqua Hill earlier. Zill and Harry kept whooping and hollering for the Ford to stay with it and she did, coughing and sputtering and blowing blue smoke, up to the top. It was about the only hill anywhere around and beyond the hill the land flattened out and ran for a long ways, with nothing more than a few little ripples here and there. Once the prairie grass had grown tall out there, but it was plow broken now . . . all broken, Dad said, and after hearing him talk I got a kind of new feeling about the flat land, and as we were bounding around and holding onto anything we could reach to keep our heads from hitting the top of the Ford, I wondered what it would have been like to have been rolling out in a covered wagon. Mom had actually ridden into Kansas from Missouri in a covered wagon, and she used to tell us how it felt, but I never had given it much thought. Probably a lot more comfortable than a Model T Ford coupe on a hot morning in June, crowded, and on a rough gravel road.

"You got some hard muscles kid," Harry said, and his fingers probed around on my upper arm. I suppose I made my biceps hard, too, maybe to show Harry that I did have hard muscles and that he'd better be careful. But he said, "Got a arm like a horse's leg. Ain't this kid got hard muscles, Zill?"

We were pounding along pretty good now having thumped through Yates Center. It wasn't a very big place, but it was the county seat, and I had never been over there before. That's how close we stayed at home in those Kansas days. Harry still had hold of my arm and I squirmed around, hoping that he'd let go. But he didn't.

"Ever done any wrestling, kid?" Zill asked.

"Just played around with it at home. Nothing much."

"Any kid of Old Sam's 'd be a good wrestler," Zill said. "Ol' Sam usta own all this country once."

I didn't answer for a moment. I knew they were kidding me, but even so I hadn't ever heard anybody say anything mocking about Dad. It really shocked me.

"What do you mean?"

"Mean about what, kid?"

"What you said about Dad."

"About ownin' all this country? Why he was braggin' himself about how he come out here . . ."

I made a violent move. I was really upset. They were just poking fun at me to get my goat. I'd been kidded plenty of times before and it didn't bother me. But I guess I was sensitive about Dad and his way of talking.

Harry eased up on my arm. It was real hot, and I was sweating. I had never felt so uncomfortable. I wanted to get out of their car, but I didn't see how I could manage it.

"Ol' Sam never told you nothin' about his gal friends, either, I bet," Harry said.

"Dad didn't have any girl friends," I said.

"Hell, everybody does, kid. An' they'll get you into trouble. I was shot in the rear over a old gal I knowed down by Coffeyville. Usta hear it said that bird shot didn't hurt none when it went into you. Heard it was goin' too fast to hurt. That's a lie, buddy."

"Ever been shot, kid?" asked Zill.

"Nope."

"Well, you got a lot of time."

"Birdshot hurts aplenty when it goes into your rear," Harry said.

Harry slewed around and got hold of my arm again. I decided that maybe he felt more comfortable when he was talking, if he had hold of something. I let him go on holding my arm.

Suddenly, Harry let out a loud whoop and grabbed

me hard. I pretty near broke my head on the car roof. I guess I hollered and slammed over against Zill and he almost lost control of the Ford. It ran off the road and into some weeds in the ditch. But the ditch wasn't deep and Zill swung the car back, skidding across the gravel. I was scared and didn't know whether to laugh or be mad. I didn't know why they wanted to tease me like they were doing, and nobody had ever grabbed me sudden like that before. Never.

I got hold of Harry's hand while the car was skidding around. Zill swore and hollered for us to set still, and the Ford straightened out for a moment, then she started sidewise again and corkscrewed down the gravel. Zill yelled and tried to get his foot onto the brake pedal, but my feet were in the way. The old car was gaining speed because Zill had forgotten to shove the hand gas-feed up. In all the excitement I near broke Harry's hand. He yelled real loud when I twisted it back. I was so upset I didn't know what I was doing, really. It all happened very fast. I've never been one to make really fast adjustments. I was a strong, country boy in those days, and I must have really put the pressure on Harry because he yelled in misery. Zill finally got his foot onto the brake and coughed the Ford down to a stop right in the middle of the road. I held onto Harry's hand. I wasn't going to let him grab me again.

"Zill," Harry yelled, "Help! He's bustin' my hand!"

Heavy dust and blue exhaust smoke caught up to us and came in through the windows. I could feel the sweat run down my armpits and down along my sides. We were really packed in there, I tell you, and I wouldn't let go of Harry's hand. It was about the only security I had. As long as I had hold of Harry, he wasn't going to do anything, but I sure couldn't see how it was all going to end. I was getting scared, and I wondered whether I had made a mistake by not going ahead and taking it all in good humor. But I knew that I had gone too far now.

"I'll twist Harry's hand clear off if he doesn't let me alone."

"Zill, make the kid let me go. He's made a figger eight outten my wrist."

"Now hold on a minute," Zill said, grinning. "Bob has got somethin' special comin'. Old Sam told us we got to teach him some things."

He sprung open the door and it squealed a little on rusty hinges. That coupe had a ruffled old pocket stitched onto the side of the door and Zill reached in there and took out a pint of stuff I guess was moonshine liquor. He pulled the cork with his teeth, took a long, long pull and breathed out hard. He stood looking into the car, grinning, and I hadn't realized until then how big he was, and I hadn't noticed how heavy his beard was ... like he hadn't shaved for three or four days. I hadn't noticed that at all before.

He reached in under my feet and pulled out a tire-iron, the busted piece of spring that was used so much in those old days to change tires. After you got the wheel jacked up you had to get one of those irons in under the tire and pry it off of the rim. I watched Zill spit and heft the iron and I knew what was coming. I really bore down on Harry's arm and he hollered fit to bust. Then Zill rapped me pretty hard across the toes with the tire iron.

"Get out, Bob." He looked really cheerful, but he hit me hard, anyhow.

My foot hurt and I was gasping with pain. I didn't know how or what to reply to Zill. He was standing there in the road holding the tire iron, and I didn't know what he would do. I sure didn't want to get hit across the head with it; things had gone a lot further than just teasing.

"I won't."

"Yes you are, too. Get outta there. You and me are goin' to have a little scuffle."

"I don't want to fight."

"Get out or I'll break your leg, Bobby."

I could see that he would really do it. He had a funny look on his face. Everybody knew he enjoyed hitting people. I slowly let go of Harry, who began to fumble for the door latch. I slid under the steering wheel since I knew I had to get out. I thought probably Zill would start hitting me with the tire iron as I was getting out, and I wondered how I could do it fast enough. I stuck my feet out first but Zill didn't do anything, so I came all the way out of the car and stood there on the running board, quite a bit above him, because the running board on those old Fords was pretty high.

The weeds in the ditch were quiet in the heat. The sun was beating down, and the whole scene, the Ford in the middle of the road, Zill standing there grinning and feeling the tire iron, and me standing up high on the running board, the whole thing was laughable almost, though nobody laughed, and Harry kept groaning on about his twisted wrist. He would mutter a few swear words then give out a loud groan. He was really overdoing it, because I was sure I hadn't hurt him.

I asked Zill, "What you want me to do?"

"Get on offa there, Bob. You'n me are goin' to wrestle. I ain't had a good wrestle-match for a long spell."

"You give ol' Bob a good lesson, Zill," Harry hollered. "You give it to 'im good. He needs a good hurting. You do it to him for me and for his ol' man."

I had never thought about Dad giving me that kind of a lesson. He had never laid a finger on me. Ever. But he had abandoned me to Zill and Harry. Maybe he did want it their way. Or maybe it just got out of hand.

"We can't wrestle in the middle of the road."

"Why not?"

"A car or something might come along."

"What do I care?"

Zill tossed the tire-iron down in the gravel and put up his hands. The heat was wavering across the fields in front of me, the way it does in Kansas, and away down the road I could see some dust rising, another car, maybe. I had plenty of reason to be mad, but I wasn't mad, exactly. I just knew that I didn't want to have any trouble with Zill. He was making a sucking sound, sucking on his lips, just waiting for me to get down so he could bust me. I never thought twice then about what I was going to do. Something just took over, that was all. I jumped into the air and kicked out at Zill's face, and my right shoe popped him on the jaw. It must have been a lot harder than I had meant it to be, if I meant to hit him at all, because he fell over backwards, sprawled out on the gravel; and I was so shocked that I was right on top of him. His straw cady came off and I grabbed his hair and pulled him over onto his face. I got a hammerlock, or what it was around home we called a hammerlock, when you bend an opponent's arm up behind at the elbow and keep lifting until the other guy hollers. It wasn't a real legitimate wrestling hold, but I didn't have the time to think about that. I guess I pushed it up pretty hard because Zill hollered loud. He turned his head over and to my surprise spit out some blood. It was the first time I had ever drawn blood out of anybody. It didn't give me any pleasure. It was kind of terrible, actually, but I had to hold onto him. I knew that if he got up, if I let him go, he would come after me, and he just might kill me as he had several people in fights. Harry shuffled near us now, sort of circling around, and I guessed that in a minute I'd have two of them to fight. Maybe then I'd have to take off running across the country to get away from them.

"What'll I do, Zill," Harry yelled.

"Pick up a rock and whack him."

Harry couldn't find a rock. He must have been looking for one, but the road gravel pieces were too little. So he limped over to where the tire iron was and picked that up. He started towards me, and I put a lot of leverage on Zill's arm again. He hollered real loud and scrabbled around in the road trying to break my hold, but I held him desperately. I must have come pretty close to breaking his arm and I yelled at Harry, "If you come after me I'll bust his arm off!"

Harry stopped and Zill swore louder than ever. There we were in a nice little standoff. Harry could have busted me with the tire iron and maybe I wouldn't have had time to really break Zill's arm, but Harry wasn't too bright and probably never thought of doing that. He just stood there, and I kept on straddling Zill and holding his arm. None of us heard the old Buick touring car, loaded with sacks of bran, coming up on us from the east side. The car stopped behind the Ford and an old Kansas farmer got out and came up and stood alongside me and Zill. He just stood there for a little while chewing tobacco and looking down at us. Finally he spit out some juice.

"What in hades is going on?"

"This kid's busting Zill's arm," Harry yelled, hopping around.

"What you want to bust his arm for?" the farmer asked.

"They jumped me in the car. It wasn't my fault."

"He busted my hand," Harry said.

"Yeah. And what were you doing to me? I should have killed you."

"We was giving you some lessons. Like your ol' man said."

"He never meant that way."

Harry limped around behind me, and I put some more pressure on Zill's arm. I was even afraid that I would bust it, and I suppose Zill thought so too, because he hollered and cussed and flopped around in the road. But I had helped Dad and others handle big hogs many times, holding them down, or helping load them into a dealer's truck to take to market. I knew something about holding onto a struggling animal, and that's what I was doing to Zill. I guess the little bit of wrestling I'd done helped, too.

Harry edged up closer to me, holding the tire-iron, and I tried to look around at him, to watch what he was doing. When I turned around, Harry jumped back a piece. But he didn't stay there. Zill kept yelling for Harry to do something, and before I could let go of Zill and tackle Harry, he came up behind me again. Harry swung the iron at me and I dodged it. He hit Zill on the shoulder, instead of me. That caused more hollering, and it might have been funny, except we were all too busy to laugh, especially when Harry came up fast again and swung the iron at me. It hit me across the side of the head. I saw a lot of stars and shooting lights. I must have let go of Zill and fallen over in the road. That's the last I knew until I came to, and I was lying in the road. The old farmer was bending down over me.

Of This World and The Land

E ven as the pioneers left a vestige of their innocence in the alteration of the land and the destruction of the pigeons, so the peoples of Europe left their own kinds of flavors and heritage in the fulfillment of their own personal and nationality quests. The stories I have absorbed from countless Wisconsin residents compete with my own personal adventures, for the early Wisconsin settlers from far away places also "came home" to Wisconsin. Much of my time has gone toward the support and creation of a literary tradition to preserve this precious heritage, a task which has created in me a deep and abiding admiration for the people who struggled through the transformation of this land.

And it was indeed a transformation. What Wisconsin is today is not very much like it once was. Wisconsin was essentially a rural state even though many settlers filtered through Milwaukee. But now the prairie is gone. The Indians are no longer lords of the wilderness. Immense highways obliterate the ancient trails. And the look across the land is filled more with industry and large harvesting and tilling machines than with hard, primitive, human struggle. The story of this transformation is epic in magnitude, and while it is essentially a tale of common folk who had a vision of how it should happen, the essence of the physical transformation is actually two-sided. On one side is the European tradition marked by sturdiness, patience, and hard work. On the other side is the Yankee tradition—ingenious, durable, and inventive. Although the two combined to make Wisconsin rich in tradition, lore, and talent, each has left its own distinctive mark upon the face of the land and its history.

I believe that the people who came to Wisconsin from Europe were for the most part people of small means, small education, but with a burning desire for freedom and opportunity in their hearts. They embarked to America from many foreign ports, came in family groups, or neighborhood or religious associations, or even were gathered together by occupation. For the most part they had two things in mind: to better themselves and their conditions and to find land. They brought with them a few choice household articles, an occasional favorite agricultural implement, and old chests packed with clothing and whatever small wealth they had. The women often carried babies or guided small children, and the old people were usually left behind in the old country.

Since the Erie Canal had been completed in 1825, many immigrants landing at New York traveled up the Hudson River and rode the mule-driven Erie Canal Packets to Buffalo. Thence by lake boat they arrived at Milwaukee, or perhaps Chicago.

It is remarkable how the foreign-born became so graphically a part of the Wisconsin tradition, and how they labored as family groups to create farms, often under the hardest conditions. A fair number stayed in cities and towns, especially Milwaukee, to become tradesmen or craftsmen, but the bulk flooded out onto the land.

They were often tricked and cheated, misled, used or abused, when they arrived at Milwaukee, and disaster usually faced them when there were no experienced members of their own nationality to guide and advise. They arrived, in most part, in penniless condition with large families. Very often their only refuge was lodging in a Milwaukee "rumhole", an early tavern which served low-grade liquor and often practiced short-changing, crooked gambling, robbery, and sometimes murder. For the most part the more than a hundred-and-fifty "rumholes" in Milwaukee in the 1840's were a bad lot, but they did save many an immigrant from losing out entirely on his dream of having a home.

Despite sojourns in rumholes and other travails, most Europeans did finally receive their hearts desire: land. They obtained the land through speculators or railroads, or companies organized to serve immigrants, or through personal negotiation, or the government. The early ones, such as the Norwegians who settled in Rock County, were fortunate in obtaining excellent lands at low cost. The crisis of 1837 cancelled land speculation in that area and the country remained open. Many foreign settlers purchased the already-started farms of Americans who came early and who, after a short time, found that the golden harvest didn't come as often or as early as the land ads had said. These Americans continued westward to open the new prairie lands of the Mississippi basin, more easily broken and better for raising wheat; or followed the gold rush to California.

But even when white settlers such as these finally came to form the lands in southern Wisconsin, they couldn't believe that the Indians might not swoop down to murder and rape. I have always felt that there were other forces more to have been feared than the Indians, namely, the land speculators who were a menace in their own right. Even government lands were not always a safe investment, and many a Yankee and European were defenseless at the hands of greedy land speculators.

The Europeans bought land only once as a rule, a home, a farm, where they worked unbelieveably hard to forge a little empire of their own. Their chief concerns were their land, their church, their animals, their families . . . not necessarily in that order. The European settlers, more than the Yankees, took care of their land. Yankees often just let their livestock loose to wander wherever they wished.

It's impossible for me to narrate the whole story of all the ethnic groups of Wisconsin. Yet I have been connected with many nationalities in search of their folk customs and traditions which, collectively, have made Wisconsin the most attractive multi-national state in the country. Pride in nationality and in family is still very powerful in Wisconsin. Old people tell me with deep feeling how their ancestors left Germany, or Switzerland, or Poland with bitter tears of parting, feeling the loss of touch with home, the unfamiliarity of the new country and the endless human struggle. It is the human struggle in which all these people engaged that is the great Wisconsin story. The beautiful appearance of the Wisconsin farm land today, for example, is a testament to the hard, hard work of immigrant peoples.

Perhaps an even better way to appreciate Wisconsin's ethnic tradition is to encounter it along the "Trail of Nations" which enables individuals to follow the settlement and to visit the festivals held at the many colorful pockets of nationality lore. There are skeptics who claim that no such trail exists, but there actually is one. It begins, rightly, in Milwaukee where each fall the Holiday Folk Fair recalls Wisconsin's ethnic traditions and where more than fifty ethnic organizations gather to exhibit folk art, present folk dances, and to nurture Wisconsin's ethnic heritage. And from Milwaukee, which has always been a gathering place and dispersal point for people from abroad, the ethnic trail leads in many directions: north, up the Lake Michigan shore through Port Washington, Oostburg, (Dutch) Cedar Grove, (Dutch) Sheboygan, (German) Manitowoc, Kewanee; (Bohemian) to Door county through Ephraim, (Norwegian) across Death's Door to Washington and Rock Islands (Icelanders). The Trail doubles back through Brussels, (Belgian) Robinsonville, to Green Bay; south through Fond du Lac, and the mixed towns in Dodge County; to Watertown (German), and further south to Jefferson (mixed), over east to Racine (English, Danes) back across country to other places in Rock County, over to Monroe, New Glarus, (Swiss), on to Mineral Point (Cornish) still further south and west to Schullsburg, Benton, Beetown: north to LaCrosse, to Genoa (Italian), inward to Vernon County places (Norwegian, Czech) on north through Polk and Pierce Counties (Swedish), to Douglas County (Finnish), and south to Stevens Point (Polish) to Portage and on and on.

The Trail of Nations has never really been marked, but it is one of Wisconsin's most treasured assets, for the Trail actually marks people—people who came seeking, who found homeland, and who stayed to make Wisconsin a place seasoned with the charm of Old World cultures.

Old World Milwaukee, as everyone knows, had a definite German look and savor. The Germans were not the only group from abroad to arrive at the Cream City, but they were certainly the largest and had the most influence on local traditions and customs. To many visitors, Milwaukee was truly a German city, with that language widely spoken in business dealings and newspapers published in German. There was a German theatre producing not only German plays but also the latest plays from Scandinavia, England, and New York, all in the German language. Some of the plays of George Bernard Shaw, for example, were first produced in German at the venerable Pabst Theatre ... the earliest productions of these plays in America. In some ways the golden era of drama in Wisconsin was the era of the German language hey-day.

Gone too is the noodled German goose, once a delicacy known in all the fine German restaurants. Goose noodling was a tradition among the old German settlers, but if the geese are gone it's still possible to sense the tradition of the thrifty Germans in the well-kept farms of Dodge and Jefferson Counties and in other localities. Similarly, I sometimes hear Welsh folks singing in country churches; watch Swiss stage festivals; see Norwegians keep alive food and dance customs. I've seen nearly all the ethnic groups in churches or at Christmas holding fast to old world atmospheres. The ethnic peoples made, doubtless, the hardest struggle to create in Wisconsin a state unique in love and sacrifice for education and a richer life. I never do get tired of speculating as to how much the early German settlers, especially those "1848" men and women with intellectual breadth, may have had to do with the formulation of "The Wisconsin Idea" and its social and humanistic implications. Personally I believe they had a lot of influence in the creation of the better life for the common man, now taken to be typical of this state.

The ethnic groups, of course, were quite different in behavior and attitude from the Yankees. The Yankee tended to be impatient. He was also inventive, always seeking a better machine to harvest crops more quickly. He took, when he could, the oak openings, the prairie lands and put his breaking-plow into the soil as soon as he could. The Europeans were more patient, willing to take longer to make a farm, and if they could clear five acres every year they were content.

Also, the Yankees and Yorkers were wheat farmers. Wheat had been a good cash crop in York State and Vermont. Wheat was what they wanted to grow in Wisconsin, and they came prepared to create habitations and farms like the ones they had back home. There are still many old houses in rural Wisconsin surprisingly like those in rural Vermont and New York. The central and western counties of New York supplied most of the Wisconsin settlers from that state, and they left New York names: Cattaragus, Lodi, Seneca, Ithaca, Empire, many others, scattered thickly over the Wisconsin country. And the Yorkers left the old, white Greek-revival houses with fluted pillars, to weather and rot in the New York hills while they came to Wisconsin to sow their crop of wheat and reap the golden reward; sometimes they recreated the York State architecture in Wisconsin.

They had worn out the land in New York for wheat, and the Vermonters had worn out their hilly lands. In Wisconsin it was better, but they cropped the Wisconsin land hard too, and by the late 1860's wheat was on the way out in Wisconsin. The Yankees and Yorkers turned to raising hops and other crops, or they just got out.

Perhaps the reason why so many people sought homes in Wisconsin, beyond the campaigns of speculator's advertisements which attracted them, was that Wisconsin provided a natural gathering place for a flow of peoples as they migrated up from the south, or from the lakeshore, or from the rivers.

From the earliest times of human habitation in Wisconsin, the Fox and Wisconsin Rivers were main routes of travel from Green Bay to the Mississippi. Myths related in the culture of the Winnebago, Huron, Menominee, Potawatomi, Sauk, Fox, and Chippewa tribes tell how they all used the waterways. And they all crossed between the Fox and Wisconsin at the portage. The Indians and very early whites, of course, were not searching for land as the later arriving white settlers did. The early French and English who occupied parts of Wisconsin first contributed almost nothing to the idea of farming. They were valuable for exploration and descriptions of the country, and in establishing relationships with the Indians. The Indians, meanwhile, had their own kinds of agriculture, and ancient Indian cornfields can sometimes still be identified. More importantly, the old Indian trails often became the first roads of the pioneers.

Harking back to my own sensibilities about the prairie, southern Wisconsin settlers in the 1830's found the Wisconsin prairie almost a flower garden. Wild grasses and sedges grew tall and thick. Flowers in yellows and purples: goldenrod, wild asters, daisies, bright orange and purple milkweeds with hairy stems, here and there brilliant lobelia bloomed cardinal red; and lilies raised orange-red bells. These were great prairies good for agriculture and requiring little land clearing.

In the new Wisconsin country there lay other kinds of land too: marshes and swales, high prairies, and well-drained forests. The trees were hardwood: oak and maple, hickory, walnut; in many places the lands were burned open, since most years fires swept the prairie lands, killing most small tree growth and leaving the sturdy burr oaks often in clumps or small woodlands. And between the clumps, on the open prairie, farms could be made. Sometimes there were hardly any trees at all upon the prairie, and here the farms could be made easily, quickly, and possibly crops grown in a first year, as soon as a little heavy-sodded land was broken.

But at times the land was more stubborn. Where there was timber the land had to be cleared, and the families worked together to make their homes and their farms. The great forest parts of northernmost Wisconsin were hardly settled at all initially, because of the deep woods, as most people thought that land was of small value to agriculture. But the rest of the people came as rapidly as the flood of settlement grew, taking their land where it was most economically feasible, or where friends were gathered, or where the land looked similar to places from which they had come in the old country. In the early days land, wherever it was located, was cheap, and every settler, if he worked hard and if his whole family worked equally as hard, could own a part of the land, and it was theirs. County by county the march of peoples showed their origin: from Vermont, New York State, Pennsylvania, Massachusetts; from Norway, Poland, on and on.

While the forested lands might eventually make better farms, their spiritual value was even greater. For as the cleared land was always fresher it has been said that land cleared by a tremendous effort would make a home more cherished by the family and succeeding generations. Early farm settlements were mostly east of a line that followed the Rock River to Watertown, and then east to Fond du Lac. Not as much early land was taken for farming in the west, toward Madison, but as the Indian "problem" was settled, the entire part of the country along the old Military Road from Green Bay to Portage to Madison and to the Mississippi was taken for homesteads. It was really, though, the coming of the railroads which opened the western parts of Wisconsin to homesteads and agriculture. For the first time farmers could get grain to market without the stress of transport in a roadless country.

The beautiful lands of Wisconsin drew the early settlers here. They arrived, a trickle at first, then a flood. They converged upon Wisconsin from nearly every place a letter, a newspaper, or an advertisement for land could reach. And the settlers, the ones who crossed the ocean with such hardship, and the Americans moved slowly across the land, walking, or by wagon, on horseback, or, later on, by the early railroads. They filtered along the Lake Michigan shore from Milwaukee, Sheboygan, Racine, Kenosha, (Southport) and other lake ports, and they spread into the back country, especially into southern Wisconsin where there were prairies and where much of the land was dry.

They brought with themselves an infusion of new blood from near and abroad; the Yorkers who stayed and their Euro-neighbors who came worked together on a new idea: to create of Wisconsin a state where the land was finally transformed to its best use. They worked it so that the hills were covered with grazing pure-bred cattle and the dairy industry was finally born of Yankee ingenuity and of European stability. It's a great story, and out of it comes today a revival of hope for a restored faith in land and people.

Even in northern Wisconsin the land transformation has been achieved. Though it was originally the 100 years of intense lumbering that caused the slashed lands to lie wounded and barren, the cutover has come back enormously; mostly because of the people, again home-seeking, who settled in the slashed lands.

Thus in the north, too, a problem has been solved. The Wisconsin land has found its use partly in agriculture, partly as vacation ground, and the whole transformation adds now to the fascinating story of land and the Wisconsin people, and how they came to be the way they are.

Travelin' West

I got up, sitting in the road, feeling my head, and looked around for Zill and Harry.

"They've went," the farmer said. "They give you a bad whack. It ain't right to whack you thataway with a tire iron."

I looked for the Ford, not really understanding what he said; but the Ford was gone. I saw my valise sitting in the middle of the road.

"They've went all right," the farmer said. "You want me to take you where you can call for the sheriff to get after them?"

"No, No." I got up feeling kind of dizzy and walked over to my valise. I leaned down to pick it up and saw the ten dollar bill lying there in the road. I don't know why they ever left Dad's ten dollars. Maybe they thought he would come after them in the court or something, or maybe they thought they hadn't earned it for something Dad wanted them to do. They had some reason for leaving it, but most likely it was just that they didn't want anything more to do with me or Dad.

Well, I wasn't going back home, that much was sure. I wouldn't go back there for anything and tell how my going away was such a joke. I was just going right on west, even if I did have a really sore head. The farmer said I could ride with him for the few miles he was going, and then I'd have to walk or hope somebody else would pick me up. He said that some guys were like Zill, just mean. He added that he had known some men who just had a mean streak in them, that was all. The guy asked me my name and said that he heard of Dad. I don't know whether he really had, or was just making talk. He let me out at a crossroads, and I walked on.

My valise wasn't heavy, and I was really enjoying being by myself, taking it easy, walking on the road which wasn't heavily traveled at all. After a while I came to a little grove by the side of the road, and I figured I'd rest a bit and give my throbbing head a break, too. There were three cottonwood trees on the bank of a slough, or a dried-up creek, and the grass on the bank was still kind of green. I went over there, sat down on the bank, and opened the valise. I was going to have one of the sandwiches Mom had packed for me. I opened the valise, a real old one made of alligator hide that Dad had owned for a long time with one end ripping out, and found that Mom had not only put in sandwiches, ham and a couple of beef ones, but had also included the little thermos bottle we had—it was full of lemonade. I enjoyed my lunch, and as I ate I never gave another thought to what had happened. Later on my head hurt worse, but it didn't bother me too much and the blood had dried anyhow. Plus, it still wasn't too late in the morning, giving me plenty of time to get a long ways west before night.

I still couldn't see any relationship between Dad and the tall prairie in what had happened to me so far. That's what he had seemed most interested in. But as I sat in the shade of the cottonwoods I tried to recall exactly what Dad had said.

One Sunday, when we were sitting and talking, Dad said that the tall grasses were the symbol of all the fruit growing and of all heat and decay and death. That's the way he put it. When the grasses browned and withered in drought and became hay, their greenness went off with the hot summer wind. And the years of the seasons revolved, he said, and the years of great growing and strong crops overcame the years of drought. It was like hearing a Baptist preacher read a chapter from the Old Testament, almost, the way Dad spoke that day. And when he came to Kansas, Dad said he knew that the days of the tall grasses were almost over. He saw all the changes come to the prairie, and he said that as time went on a lot of the plants that had been on the fields when he came disappeared as the plows broke open the sod. Then the cattle came upon the land and when they did, and grazed upon the grass, the prairie flowers began to go. He said the prairie was a sea of violets and scarlet painted cup and something he called alumroot and wild lupine. The little prairie roses, he said, were across the whole prairie world in the spring; a great rug of roses in the spring and they came out five-petalled, pink, with a yellow center, and they were there amongst the trees, and in spring the dogtooth violets and the Easter lilies came in the shady, wooded, rocky places and on the sides of the little cliffs along the streams, the wild columbines grew amongst the little crannies. He said he walked out on the land and in the ravines and he thought he was in a paradise; now he said, there were a few of the old plants left, especially along the railroad track where the growing things weren't much disturbed. That's about the only place you could see the real prairie as it was, he said, except in that old burying ground on the river.

My head ached a lot, and there was a big bump now above my ear. Harry had hit me with the flat side of the tire iron. I guess I could have been hurt worse if he'd have hit me with the edge. I couldn't believe he'd wanted to hit me hard anyhow—if he had there would have been a larger cut, and I might have had to get stitches and all that. Funny thing, I wasn't really mad at Zill and Harry. I even thought about laughing, yet I was surprised that they done what they did. It was as if they didn't care whether anything was right or wrong, as long as they wanted to do it.

I started out walking again, and after a while a young short guy in a Dodge sedan came along. He stopped, yelled at me real friendly, and invited me to ride along with him. He said he liked taller guys, and that he was on his way to a religious meeting at Estes Park, Colorado. He was a YMCA man, worked for the Kansas City, Missouri "Y" and was on his way out there to be part of a bunch who were working on a plan where there would be peace for everybody in every country. He said that it would all be a Christian world one of these days, and then there wouldn't be any more trouble, and times would get better because everybody would love and care about everybody else. He asked me where I was headed, and I said I didn't know, but if it was all right with him I would just ride on for a ways.

As we rode over the straight gravel, with stones banging up and clacking on the Dodge's fenders, he told me that he figured bad trouble was abrewing. The World War that had ended in 1918 just wasn't anything compared to the hell that would someday be let loose on the world. It was foretold in the New Testament that fire would come out of the sky and lap up everything, he said, and all the wickedness of the world would be burned up. He figured that these hard times, with everybody out of work and all, were just the beginning to a time that would lead right up to the mouth of hell.

In fact, he said he knew a prophet in Kansas City who predicted how the old USA would come mighty close to bein' done away with, burned up, scratched out. People would lose their morals, and there would be nude women in all the theatres, right on the movie screen, and on the streets, even. The prophet guy said the day was coming when people would do almost anything right out in the daylight, on the street, in the park, on the stage. He said that there would even be laws passed that would make it legal to have pornographic books in stores, and these laws would weaken the government until finally there would be a big explosion and then a great leader would come to save the country.

He added that he believed, personally, that this leader, the prophet the Kansas City fellow was talking about, was really Jesus Christ himself; but a guy he knew said no, that it was probably Alf Landon of Independence, Kansas who was coming on strong in the Republican party and who would get the country back on the right track if he would get elected president some day. Then he gabbed on about how there were forces in the world that were shaking things without folks knowing. "Influence," he yelled once. "Influence is what will get you there." "Where?" I asked. "Wherever you want to go. You got to be on the inside."

This YMCA guy talked all the time, seemed like. He didn't speak nearly as interesting as Dad, either. I just kind of half-listened to him. Anyway the YMCA guy had it all fixed up good. He said there were just two kinds of folks; good folks and bad folks. He could tell by looking close at me that I was one of the good kind and that I had never done any wrong things. I asked him how he knew that, and he said that there was always a kind of special look to a guy who had been raised a Puritan. He could also tell by the way Puritans talked and shied away from subjects that weren't totally pure. He said that he hoped I would stop by the Kansas City, Missouri, YMCA some day, and if I did he would show me around and introduce me to guys who could maybe help me. He added that he knew a guy in Kansas City who was an expert on handwriting and could tell right off what a man was fitted to do and what his course in life was likely to be. That interested me because I thought the handwriting guy might tell me what Dad wanted me to be looking for. Well, I never thought I would ever actually see this YMCA guy in Kansas City, anyway.

We rode on and on. The YMCA guy said his name was Charlie Gribble. He talked most of the time, all of the time. I didn't feel like talking.

Through the hot, dusty June afternoon we rolled west. We passed a lot of guys out on the road, too, and they all seemed to be heading west. Some of them carried bundles or maybe an old suitcase, and the Y guy, Charlie, said that in Kansas City times were sure hard, and that there just wasn't any work for anybody.

There seemed to be an atmosphere about the Depression that plunged into the hearts of everybody. It was certainly like no other time America had experienced. There were wounds upon the land caused by the erratic seasons, by the strong winds, and by puzzling floods at certain times as well. The drought drained the moisture out of people as well as out of the land, and when the wetness returned it was in sudden spurts, far-spaced. I felt the spirit of the Depression as we drove, and would have liked to express it in words, but it was a spiritual thing, an unutterable misery of silence.

"Unless there is a change of president," Charlie warned, "there will, before long, be a revolution in the country." Folks were talking that way in Kansas City, at least. He hoped that there would be a peaceful change and that Franklin D. Roosevelt would be elected president. He thought the Democrats would have a better chance of cleaning house in Washington, and that some changes could be made to put guys back to work. Otherwise, every man in the whole country would become a hobo, just drifting around; graft would get worse and worse.

Even though he talked non-stop, Charlie also seemed real interested in me and my finding a job. I'd never had to find a job, really, and always had plenty to eat at home. I heard what Charlie was saying, but it didn't mean very much to me. I was a lot more interested in the kind of country we were going through. It wasn't like our eastern part of Kansas; it was a lot flatter and you could see a lot further. Mom had always said that Kansas was the prettiest state in the whole nation. She was always quoting a poem called "The Voice of the Prairie," which we all, Dad included, liked particularly well. He sometimes asked her to speak the poem at the dinner table, and when she came to the part about "*the voice of the prairie calling, calling to me,''* she would sometimes stop and tell how one of her relatives, Uncle Lloyd, and his family had gone out to western Kansas and got a homestead and built a house out of the prairie sod. Uncle Lloyd had later became a banker, but he always wanted, she said, to go back to western Kansas and live in that sod house. He told a minister once that if he had to make a choice of going to heaven or to western Kansas, he really didn't know how he would choose.

Well, the Kansas land was pretty flat; you could see the heat shimmer a long, long way, and the windmills, more and more of them, as we went on west, sticking up here and there on the flat lands. And there was a feeling about the whole country that I couldn't describe; it was widening out and opening up. There were still just about as many farms and houses; but a real difference from eastern Kansas was the way the land looked in browns and greens and then the sky taking over. I could sure see what Mom meant about Kansas, and I sensed that maybe the country did have a voice like her poem said. I suppose a lot of people would have said that Kansas was just hot and flat and would want to get across it as fast as they could. But if you're born and raised in Kansas, you sure get a different idea.

When we came to the outskirts of Wichita, we passed a crowd of people gathered in an open field. Once we saw they were crowded around an airplane, Charlie stopped and said we should go over and see what the excitement was about. My head had just about stopped hurting; the lump hadn't gone down, but I felt all-right. We went across the field and into the crowd. A big guy was standing beside the little plane and was giving a lecture about how fast it would go, how it would roll and climb. Charlie asked who he was and somebody said he was a flyer from Kansas City named Art Goebel. We stood and listened to him for a little while before he finished talking. Then Art Goebel started up the plane's engine, got in, and the crowd hurried back out of the way. He gunned the motor, and the little ship traveled down the field only a hundred yards or so, and then seemed to spring right up into the air. It climbed very fast.

We all cheered, and people all around me were talking about how Wichita was going to come into its own pretty soon. They were going to make airplanes at Wichita, and everything there would be fine, if just Herbert Hoover would get reelected. Charlie heard that remark and decided to stay and argue about it. He walked right up to an old man who was wearing overalls and a straw hat, and said, "Say, didn't you ever hear of Franklin D. Roosevelt?"

"I heard of Teddy," says the old man, "but who'n hell's Franklin?"

"Savior of America," Charlie says.

"Christ is the only Savior we recognize out here in Wichita," the old man says.

"Yes, Christ is the *big* Savior, but Franklin D. Roosevelt is the Savior of America."

"What's he done to prove it? Ain't the country in a hell of a fix?"

"And who put us there, friend. Herbert Hoover."

"It weren't Hoover. Was the Communists."

"The commies never had a thing to do with it. It was greed. Just plain greed. And our morals got rotten. That's what it was. Don't you know what happened to Sodom and Gomorrah? Do you know what it's like in Kansas City?"

"Hey, are you a preacher?"

"No, I'm not a preacher. But if I was one, I would tell all you people that you are going to hell. Roosevelt knows that. He'll take the country into a new day; the Democrats will do that."

"Ain't Roosevelt going to hell, too? Same as us?"

And so it went. Charlie really enjoyed the discussion. But the folks got tired of arguing after a while, and we set out going west. Not far outside Wichita we began to pass larger and larger wheat fields. The grain was mostly golden ripe, but here and there in the fields there were still some green spots. I could see the wind start at the far edges of a field and cross in strong, circular billows until the whole field would seem to be matted with bending stalks of wheat. I don't know what it was about the wheat and the wind, but I got a feeling as I watched; maybe it was the color, or the hot kind of dust-colored sky, or the way the land was opening out. I felt something, that was sure, like I wanted to go out into the fields and stand and take hold of the heads of the grain. Maybe it was like the grass of the prairie calling to Dad and Mom. It was all tangled up inside of me, all that feeling, and I still had a headache, too, and maybe that was part of the strange way the whole country looked to me. Anyway, Charlie never stopped talking.

"I believe in God, my friend. I believe in One Creator of Everything. How about you?"

"I guess I do."

"Chripes, you got to *know*, son. Hey, are you saved?"

"I dunno. I been baptized."

"You were? Tell me about it."

Well, I sure wasn't going to tell any stranger what happened in the church back home with they baptized me. I wasn't going to say a thing about it, but it sure ran through my memory. I had figured Dad was going to spare me from being baptized because he didn't hold much with going to church. But he never said a thing to stop Mom.

It was a cold Christmas Eve and the small church wasn't heated very well by the Round Oak stove that stood in a front corner. The baptistry was opened at the side of the pulpit. It was a covered tank set into the floor, about the size of a small, stock-watering trough. When they were going to baptize somebody they just took off the cover and then you could use the wooden steps leading down into it. Mom had laid out my new long underwear. "I want you to look clean, at least," she said "when you go down into the holy water."

"What will I wear?"

"This underwear, of course."

"Oh, no."

"Of course. Everybody does. When Mr. Benson up at the bank was baptized, he went down in his long underwear."

"In front of all the people?"

"Certainly."

"I don't want to."

"Now no more foolishness."

"I wish I wasn't being baptised."

"Hush."

But it happened. They brought me out of the Sunday school room, where I had undressed, into the full view of a couple of hundred folks who were in church for the Christmas Eve Service, and the preacher motioned for me to enter the water. I went down the steps with the cold water creeping up higher and higher on my long underwear until it was above my waist. At least, I thought, they can't see much of me now. Then the preacher came down the steps in his best suit and I could see the large, gold watch chain across his vest. I thought about how unfair it was that I had to go into the cold water, but I didn't think long because the preacher grabbed me by the shoulders and the head and pulled me over backwards. All I could think of then was that it was Jim Rayburn who had got me into it.

For Jim had come to our town and set up a large, wooden tabernacle in the courthouse park. And there, every night for a whole month, he preached and raved and told how he'd been a pro ball player and had seen a vision one day and become an evangelist. Always Jim's success was great and after each sermon people flocked, really ran, up front as the congregation sang the revival songs: "Throw out the Life Line" . . . "Just like a tree . . ." and they were converted.

Even then I wondered about that minute when they were converted, whether all the people really felt a great new change in their lives, or whether they walked up just because everybody else did. I wondered whether it was really possible for one moment in all of the time in a person's life to be so immensely important, so far outrunning the other countless moments a person knows, like when they walked out in early spring, for instance, and went into the woods, where they found, beneath the damp and quiet, last year's leaves, the first dog-tooth violet blooming, or the first Dutchman's Britches growing in the shade, or later, the first of the yellow wild violets.

But Jim Rayburn's business was the conversion of souls and not the discovery of early wild flowers. So when, under Mom's pushing, I walked, hidden among a flock of converts, to the front of the tabernacle, I wished I wasn't there. But I was, and I imagined that I really thought I felt a mighty spiritual change when Jim put his arm around my shoulder, and said in a confidential voice, "Boy, so you want to be a Christian?"

"I reckon so," I said. And Jim passed me on as saved. This led to my being baptized on Christmas Eve and Mom was very happy; but as I left the tank, dripping water onto the carpet and shivering desperately, I remember I kept thinking: "How do I know? I don't know. I don't know anything about being a Christian."

But to Charlie I said, "Sure, I been baptized. Can't recall much about it."

"Well, you were probably too little to remember, I guess. But the important thing is you been saved. I see these Kansas City bums on the street all the time. They'll hit you up for a dime anytime. I always wonder where those guys would be now if they'd done things different. Had a faith. Been baptised. I keep a little Bible right here in my pocket all the time, so I'll never forget that I been saved. And I have to watch myself, too. All the time. It ain't easy when I face temptation, I'll tell you that. But I have made myself strong. You remember that, friend."

"Sure, I will."

It was getting dark when we came upon a small city. There was a sign that said: "Pratt, Kan. Pop. 3,000." Charlie said Pratt was one of the bigger towns in that part of Kansas, and I could sure tell that it was right in the middle of the wheat harvest. The fields came up to the edge of town. I suddenly made up my mind that I would get out. I didn't have a real reason, except that I was feeling miserable and hot and my head hurt. Charlie had been nice to me—we had stopped at a restaurant a piece back and he staked me to a sandwich and a glass of milk. I offered to pay him for the ride, but he said I could pay him by saying my prayers every night. I didn't tell him that I never had said any prayers, except in church, and I opened the Dodge's door and got out.

He was going to drive on through the night. I could have gone along with him; he asked me to, but I wanted to stay in the wheat. I felt, somehow, that I belonged there. He hollered goodbye and told me to be good and to come and see him in Kansas City where he had connections. I thought he looked kind of wise when he said "connections," but I didn't give that any thought. I was suddenly out there on the main street of Pratt, Kansas, and I didn't have any good idea where to go or what to do.

Removing The Red Menace

Some years ago, when I was working on research for my Horicon book *Wild Goose Marsh*, I spent a good deal of time in the Horicon Marsh area. My hope was that I might find Winnebago Indians living there who could relate to me tales of the fabulous Marsh where their ancestors had hunted and foraged for centuries. The Marsh, I knew, had been a chief provider of food for the Indians—abundant wildlife, wild rice, cranberries, great fish easily speared or caught, etc. But I found no Indians at all. Their trails were all but obliterated by agriculture, only a few traces across the foot of a meadow remained. I could tell that they had been there alright by the mute branches of a large oak tree, branches which were bent in the tree's youth and later tied by the Indians with vines or rawhide to mark a trail across the Marsh. But except for the trail tree and the many effigy mounds that still remain, there is almost nothing of the Indians, nothing that was of living flesh and memory. When the white settlers came they found no comfort in close association with their red brothers, so little by little the Indians in southern Wisconsin were crowded back and out, or were dispersed in forced migrations west and north to Iowa or Minnesota. Narcisse, the son of the famed Milwaukee pioneer, Solomon Juneau, led an early migration of the Winnebago from the Horicon Marsh area to a reservation in Iowa. The people did not want to go; some drifted back, but the country of plenty was never theirs again.

The Black Hawk War was the political-military event that terminated the "Redman problem" in southern Wisconsin. The conflict itself was hardly a "war." A few whites and several Indians were killed, but it was important primarily because it opened the way for white settlement.

Treaties to gain cession of Indian lands were being constantly negotiated, and before 1832 when the Black Hawk confrontation started, white settlement in Wisconsin was limited to patches along the Lake Michigan shore and the southwest where Americans and some Welsh and Cornish were mining lead. The miners, and such farmers as there were in the region, joined with Henry Dodge and other military leaders to chase the Indians out. It was action inspired by fear, of course, but it was political, too, for the basic reason behind the "war" was to aid white settlement.

The whole sad story of how Black Hawk led his ragged band out of Iowa and Illinois and into Wisconsin, fleeing from Federal troops, is well known. He and his people came north as far as the Horicon Marsh, hid there, and were coming out, trying to get west to the Mississippi, when they were discovered. The pursuit west along the Wisconsin River, and the final slaughter of the Sauk Indians at Bad Axe (there is a little Mississippi River town actually named "Victory") is not one of our more glorious Wisconsin episodes. But the "Red menace," so-called, ended there, and the Indians never again re-emerged in any significant way.

And yet their memory, or rather their presence, lingers. At Madison, along the shore of Lake Mendota, just beyond the location of the former University of Wisconsin low-cost summer session tent colony (a location now recalled by only a few old-timers), is a small cave known for many years as "Black Hawk's Cave." The name came from the belief that in the month of July, 1832, the noted Sauk chief, Black Hawk, during his memorable retreat across the present site of the University at Madison and north, to the Wisconsin river, hid in or visited this cavern. This is, of course, a mere myth, as the old warrior and his fleeing Indian band were being too closely pursued by the military to seek even temporary security in any cave. But this legend persists despite the efforts of local historians and others to discredit it. The cave must be approached from the water and every year curious persons approach it by boat and enter it, believing that it once harbored the Sauk Indian patriot of pioneer days.

All along the line of Black Hawk's famous Black Hawk War retreat, from the Four Lakes region to the Wisconsin River and on to the Mississippi River (where on the Bad Axe battleground on a "Battle Island", August 2, 1832, his force was all but annihilated), hundreds of stories and legends about this chieftain have come into existence in the past one hundred years. There are springs at which Black Hawk was supposed to have quenched his thirst, heights from which he watched his pursuers or directed his fleeing band, places where he erected hastily constructed "fortifications," or secreted loot, or held conferences with traders or friendly settlers. Practically all are myths.

At Wisconsin Dells lies a tree in whose branches Black Hawk supposedly hid at the time of his capture. In another tree at Prairie du Chien he is said to have secreted himself during an escape from Fort Crawford, where he had been a prisoner. The constriction of the rock walls of the Wisconsin Dells at the Wisconsin River Narrows is also known as "Black Hawk's Leap"—so-called from a fanciful belief that here he had jumped the river, from bank to bank. The local folktales concerning these Black Hawk "landmarks," despite their falsity, will endure for many years to come, though they are without fact.

Similar legends and stories occur at different places in the Rock River and Lake Koshkonong regions, along the line of the march of Black Hawk's band into Wisconsin, from the present site of Beloit to the Horicon Marsh region.

But now the Redmen are all vanished from places such as the Marsh. No old Indian man or woman is left there to tell the tales of their ancestors . . . and only a handful of the legends have ever come down to us.

So what has white, European Wisconsin to show for over 300 years of contact with the Indians? Most notably, mutual hostility. Some whites had viewed the Indians as a means for financial profit; others were interested largely in the Indians' spiritual salvation. But most whites came to want control over the lands which the Indian occupied and all the commercially exploitable resources associated with this territory. As a result, most Indians were either killed or driven off if they refused to cooperate with the white settlers. And we, for our own part, are not only minus their history, but we are without their company as well. As the Winnebago Reuben Snake, Jr. has said: "Being Indian is feeling that Grey Wolf, Thunder Chief, and Smoke Walker are more beautiful names than Smith, Jones or Brown . . . Being an Indian is forever!" Horicon Marsh speaks these same words, but I am not Indian enough to understand them.

The Hotel

Pratt, Kansas, sure wasn't much of a city. It was a little bigger than Iola, maybe, but nothing to write home about. A lot of the town's buildings needed painting and fixing up; the streets were wide and there were some cottonwood trees growing along the side streets and around a little park on one corner of the main street. There were lots of cars, mostly Fords and Chevys parked along Main Street, and some of the stores were still open. A lot of the people on the street were men and boys, guys like myself, looking for a job in the wheat harvest. They were all dressed in work clothes, or in suit pants that'd seen better days. Most of the men wore hats, old felts or straw hats, some with the stiff brims and flat crowns same as those the city guys wore in Iola, but seedier looking. There were also a lot of people who looked like farmers, with very tanned faces, creased and furrowed. But all of them seemed real worried to me, and there wasn't any laughter, the kind a crowd of men and boys would generate, standing around on street corners. The Depression was taking its toll allright.

I walked up and down Main Street, wondering what I should do and where I was going to spend the night. I didn't see how there would be enough sleeping room in town for the crowd that was hanging around. I wondered where they'd all go when night really set in. I supposed they'd sleep out in the park, or maybe they had cars they'd crawl into. The large mess of men, and the uneasy feel of the town as dark came on, gave me a restless and uncomfortable feeling. I passed a line of guys squatting back against the front of a store which was still open. They were just squatting there, not saying much, and they looked ready and willing to go to work if anybody offered them a job. I got a feeling for hard times that I'd never before felt.

I guess I was too nervous and scared, possibly because all the troubles of the world seemed to me to be right there in Pratt, Kansas. The noise of the cars on Main Street, the call of a guy to somebody across the street, the desperate faces—it all added up to unhappiness and loneliness.

The crack across my head didn't bother me too much, but I wondered what would happen if I came across Zill and Harry in Pratt. They might be here, actually, because they were ahead of me when I was travelling in the Dodge. I really wasn't mad at them, I just didn't understand what was going on.

Counting the ten bucks that Zill had thrown down in the road, I still had fourteen dollars. Dad hadn't had but a dollar, he said, when he'd left Illinois, so I guess I should have felt rich. I went into a little counter place and had a bowl of soup and a piece of rasberry pie that only cost fifteen cents. I sat at the counter and had to hold my valise on my lap as there was a fellow squeezed on each side of me so close that I could hardly eat. I got out as soon as I could, and continued walking around. I passed two hotels. One was on the main street and was a very fancy-looking place, with a big lobby and nice chairs set out on a wide front porch. I could see men and women sitting in the lobby, looking as if they had the money to stay in such a fancy place. I didn't waste any time thinking about putting up there. What I really had in mind to do was go to the park and find a corner there to lie down.

But as I went down one of the side streets I came across a little hotel. It was sort of a square, old brick building, with no porch or anything, but flush to the sidewalk. There was a sign hanging in front of the place, faded-out mostly, which said: "Corina Hotel" in mighty poor lettering. The evening wind was swinging the old sign a little bit, and it made small, rusty sounds.

The place didn't appeal to me. I could see inside and there were several men standing and sitting in the small lobby, not a dressed-up crowd like in the lobby of the bigger hotel. These guys looked really seedy, like harvest workers out of a job. I finally decided to go in and see what the place was like and what they wanted for a room. I was really bushed and desperate for a bed. The lobby was tighter and smaller than it looked, even from the outside. There was a counter at one side with a couple of bare, forty-watt bulbs hanging over it that let out a little flyspecked light. There was a bulb on the ceiling not much bigger with hundreds of flies buzzing around. The guys in the lobby weren't saying much, just sitting or talking low. The place smelled rancid, too, sour and moldy and sort of like urine. I was about ready to turn around and walk back to the street, thinking that I'd prefer the park or even a country road to what was there in the hotel. But then I saw this woman. She came out of a side door behind the desk and started to fuss around with some papers. I felt kind of silly, walking in there and standing around; some of the men were looking at me. So, I walked over to the counter and stood there while she fiddled with an old adding machine. She added up a few figures and pulled down the lever for the total. She never came right over to speak to me and acted like she didn't care anyhow.

She was a large woman with a bit of rouge and a sticky-looking green dress. I couldn't tell what kind of stuff the dress was made of, but it wasn't very clean. She had a short, fat neck and large shoulders and arms. There were little rivers of sweat running down her neck, out from under her black hair. In the yellow light the sweat glistened like rain on a dirty window. As I leaned against the counter I could smell her, too. She had a kind of worn and musty smell—perfume, maybe, and a lot of other things. Her odor was like a dog that gets wet and smells what my Mom used to say was a wet-dog smell. This woman's face, as far as I could see, never changed at all, as if she were wearing some kind of Halloween mask. And her lips never came quite together. I don't know how old she was. Maybe thirty, maybe older. She wasn't any high school girl. I knew that. I said, finally, "You got a place to sleep?"

"Maybe."

"You got a room?"

"What do you want it for?"

I had never thought much about such a question. Maybe I should have, but I didn't. I never thought much about anything. Her attitude made me kind of angry.

"A place to sleep."

"Ain't got no room. But I can let you sleep in the hall."

"Where?"

"Upstairs in the hall. Take it or leave it."

I didn't like her, and I sure thought she didn't like

me. She was still sort of smiling. That never changed, but her mouth opened up a little wider.

"Give me a quarter. I'll let you use a blanket to sleep on."

I didn't want to sleep in any hall, but I felt the guys watching me and I didn't know what else to do. I gave her a quarter. She reached onto a shelf behind her and took off an old brown blanket. I didn't want the blanket either, but I took it.

"Upstairs," she said.

I went over to the stairway. It was pretty narrow and dark with a bulb hanging from the ceiling at the top. There was a little landing at the top of the stairs and then the hall turned and ran straight down the middle of the building. It wasn't wide enough to lie out straight across it; but there were guys lying up against the walls all the way down the hall. There was a little aisle down the center so you could get by without stepping on anybody. The air was very close. Stifling, in fact, and there was a smell of dirty feet and dried sweat. Back down the hall a kid cried as his father tried to dry him up. I figured the kid must have been pretty homesick.

"Shut up," the father said to the kid.

"I want to go back home."

"Now be still. Tomorrow we'll get us a job in the harvest. You'll feel better then. Some home-cooked grub will make you feel a lot better."

"No it won't."

"Where you from?" a guy lying next to the father asked.

"Kansas City. God damn, I stood all day last week out at the Armour Packing plant. They only took on two guys all day. One was a Black guy."

"Well, they need them Negroes in the slaughter house."

"I'd even work there. It's that tough a time. Shut up, Walter. Go to sleep."

The kid sniffed and continued to cry. I really felt sick. I never had been much for mixing in close with a lot of guys, and I couldn't see any place to lie down either. I didn't want to touch anybody, and I didn't want anybody to touch me. I wanted to sleep outdoors, away from the odor and the feeling of fear and unhappiness. I turned around, went back down the stairs, walked to the counter, and shoved the blanket back at the woman.

"I won't sleep up there."

"What's the matter? Ain't it nice enough for you? A guy like you got to have a nice white little bed, huh?"

"Give me back my money."

"Nothing doing."

She stood there and laughed at me. I didn't know what to do. I should have turned around and walked out, but her laughing made me angry. I really wanted to reach across the counter and pull her over onto the floor, but it wasn't in me to do it.

"Give me my money. I'm not staying here."

"You ain't getting your quarter back, honey. But if you got some more money I might give you a place all to yourself."

"How much?"

"I got one nice room I been savin'. You can have it for a buck and a half. Give me a buck-twenty-five, I'll credit you with the quarter. How's that sound?"

I pulled out the ten dollar bill. I shouldn't have showed her I had a ten, but it was the first thing that came out of my pocket. She looked at the bill, as if she hadn't seen a ten all day. Maybe all week. Some of the guys standing nearby saw it too. She gave me change without saying anything. I put the money in my pocket.

"Number seven upstairs. The door ain't locked. Walk in and make like you was home, honey. And I just hope to God there ain't somebody already in that bed."

They were laughing at me, everyone within earshot and many of the fellows made remarks. I went fast up the stairs and found number seven back at the end of the hall, off by itself. I pushed the door open, and the smell was even closer and more raw than out in the hall. I found the light by leaving the door open and pulled down the broken chain. The wallpaper was dingy and full of dead flies. There were about a thousand more flies on the ceiling, and the old bed seemed to be suffering from a broken back. I put my valise on the floor and sat on the bed. Some roaches came out and scooted across the room.

I sat there for a long time, trying to make sense out of it . . . everything that had happened during that long, long day. All I could see was a whirling of land, of wheat, and of heat across the fields; of roads, straight and dusty. I was in the middle of a whirlpool. I hadn't ever seen a real big whirlpool, but I could imagine how the water would swirl around and around and suck at you and take you down. Sometimes there were little whirlpools in the Neosho river back home when it was in flood, and the brown water would start to go around, and if there were any little sticks or trash floating, they would turn around and around in the pool. It was like that there in the Corina hotel. Colors, lots of them, dirty yellows, and browns and greens, and people too, wandering along, not going any place—they seemed to be caught up in the whirlpool. I couldn't get the spinning to stop. I guess it was partly the whack I had on the head or something. I took off my clothes, dumped them on the floor, and lay on the bed.

I knew I was awful tired. It had been a long, long day, the longest I could ever remember. I didn't like where I was, and I couldn't figure out why I was there. Last night I had been in my own bed at home, and it surprised me how fast things could change; whole habits of a lifetime altered so lightning fast. And now a foreign place, different, unfriendly. A dirty bed with dirty sheets. There was a special sour odor about the bed that was different from the smell of the room, sort of like a bed with a mattress that somebody has wet night after night. I hated it. I felt lonesome and sorry for myself. I finally fell asleep laying on my back because the lump on my head was on the right side, and I usually slept on my right side.

At first I thought I was having some kind of a nightmare: you're in a dream, fixed in there, and something heavy is holding you down. In the dream you are thinking about Dad, and he is telling about a nightmare he has over and over when a man without any face is sitting on his chest and he can't breathe. You don't have any strength to fight back. You want to fight and scream and get away, but you are being held right there.

I've had that same dream a number of times since, where you can't move or get loose or lift your arms or legs; but that first time it happened wasn't like the times since. I kept hearing far-off sounds and feeling the heat—that was the worst part of it, the heat that was burning me up. But it was the smell that woke me up, finally. I remembered instantly what the smell was, the musty room, and then I was able to move my arms. I still couldn't tell whether I was asleep or awake, but I could move. And I heard words, too, a guy saying, "Hold onto him. He's wakin' up."

Then hands grabbed me, and another hand was clamped hard over my mouth. I struggled, scared as could be, but they were strong, whoever they were. And they were silent too, I heard somebody say, real low, "You listen. You lay here and it'll be all right. If you yell or foller us we'll kill you, kid." At first I thought that the voice sounded like Zill, but then I knew it wasn't. "Come on," someone else said, and I heard them go out. I waited there on the bed for a long time. I was breathing fast, really scared. It struck me that I might have come close to being murdered. And one thing I was sure—I'd been robbed. I finally got up, felt for my pants, and eventually found them over at the other side of the room. Every cent I had was gone.

Trembling hard, I tried to wash up a little at the dirty basin that stood in the corner. Washing didn't seem to do much good; I couldn't get off the foul smell. But I quickly got dressed and out of there, passing several guys still lying asleep in the hall.

I guess it all had happened right before dawn, because the light was coming up as I went outside. I walked to the Pratt railroad station and hung around there until it got light, then I walked back over to the little park. My stomach felt queasy; I knew I better have something to eat. Although I had no money, there was still a sandwich left in the valise from the lunch Mom had fixed only yesterday. I ate the sandwich and felt better. An old guy who was up early, sitting on an adjacent park bench, told me that there was a Federal Government employment office up the street aways. He said I ought to go up there and ask for work. I thought maybe I would when it opened up. I plopped down on the grass and fell fast asleep.

SYMBOLS

An Academy member whom I loved dearly was the great Wisconsin craftsman—wooden bowl maker without compare—Harry Nohr of Mineral Point. He would often drop by to visit, for we were old friends. His stories of his adventurous life, of his love of art and wildlife, made him innumerable friends. One of his best friends was Gordon McQuarrie, wildlife writer for the *Milwaukee Journal.* Nohr, McQuarrie and some others once characterized themselves as "The Old Duck Hunters" and when McQuarrie died, some money was left for an award to a person who had done the most to encourage better wildlife management and environmental regard in Wisconsin. While Harry Nohr lived, he managed this award.

Harry was always searching for native woods that he might turn into bowls so thin and so beautifully treated that no craftsman could equal them. He tramped the woodlands throughout nearly every state for burls (growths on trees) that he could obtain since a burl turned into a bowl has fantastic charm. I knew Harry Nohr when he was the postmaster at Mineral Point, and later when he was retired and devoted his entire time to finding beautiful woods and turning them into bowls. Examples of his work are in most of the great museums. I have acquired several of his bowls, and when Harry died suddenly in 1977, I began to reexamine what it meant to own a Harry Nohr wooden bowl.

Over the years I have become intrigued by what appears to be a mystical relationship between objects and persons. There is a symbolism that grows and develops around objects that has to be the result of a close association between object and individual. The object often becomes the symbol of a tradition, of a way of life, of a feeling that actually waxes important in the routines that all of us follow, or in the rituals that support our struggles to find happiness, peace, or satisfaction in values that are meaningful to us.

Objects that attain a symbolic status are almost always those which have been with us or near us for some time or with which we associate intimate experiences. We often act as if we believe objects can influence us in exploring a particular lifestyle; or they arouse memories, or we prize them for many other personal reasons.

I am sure that the modest collection of Harry Nohr bowls which Maryo and I display in our home is an excellent example of what I mean. The bowls, mostly in our living room, have meanings for us almost beyond my ability to articulate them, and each bowl arouses its own kind of response.

There is a catalpa bowl that rests on the top of a Civil War period desk. Both desk and bowl have fascinating stories, and have become part of our family legend. The desk, no doubt hand-crafted by a country carpenter, is created of several kinds of wood. It is pigeon-holed with a narrow writing shelf, slanting, and doors that open to disclose other storage places for documents. The desk belonged to my wife's great grandfather, the business manager for the famous Tredegar Iron Works of Richmond, Virginia, the foundry which made most of the heavy armament for the Confederate Army and Navy. For many years, Great Grandfather Anton Osterbind, a Prussian immigrant, sat at the desk, and over it and around it flowed much of the ordnance paperwork of the Confederate war effort. In a small drawer, when the desk was shipped to us from Georgia where it had been owned by another Osterbind relative, was a railroad spike made from the armament of the mighty ironclad, Merrimac. Jeff Davis' government had the spikes made for sale to the public to raise funds to support a desperate army, low on supplies and cannon. The word Merrimac is stencilled on the spike.

I sit often at the old desk trying to recreate what went on: to imagine the forgotten voices that spoke, that made decisions. The old spring-less desk chair is there, too, very uncomfortable. And on top of the desk is the Harry Nohr bowl of catalpa wood, turned and shaped by Harry at our special request, and delivered to us in person in, I believe, 1966.

Behind that bowl is a story, too. We had a large

catalpa in our front yard that suddenly, in 1964 or 1965, showed signs of decay and disease. We loved the tree, for its blossoms were, we thought, more plentiful and more beautiful than those on the other catalpas in our neighborhood. We were desolate when it became apparent that the tree, 70 to 80 years old, was dying. Our neighbor next door, a noted physicist, Julian Mack, stood with me often, looking at the tree, feeling as keenly as we the impending loss. Julian was a remarkable man, noted in nuclear research, but beyond his scientific knowledge and achievements he was a warm and dear man, a splendid neighbor, interested in all that went on involving trees, wild animals, or his friends' best interests.

When the catalpa finally went, Julian came across the yard to tell me that he had just talked to Harry Nohr. Julian knew Harry well, they were good friends, and he, like I, often stopped at the Nohr house in Mineral Point to swap stories or to glean information on local matters. At that time, University Extension wished to use Mineral Point as a study center and Harry had definite ideas about his town, and how it ought to realize its potential as a cultural center for southwestern Wisconsin.

Harry had run into some local road blocks on this point. He tended to be impatient with the community for not moving fast enough. Anyway, Harry came to Madison on the day that the old catalpa was cut. He brought his station wagon, and Julian and I helped him load in several large pieces of the tree. We had no idea at the time what kind of result Harry would produce, but Julian made a special plea to Harry to create some bowls. He said that bowls made from the catalpa would surely have a special atmosphere of spring, of white blossoms, and, he said, of hope.

Julian never mentioned to us that he was dying of cancer, but he died before the bowls were finished. He never did see the beautiful bowls that Harry made of the wood of the catalpa; but in demonstration of what he meant by hope, Julian willed his eyes, so that some handicapped person might have sight. I have often wished that I knew who was the benefactor, so that that person might see our catalpa bowl.

Harry brought the bowls to Madison when they were finished. We obtained one, a lovely, light color, grained with intriguing patterns. Ours took an immediate place on the cherished desk, and became a symbolic object; for whenever I notice it the stream of memory begins. I think of the great occasions when Harry and I met, and the appreciation I had of his humor, and his unusual observations on life. I think of Julian, too, and of our meetings in the front yard, and of the reality of good neighbors.

We also own a great black walnut bowl that Harry turned from a burl—a burl which, he told us, he had obtained under great difficulty and was probably one of its kind. We believed him, because Harry never said anything about one of his bowls that wasn't accurate. He might, occasionally, spin a tall tale—what storymaster does not? But where his bowls were concerned he never stretched the truth. Maryo, who was exceedingly fond of Harry, told him one day that she earnestly wanted to own one of the greatest bowls he ever made, and Harry called her one evening to tell her that he had a wonderful black walnut bowl—in his opinion one of the finest he had ever turned. She instantly said, "Harry, please hold it for me."

Eventually we got the bowl paid for; it took some time. Typical of Harry: at Christmas that year (1976) he called me. We had paid something on the bowl, not all. He said, "Laura and I are coming to Madison to spend Christmas with the Klus family. We are bringing the black walnut bowl. We want Maryo to have it for Christmas."

It was, of course, her best Christmas present; and the bowl, now completely ours, rests on a table under the portrait of a great Nashville woman and close friend, Jane Inge. On the table too, are the Boehm Canadian Geese, the family group commissioned by President Eisenhower. Canadian Geese are very special to me, as they were to Harry. The bowl, the figures of the geese, the portrait—all comprise a symbolic corner and remind me of the geese at Horicon Marsh, of Harry the sportsman, and of Harry and our Tennessee friend, Jane Inge, humanists. Owning a Harry Nohr bowl is a wonderful and responsible experience. The symbolism does increase.

The Office

The U.S.D.A. employment office at Pratt was very crowded when I arrived. The office itself was inside a long, wooden building, and the room too was long and narrow with a desk at one end and benches along both sides. Today, the benches were filled with harvest workers looking for a job. In fact, the desk was almost hidden by five or six guys hovering around it, trying to find out, I guess, from the clerk or whomever, whether there were going to be any jobs that day. I could barely see the fellow behind the desk. He looked heavy, with several folds of skin hanging down from his neck, gray-haired, and he wore a white shirt. He was sitting there with a cold cigar in his mouth, trying to answer questions.

The racket in the room was deafening until a young farmer came in and walked quickly toward the desk. He looked a lot fresher and cleaner than anybody in the room. The workers must have realized that the farmer was looking for help, because they all stopped talking. Even the guys at the desk turned around to look. The farmer, meanwhile, elbowed his way up to the desk, and I heard him say that he was looking for three good men. Immediately everyone in the room thought that he was a good man and could qualify. I know I did, even if I was beat; I still knew I was a good hard worker. I figured I didn't have a chance, though, with forty or more guys in the room all needing work, some worse than I did maybe. But I didn't have any money and didn't know how I was going to eat, so I too was desperate. The guy at the desk talked a while with the farmer, then yelled, "He wants two tractor drivers and a combine man."

Well, you never saw a flock of old hens fly, push and

scramble onto a scattering of shelled corn, more'n those harvest workers did on the farmer. They were onto him all at once, and the whole crowd was yelling and whirling around, trying to get him to hire them. Pretty soon though, the farmer busted out of the mob with three guys. I never could see how he chose them. Then it again got quiet in the room. The harvesters returned to the benches, looking more hopeless than I felt myself, and that was pretty hopeless.

I didn't see how anything could happen in that employment office that was going to be any good for me. But I hung around for a while, watching and listening, standing up against the wall, even though I wanted to lie down somewhere. My head hurt bad, and I drew my fingers across the lump, feeling the edges of the place which had hardened and crusted. I wondered what Dad would have done to find a job here in the harvest fields. He claimed he had worked his way across from Illinois to Kansas, and I knew some of what he did, but I bet he never was in a room with forty or fifty guys all out of work and desperate. Maybe it was this kind of hard times that Dad wanted me to experience for him, but I didn't really believe that any more than I believed that he thought I'd learn much about the prairie grass in a dirty bed with some thugs holding me down and stealing my money.

About eleven o'clock a tall, old farmer-woman came in. There is something about a woman who does farm work that gives her away. She walks rather free and easy, but firm, as if she owned the world, and was used to driving mules, or working alongside men. I had seen some women back home who were like that. There was little interest among the men in the room when she came in, nothing like there had been when the young farmer had come. I guess nobody thought that a woman would come into the employment office looking for harvest hands. Most city guys believed women stayed around the house all the time, and most of the men in the room were probably from cities. I know that Dad felt that women weren't supposed to do hard stuff like men, but he sure was glad to have Mom help him with the milking and other chores. Supposedly all the public stuff that women were supposed to do, Dad said, was to defend folks' morals and maybe help lead the WCTU. He never was really sure that Kansas women ought to have the right to vote, and he and Mom sure had some hot arguments over that. He never did go to church, but he had read the Bible and he said that there were plenty of places in the Bible where God told how to treat women, making them your handmaids and all. He said he didn't hold with that himself, but it was there in the Bible and he wanted Mom to think it over, since she was such a good church goer. She got riled up every time.

Well, this lady entered the employment office anyhow. I thought I hadn't ever seen a bigger woman. Everything about her was big. Maybe she wasn't quite as tall as I was, but she came pretty near it. She had long arms and big hands, as heavy as a man's, and the sleeves of her shirt-waist were rolled up. Her forearms were burnt dark brown. She was wearing bib overalls. Her face was large and wrinkled and her eyes were crinkly, as if she was going to laugh any time. Her gray hair hung down on both sides of her face and was put up in a knot at the back of her head, about like Mom wore hers. She carried an old felt hat that reminded me of Dad's.

Her mouth was clamped shut, a straight line right across her face. She seemed like a strong woman, and she'd had some hard times, you could see that. But there was something about her, sort of daring the world to be as big as she was. I just stood there and looked at her; maybe she saw me as she walked past.

The guy at the desk knew her. He glanced at her, looked down again at his papers, and says, "Howdy, Mrs. Settles. And what can we do for you?"

"Why," she said in a loud, man's voice, "Why, I want a man to help me in the harvest. I want a man who'll work and not cheat me. I want somebody who'll do the chores and do what he's told. You got somebody?"

"We got plenty of men who want work, Mrs. Settles. You can just about take your pick."

"I got six milk cows. He'd have to do the milking. My regular hand is on the tractor, and I'm sitting on the binder. I need a strong worker and a general worker, one who can shock grain."

Maybe there weren't any workers who knew how to milk, I'm not sure why, but whatever the case nobody came running. I didn't move either, and I don't know why I didn't. I knew how to milk, and I'd shocked plenty of grain, oats mostly, back home where they didn't use combines much. I didn't move and didn't say anything, mostly because I was too bashful to speak out in front of the others. She turned and looked over the guys in the room; her eyes went past me but when she got to the end of the benches on my side, she looked back again and motioned for me to come up to the desk. Maybe it was because I was taller, or maybe because I was younger. Anyway, she motioned and called to me to come up. "You, tall one. Come up here."

She was even larger up close. She stared at me a little while, then she said to the guy at the desk, "I want this one."

"You sure, Mrs. Settles? He's maybe too young.

"He's old enough."

"Yeah, but maybe you'd better take an older man."

"I want *him*."

The guy sighed; I thought it was because there were so many older men wanting work. But I guess he knew she would have her own way.

"All right. Whatever you say, Mrs. Settles. What's your name, son?"

"Bob Gard."

"You got a terrible bump on your head," Mrs. Settles said. "How'd you get that?"

"Had an accident."

"Have to put some salve on it."

"You ain't even asked if he can milk cows," the desk guy said.

"I knowed he could," Mrs. Settles said. "I knowed it right off. He's a farm boy."

"Let us know if he don't work out."

"I'll do my own knitting."

"He might not be any good."

"I suppose you'll tell all the world that old Mrs. Settles hired a kid, when she could of had an older man."

"Oh, no. It's your business, Mrs. Settles."

She strode out of there, and I had to hurry up to keep alongside her. I sure was elated about getting any kind of a job. Mrs. Settles was driving an old Ford truck, about a 1920 model, that seemed to be barely hanging together. The springs in the seat were coming out, and she had two or three old gunny sacks spread out to keep the springs down. She wouldn't let me crank up the motor. She said it kicked only once in a while, and she better do it herself. It turned right over, and we headed out of Pratt through what I discovered to be some of the greatest wheat country in the world. The wheat went on and on, without any breaks; up and over the little rises, yellow, yellow in the hot sunlight, with the wind stirring the wheat a little, making it swell against the shimmer. As we got further out, we passed less traffic, until finally it seemed we were all alone in the middle of a yellow world. Maybe it was like that for Dad in the middle of the prairie. I felt as if I was feeling something akin to what he had, and I began to get excited. It was all different, so different from anything I had ever felt before. I had spent a lot of times on narrow roads through high corn, and I had always felt excited by the atmosphere of loneliness which I got from that. But this was like I was completely alone, although in the wheat it was a loneliness with a lot of color, and you could see above it, out over the whole land. It was as if me and the land were brought close together and yet the edges of the world had been knocked out, someway, so it all belonged to me because I could feel it so deep.

The old Ford chugged along, the gravel hitting up at the fenders in back. Mrs. Settles didn't drive very fast, so there was plenty of time for me to say something to her about the way the wheat made me feel, but I couldn't. I couldn't say anything, and then I didn't need to because she started in to talk. Maybe she knew I was thinking about the wheat fields, I don't know. Anyhow she started right in talking as if she knew.

"I've seen 'em go into it, during the early years of this century, those first big wheat combines, with platforms and a cutting sickle thirty feet or more long, and no tractor, no big steamer to pull it, 'cause they wasn't practical and couldn't travel fast enough to run the cutting bar. But the horses pulled the first ones. Twenty-five or thirty horses hooked together with lines on the lead team. What a sight! Oh, how I wish I could show you something like that. Everything's smaller now, and there's not much of a show to it. But back then! Fields two or three sections big, and the wheat so yellow and ripe. Here come the great machines biting into it, and the horses laboring on the sides of the hills. Oh, the men took to harvest those days; how they worked! And the threshing crews! When they cut the wheat with binders and stacked it up and then threshed it out. Those crews would eat everything in sight, and some stuff that wasn't in sight, too. This country ain't the same, and the men don't seem to be the same. Too small! Too small-thinking. They think everything has to be little and niggling. You believe in God?"

She sprang the question on me so fast I didn't know how to answer it.

"I guess."

"Well there is a lot of hollering about God around here, and how He's got everything set up good for a lot of these folks. But I never pay much attention myself. I got plenty to look at and plenty to think about, and I do things for myself. I've seen so terrible much. . . . I saw it all happen. Me and my husband . . . you look somethin' like him, when he was young, I guess that's why I picked you out. He was tall like you. But we seen it all. Them early reapers, and binders. We seen them cut it with the headers that just lopped off the tops of the wheat, loaded her up for stacking and the threshers. And we saw the first combines come, after those horsedrawn ones, big outfits, big as a railroad engine. And the threshers! That was the big thing here. Nicholson-Shepard engine with wheels near as tall as you, and a Red River separator; down the roads they come, you could see 'em comin' a mile away, black smoke belchin' out of the tall smoke stack. And how they could get things up for the threshin'! Dug in the wheels of the engine and the separator so they couldn't move, and spread out the belt. Such a belt you never seen! Eight-twelve inches wide and thick, and over the flywheel and onto the pulleys! How the wheels and gears did move when they set her going! And the men and wagons and the dust and heat. You never seen anything like a big threshin' rig in action! Excitin'! And the women in the kitchen making grub for those hungry threshers, meat they had to get that day from town, from a store that had a big ice box, because you couldn't keep big hunks of meat like that at home, not for more'n a day. And potatoes and gravy, a barrelful of it; and any vegetables you could get, and biscuits by the wagonload, hot, right out of the oven; and jam and preserves, and butter, and pies until hell would of run over with 'em. Always a lot of mulberry pies because them berries was plentiful. You hungry, Bob?"

"I sure am." How could I help being starved with her talking like that?

"You look it. When we get home I'll feed you. I ain't much of a cook, but there's plenty of it! But I tell you they do it smaller now. Little combines and tractors. But I do what I can to keep the romance of the big, big, harvest. I ain't got a combine myself, but I bind wheat. Got an old McCormick binder and a tractor to pull it. There's still a few threshers who will come around and I want to keep doing it the old way, even if it ain't big anymore. . . . The wheat to me is the meaning of it all. People and wheat. That's what we busted up the prairies for. For the wheat. Kansas can feed the whole world. And does. Now we got hard times; but them times will change. You can bet on that. . . ."

"You ever see wheat stubble after the crop is off? It's something that calls and calls to me. I can't wait to get a plow into the stubble. It keeps on calling, next year! Next year! You ever heard that call yet?"

And she kept on talking, and the more she talked about the wheat the more I wished that I could hear Dad and her talking together. I sure would have liked to hear them go at it; his talking about the prairie grass, tall and waving and all, and her talking about the hills and spaces of golden wheat.

We drove up the long lane to her farmhouse, a simple structure once painted white but faded bad now, with a little porch on one side. There was an old barn and sheds and a grainary, and old wire fences around the place all kind of leaning over towards you. There was a mail-order house windmill still clanking in the yard, pumping water into a big cement tank. There wasn't much sign of life except for some milk cows standing along a fence inside a little pasture where the grass was turning brown.

Mrs. Settles took me into the house. It was badly cluttered with old furniture and pieces of machinery and magazines and newspapers. There wasn't any order at all, but it was kind of easy-going like she was. She made me sit in a chair in the kitchen while she rubbed some kind of salve into the bump on my head. It stung, then felt better, and she got me to tell what happened when I got hit by Harry. I told her about leaving home, and she said I had better send a card back home and that she would give me one later. She said she understood why Dad had sent me away, and that if she had a son, she would maybe send him away, too. She would have wanted him to taste the big, free harvesting days, because around here the old joys of the real harvest were about over.

"Some men nowadays don't want to work!" Mrs. Settles cried, "They don't want to get dirty, and feel the dust and smell the smoke, and they ain't hardly anybody who can build a good stack of wheat anymore. And most of the horses are gone. Engines! Tractors! We got to have 'em, but it ain't the same freedom. The bigness is gone. The joy is out of the hearts of the men; it's gone. But I'm fighting for freedom. It's all I have left. Freedom to do what I want, when I want."

After she fed me cold chicken and homemade bread and coffee, we went to the field for the afternoon. She sure wasn't one to waste time. The hired man was a thin-necked guy named Sam. I never did know his last name. He drove the Hart-Parr tractor, and Mrs. Settles rode on the binder. Her wheat didn't look as good as some we'd passed on the way out from town. Her land seemed thinner, somehow, and sandier. She said I didn't have to work very hard since I had a sore head, but it seemed all right, and after the good food, I felt pretty well. I worked hard, shocking the bundles, since I knew how to do that and how to work in the opposite direction that the grain was cut, so that the butt ends of the bundles would all be in the direction I was coming from. It made them easier to grab. I worked hard the rest of the afternoon, and I was glad to do it. I felt pretty lucky to have a job, as a matter of fact, though Mrs. Settles hadn't said a word about what she was paying.

Late that evening I got the cows into the barn and milked them. After I had finished the milking, I took the milk up to the farmhouse, and Mrs. Settles strained it and set it out to cool. We had a good supper. Sam came and washed up on the side porch and ate plenty, but he never said a word all through the meal, which was fried meat and potatoes and a big raisin pie.

But all through supper Mrs. Settles kept talking about the old days and the big harvests, and how those old-time harvesters could eat. After supper she fixed me a bed out on the porch. I never was more tired in my life. I heard the western Kansas wind soughing through the silver maple trees and through the black currant bushes, and I went right to sleep. I never even thought about the Pratt hotel or the robbery or anything. All that seemed far away, somehow, real far away. . . .

The Symbolism Increases

For me symbolism can spill into other kinds of objects, too. The Academy owns several of the great prints by the Wisconsin wildlife artist, Owen Gromme. One of these pictures is of Canada geese coming in for a homing on the Horicon Marsh. Looking at that picture never fails to stir me. The mysterious symbol of the wild goose has always been important ... I cannot forget that my Dad had told me that he'd followed the wild goose cry when he was a lad, and wandered west to the great unbroken prairie lands, and how the longing never left him to go further, to see more, to find more and more of the wild unbroken land. He told me to wait for the wild call, and I did and I suppose it's there in me now by heritage and inclination.

Since it is the Horicon Marsh in Wisconsin that is the chief spring and fall time setting for the mighty flocks of Canada Geese, it is natural that the Marsh has had a symbolic meaning for me.

The Great Marsh was once more than a hundred square miles, in shape roughly oval, surrounded by a forest of oak, maple, ash, elm and hickory, and to the west the prairie spread widely, with oak openings where the fires had burned away the tenderer, less hardy growths and where the prairie grasses waved higher, at times, than a horse's back. And before the white man arrived the Marsh breathed under the leavening seasons, tossing wild grasses and rippling waters, with water anemone floating so brilliant; and the water lily on the blue, clear mirror. On hummocks the wild roses felt the gentle winds that moved the snapdragons and stirred the purple vetch; and deep in the bogs the winds turned forwards and backwards the yellow thrusts of the wild marigolds. Yet it was a tree there that impelled me to produce a book about the Horicon Marsh.

It started when I visited Horicon, Wisconsin, at the invitation of Kathleen Karsten, back about 1952. I made some kind of an informal talk that evening, I remember, to a group of local ladies. Then I was taken to dinner at the Rogers Hotel in Beaver Dam. During the pleasant meal I was told by Kathleen about a wondrous tree that stood near Horicon, near the Great Marsh, and that it was a trail marker tree ... one which the Winnebago Indians had tied with vine, certain branches to point in the same direction, and so to mark an important Indian trail up and through the Marsh. The story, as she told it, fascinated me, and I expected some day to use it, but I didn't really come back to her yarn for many years. Then, one afternoon in 1971, driving along beside the Marsh on Highway 28, I had an impulse that the time had arrived to tell the greatest wetlands story in America ... for so I had come to believe. I was amazed to find that very little popular literature had been written about the Marsh, though the lore about it and about its wildlife in oral terms was immense. Also the Marsh had become one of the truly fascinating wildlife shrines of America, especially since there is now a greater congregation of Canada Geese at Horicon in spring and fall than at any other North American refuge. Despite the fact the Federal Refuge people are hazing the birds daily and attempting to reduce the flock, millions of visitors arrive yearly in the Waupun area to view the wonderful birds and to watch them feed and at rest. Actually, nobody knows much about the Marsh or why the birds are there, or about the unlikely chain of happenings that created finally, out of years of struggle over the fate of the land, a refuge for the geese and a real chance for them to discover their mid-America haven.

The strange part of the story comes now. I was visiting in Mayville, Wisconsin, in March, 1972, with my friend Ed Mueller, local Mayville photographer, and during lunch I started to tell him and his wife Dorothy about that 1952 visit to the Marsh, and how Kathleen Karsten had told me about the Indian tree. Ed said he knew a fellow named Willard Bartelt in Horicon who ran the city dairy and said that Bartelt might know where that old tree was located. If he did, Ed said, we would go out and photograph it ... for I had remarked that I wanted to begin and end the book with some symbol that might have significance for both the old days and the new.

Ed called his friend Bartelt who said that *he* didn't know anything about the tree but if we would call back in a while he might find somebody who did. Meanwhile, I called the home of Kathleen Karsten to find out whether she remembered the incident that happened twenty years before, and whether the old tree she so beautifully described was still standing. There was no one home at the Karsten's.

Then we called Willard Bartelt again, and he said: "I have Dr. Karsten here. He is eating lunch here today. He will talk with you." Funny thing was that it was the first time Dr. Karsten had eaten lunch at the dairy for many months. Kathleen just happened (if that's the way you want to look at it) to have gone to Fond du Lac shopping. It turned out that in the intervening twenty years since I had first heard of the tree from Kathleen, Dr. Karsten had purchased the farm on which the old trail tree stood. He was as excited as I when I reminded him of the long forgotten incident, and of the tale told me then in his home. He got his Scout, for the land was mushy still in the early spring, and drove Ed Mueller and me out to the location of the old tree. There it was . . . at least two hundred years old, we thought, a weathered and beaten old fur oak, some of the branches dead, but the two Indian vine-tied ones pointing out unmistakably, together marking the ancient roadway of the Indian peoples. And we stood there for a while and marveled at the way chance works things out, or the fates, or the Indian gods who *might* have decided that it was time for us to tell the Horicon Marsh story.

Anyway, Ed Mueller did take the picture of the tree while Dr. Karsten and I exchanged pleasant reminiscences, and that trail tree became immutably fixed for me in the folklore of the Horicon Marsh. I only wish that the Indians who tied the tree branches to point the trail were still around to tell their tales, but they have vanished. I suppose they will never return unless events occur again in the same way, which maybe they will, and another Ice Age begins, and new marsh areas are created, and migrating red-skinned peoples come again to enjoy the luscious plenty that, little by little, grand Nature, a part of the Great Spirit's plan, provides for us all, if we will but wait, take care, listen, enjoy, tolerate, preserve, and have faith.

There is much more that I have learned about the

Marsh, and come to know and appreciate, but it is the wild goose which sends me again and again to listen, floating in a silent canoe on the Marsh ditches in early summer hearing the redwings, the coot away back in the tall grasses, seeing the swallows and kingbirds flashing above the blue ditch waters. Further in, I hear the splash of landing ducks, cries of herons and egrets from the islands where they still nest. It is easy, in a canoe, to listen and imagine how it all was. And for me it was all caused by the cry of the wild goose, for that is what first sent me to the Marsh where I learned that I too was a poetic instrument; and that I would never again be content until I understood the secrets of the Marsh and the siren-calls of a great and forgotton time of wilderness.

Little by little I learned. I walked the edges of the Marsh with Edgar Mueller. He too was a searcher and confessed to me that the wild goose had taken him in thrall, that his camera must record the birds in all their mystery, in all their habits of flight and rest. He called my attention to objects that I might not have noticed and that were also part of the story: a weathered and sagging old gate, entrance to a once-cherished marshland farm and a reminder of the great controversies first caused by the flooding of agricultural lands by the dam at Horicon in the mid 1800's.

But the great flock of Canada geese with which we are now familiar has not always spent fall at the Marsh. Until the 1940s there were virtually no geese in the area. They began to come when the refuges were created and abundant corn was planted. Migrating flocks were decoyed into the Marsh area. In days beyond human memory, though, the geese were there. Geese and ducks once nested on the many wetlands throughout the whole prairie area. With white man settlement, however, and the breaking of the prairie lands, the wetlands grew fewer and fewer and the water birds moved north and further north. Now the Horicon flock nests in the James Bay region of northern Canada. Through years it has expanded and expanded. The thousands of Canadas are, in the fall, one of the unforgettable and poetic sights of the Upper Middle West. Is the flock now too large?

Devoted friends of the Canada geese do not want the birds disturbed by those professional wildlife experts who hold that the flock has expanded beyond good scientific management. Their recent goose-hazing project to reduce the flock drew a great deal of criticism, and a certain bitterness has grown between those who, more pragmatically, want control and limit. It is sure that a vast amount of corn is required to feed approximately 200,000 geese, each one of which is capable of eating a pound of corn each day. It is said that a disease will eventually kill the flock; that it is impossible to care for so many; and the Marsh farmers have never been very happy about raided grain fields. But the roar of airplane motors as the flock is dispersed and hazed is abhorrent to many persons, like myself, who have cherished the Marsh as the great stop-over of the Canada goose. The Marsh, the birds, represent one great thing that adds to the lure and lore of Wisconsin. What will eventually happen to the flock? I do not know.

The cry of the geese is timeless, however, and will never be stilled. I am aware of the problems of today, but I find the lore of bygone days more interesting. The whole story of the once-wilderness, the red men, the coming of the white, the change-over to a method and economy of a new time ... the great hunting days of the Marsh ... in the goose symbol I find meaning for all.

I feel some of that meaning in winter when I visit the Marsh and receive a sense of the endlessness of time ... the cry means that endlessness, too, emphasized by the bending reeds, cattails, so brown and sear in winter, the snow covered muskrat houses, and the tracks of foxes in the pure snow. I know that I can, at least, follow the wild goose to the Horicon Marsh, and there relive the tale.

Above all I love the concept of the primitive, and how it all was in ancient, unrecorded days. I can only wish though, that our unbroken prairies were back, and that the geese and ducks and cranes were nesting again upon primitive Wisconsin wetlands. I wish so much that the wild goose call could transport our national hunger for the wild and the primitive into real manifestations of such things. I believe that my hunger for the search, for the restless movement to new things and new ideas, is basic to us as a people. I will always cherish and keep my wild goose symbol, and listen endlessly for his cry in evening or at dawn. And my eyes will always travel upward to watch the flocks as they fly, heading only they know where, and I'll feel sadness in their going, for perhaps the restlessness and seeking belong to another time, when there were vast, lonely lands and abundant foods, and far, far fewer human beings to be affected and strongly disturbed by the note of the wild. As with Harry Nohr and his bowls, the symbolism here does indeed increase.

Mrs. Settles

I worked very hard in the Kansas harvest for several days. Better yet, I was feeling real comfortable at Mrs. Settles' place. I wasn't getting top money, she was going to pay me thirty cents an hour, but it was all right with me. I was sure earning it. And although I had quite a bit coming, somehow the money wasn't too important. I was really getting to know Mrs. Settles well, and she talked to me friendly and easy. By now I would have done just about anything for her.

Several times Mrs. Settles took me out to a far end of the big pasture to show me a windmill her husband had built. It was tall, made of wood, with a wooden ladder and a high platform. She said he had made the platform specially large so he could climb up there and look across the flat Kansas lands. He liked to do that at sunset, she said. There was something about the wooden windmill that really got me. I could stand and look at it for a long time and see something different every time I shut my eyes and looked again. It had a huge wheel at the top which was different from any other windmill wheel I'd ever seen. This one had many sections of blades, each turned at a different angle. She said he'd made the wheel himself and that it was better at catching wind than any of the commercial ones from the mail order houses, Montgomery-Ward or Sears-Roebuck. He'd never bothered to patent it or anything. But that was his way. He just liked to fool around and make stuff, and the neighbors hadn't understood him, especially since he had a little problem with whiskey. The old windmill hadn't been running for a long while, but I never did get tired of going out there, alone, in the evenings, to study it.

One evening after supper we were sitting in the

kitchen, Sam was yawning and I was about ready to turn in too. We heard somebody drive up in a car, and Sam went to the door to look out. He never said anything, but he got his hat and went away. In a minute there was a knock, and when I opened the door there was a funny, dried-up little guy standing there, bald headed, with his straw hat in his hands, and a white shirt opened about half-way down his chest. He was getting on in years, there was some gray hair still around his ears, and his Adam's apple stuck out about as far as I ever saw one. When I opened the door he started to come in, then he stopped in the doorway and looked into the kitchen.

Mrs. Settles saw him standing there, and for a minute I thought she wasn't going to say anything, or ask him in at all. But pretty soon she cleared her throat loudly and says, "Come in, Reverend. Come in."

He came part way into the room and stood by the table, turning his straw hat around in his hands. I could tell that they knew each other all right, and I could see that they weren't very friendly. Mrs. Settles didn't do much to help ease things. She said finally, "Reverend Somers, this here is Bob. He's the young man who's helping me in the harvest."

"So I know," the Reverend said.

"Well, Reverend, you might as well sit down. Just take a chair. You come to chat with me, I suppose."

"Yes, ma'am. I came to have a talk."

"First time you ever been here, ain't it?"

"Once before. You recall that."

She cleared her throat again. "Yes. I recall. When Horace died, and I threw you out."

"I tried to reason with you."

"Nobody can reason with you, Reverend. You ain't the reasonin' kind. You got only one point-of-view."

"You oughtn't to say that, Mrs. Settles."

"I'll say whatever I please."

They sat a little while, and I sure didn't know what was going to happen. She was bigger than he was, and I knew well how strong she was—if it came to a pushing battle I was certain who would win. You could just feel them disliking each other.

"You got to let him go."

"Let who go?"

"This young man here."

"What in tophet for? He's a good worker. I like him."

"You're ruinin' his life."

"Ruinin' his what?"

"You'll be the ruin of him and all his kin and all that they done, and all that they will do."

She got up and walked around so she could stand over near him. She stood there looking down at him. "Now you tell me how I'm ruinin' his life."

Reverend Somers got up too, and they stared at each other.

"You're teaching him to disbelieve in God. Ain't that why you hired him out here? To get a young man to ruin, with your infidel's slobbering?"

"Slobbering?"

"You holler out that there ain't no God."

"I say what I want. And I ain't slobbering."

"You are a blasphemer. God will come to punish you with fire and tempest. You are the only one. The *only* one anywhere hereabouts who don't believe in God."

She grabbed him by his shirtfront. Maybe she got hold of some skin, too; he gave out a loud holler. I figured she was going to slug the Reverend, and I didn't know what I should do. In a way I felt that he needed help more than she did. And I felt pretty funny about being talked over, too. I didn't know that anybody cared what I did except Mom and Dad, maybe. I never figured anybody would talk about me, or care where I was working or whether I believed in God. That sure seemed like my business.

"It's my right to do and say what I want," Mrs. Settles said holding onto him. "Ain't you never heard of the U.S.A. Constitution?"

He jerked around, trying to get loose. His shirt tore a little.

"Yeah. You say what you want, even if it ruins a young life. Folks here ain't going to stand for that, Mrs. Settles, and neither is God."

She started to haul him toward the door.

"Git out!"

"You best come to church," he yelled, "and fall down to your knees and ask for God's forgiveness."

"When I come to church," cried Mrs. Settles, "I'll come because I got a good reason. I won't be there because you or anybody else told me to come. Now git! And don't you ever come back. I sure got a mind to lay a board to you. And if there is some others who sent you, tell 'em I don't need 'em. They ain't going to do my thinking for me. You look in the Constitution of the U.S.A.—it's right in there. Everybody's got a right to think what they sees fit."

"There ain't no constitution in heaven. God's law prevails."

Mrs. Settles shoved him roughly out the door. She came and sat back down at the table, breathing hard.

"You believe in God, Bob?"

"I sure try to."

"Well, whether you do or not, it's your business. Nobody else. You hear? Nobody!"

She looked so fierce, I figured maybe she would set in on me next. I got up slow, yawned, and said I was tired and had to go to bed. I would have liked to hear her talk some more, but I was afraid to set her going. It was like Dad when he got started; he would just keep going on and on. All you could do was get up and leave. And sometimes he went on talking even after you left.

Mrs. Settles just sat there at the table.

On Monday when we had about finished with her harvest, Mrs. Settles asked me if I would mind going to a neighbor to help him for a few days. She said the neighbor was one who didn't approve of her or of the way she thought, but his helper on the wheat truck was sick, and he couldn't afford to hire anybody else. She wanted me to go over and help him and even offered to pay me herself. I wasn't going to take her money, but I said I would go.

I got up early the next morning, and she drove me over in the truck. The guy, name of Ray Ellefson, was out in the yard fooling with his Chevy truck motor when we drove up. Ray didn't seem too pleasant when he greeted Mrs. Settles, not even when she told him I had come to help. But he didn't refuse. He said something like thanks, and asked, finally, whether we'd had any breakfast. Afterwhile he got around to asking Mrs. Settles to come into the house, but she said she couldn't and finally drove away.

Ray didn't turn out to be such a bad guy either. After Mrs. Settles had gone, he warmed up and said he was grateful to me for coming over, and he'd make it up to me. He seemed to be embarrassed, or guilty, or something about Mrs. Settles. He showed me around the place, and I met the tractor driver, a young fellow from Pratt. I was going to stay at Ray's place as long as he needed me. He took me to the barn where the Pratt kid, whose name was Quinn, was finishing up the chores. They showed me where I would sleep up in the barn loft, on a cot. My bed was already made up with clean sheets.

"I reckon Mrs. Settles told you I was so hard up I couldn't afford a wheat scooper," Ray said.

"That's about it."

"Well, everybody's hard up. But I ain't that bad off. I'll pay you myself. Mrs. Settles has always sort of looked after me and my wife."

He cleared his throat, and I got the idea that he was caught between what folks thought about Mrs. Settles and what he thought. The three of us walked down the road to a field that Ray was figuring to start cutting this morning after the dew was off. A couple of little kids, a boy and a girl, came running after us, puffing the dust with their bare feet. The kids came up to Ray, a tall and husky feller, and took hold of a hand on each side. We walked into the field a little ways, and he broke off some heads, rubbed the grain out of the hulls, and chewed them. He told us that he'd seeded his field late and that it was ready to cut now.

"We'd better go back to the barn and get ready to work."

I was hoping that he'd say more about Mrs. Settles and what folks were thinking about her, but he didn't talk about her at all. And he never did again, really, not while I was helping him.

The kids were now holding my hand and Quinn's. I hoisted the boy on my shoulders, and we walked along laughing and having a big time, until we got back to the house.

"You better come in and meet my wife," Ray announced.

The kitchen at Ray's place was low and cool. There was a large, round table covered with a white oilcloth. A tall woman came into the kitchen, and she was holding a baby on her breast. Her face was already wet with sweat, and she kept brushing the black hair away from her eyes.

"What's your name?" Ray asked.

"Bob."

"Vera, meet Bob. He's goin' to help us with the scooping."

"I'm glad you got somebody so fast."

"Well, I wouldn't have if it hadn't been for Mrs. Settles."

Vera didn't answer at all. I figured they must really like Mrs. Settles but were afraid of what folks would say.

My job was the wheat truck, the unloading of the bin on Ray's Baldwin combine where the wheat was collected. Ray rode the combine, his hand on the big lever that raised or lowered the platform. Quinn drove the Allis Chalmers tractor. I waited the arrival of the combine when it rounded the field and stopped near the place where it entered. I backed in the large Chevy truck placing the end of the body under the spout on the bin, and, coming around, opened the sliding door at the end of the spout. The wealth of the pure grain spewed out in a glorious stream into the truck body, as I kept it scooped away. There had been enough rain earlier in the spring and moisture through the winter, so the harvest was good. But grain prices were extremely low . . . hardly fifty cents a bushel. One partial round of the large field had filled the truck box, and, once filled, I eased the loaded truck away from the combine. My job then was to haul the grain to the farm where I scooped it out into a grainery, because Ray wasn't selling his wheat at the moment. He meant to keep most of it until winter, to see whether prices might rise. Some experts were saying the low prices would cease by winter, and then the country would get back on an easier track again.

Round after round, all day, everyday except Sunday, the combine roared through the wheat. I could throw off a hundred bushel-load of wheat in record time, and was always waiting for the machine when it rounded the field. I prided myself that the combine never had to wait for me.

When I was waiting for the machine, I sometimes walked around the field, curious about the many plants and weeds that grew in the field edge. I wondered how many of the plants along the fences had been there when the country was open plains. I recognized some of the plants that were the same as back home. I wished that I had as much knowledge of the land, the soil, and the ways of prairie plants that Dad had. He never went to a formal high school, but he knew a lot more. He knew about the insects that burrowed into the top layers of the earth for the winter, and then came out the next season, opening the earth to the air and helping it to grow better crops. This produced taller grass, and the prairie flowers bloomed wilder and more full. And Dad told how the buffalo, sharp hooved, tramped down and broke the dead stalks, preparing the way for the growing of the new grass, while the places where their hooves had cut made a bed for the grass seeds.

Apricot trees were growing wild and plentiful, and the fruit was beginning to get ripe. Often I ate the apricots and wondered whether possibly Dad might see some change in me for I'd found at least something . . . a tiny niche that I had made myself. But I didn't know where I'd go or what I'd do once the harvest ended.

The harvest at Ray's place went really well. We were ahead of schedule, and Ray's spirits were very high. He said he'd make enough on this harvest, even with the low prices, to pay the interest on his farm mortgage; things looked some better than they had the year before. He never said anything about Mrs. Settles, and the way he talked about himself I figured that he must be better fixed financially than she was, and I began to wonder whether she had sent me over to help Ray because she couldn't afford to pay me anymore. I guessed I wouldn't ever know. Ray told me he would pay me himself.

The food at Ray's was good, and the beds that Quinn and I had in the hayloft were great for sleeping. I kept thinking I'd go over to visit Mrs. Settles, but I didn't get around to it.

One morning when we got up there was a strange, dry look to the sky, as though the air had dust sprinkled through. The sun, by ten o'clock, became desert hot. Ray said he expected a storm before the day was out; he hoped it would hold off a while because we were getting along so good that we'd be finished long before the middle of July. As the day went on it was easy to tell that a storm was coming by the way the insects acted. The large sweat bees usually buzzed around real fierce, and the smaller insects moved fast as lightning when they were swatted, but this morning they hung and buzzed and dipped. And when they lighted it was as though they were drugged; you couldn't hardly knock them off.

When we went out to the field after dinner the sky had turned light yellow and the sun had disappeared behind light, high, and very fast-moving clouds. There was no wind on the surface of the earth, and it was so still that I could hear the young chicks chirping under the black currant hedge nearby. The air was sultry. It was sure difficult to breathe.

I had hauled three loads of wheat after the noon meal and the combine was stopped on the near corner of the field. The motor hadn't been running well, and Ray was fiddling with it. I walked over to the machine to see what I could do to help. Ray was filing the points when the entire countryside suddenly turned dark. "What's the matter," Ray said from deep inside the machine.

"Somebody turned off the lights," I said, laughing, and my laugh sounded hollow to me and far, far away.

"I ain't never seen anything like this," Quinn cried.

We stopped working on the engine and stared up and around at the sky. In the southwest it was black as night except for a tiny edging of white frill above whipping clouds.

"Don't like the looks of this," Ray said, swinging down from the combine. "We better make for the house, boys."

"I'll bring the truck over," I said. I started to run toward the truck when a faint breeze whispered into the wheat. It was ice cold at first, then it turned hot. I whirled around, and then we heard it . . . a low roaring that shook the earth. For an instant there was just the low rumble and the faint chirping of chickens from the far-off farm house. Then Ray grabbed a shovel off the side of the combine and started to dig in the sand under the machine. "She's a twister, boys," Ray yelled. "We'll never make it home. Dig in!"

The roar was terrific now, and we could see the storm coming: a huge black and yellow thing with an evil, big body and a tail that was whipping around and whirling up everything it touched.

I dove in under the combine, and the three of us scrambled together in the shallow hole Ray had scraped out. We clung together, and I heard Ray praying that God would take care of his wife and kids. There was a sucking sensation . . . the air seemed completely drawn out of our lungs and our bodies felt light and poised like arrows on taut strings. Then there came a hell of a roar and a smash and a clatter. Buried in the sandy earth with the terrible noise concentrated all around us, I flashed on many things: a field of blue flowers somewhere . . . I couldn't recall just where, along a railroad; a tall haystack I had climbed one time as a child; a woodland where I crept away when I was troubled; Mom frying pancakes. I also remembered a story Dad had told about his walking on the prairie in the early days when a hurricane-like wind suddenly began to blow. Dad had laid down in the tall grass, and seized hold of it with strong hands. The wind, Dad said, had flopped him up and down like a woman shaking a tablecloth. But the grass saved him. The thought of Dad bouncing up and down like that in the grass made me want to laugh, even though I was plenty scared. I also wondered what Mrs. Settles was thinking, if she saw the storm, and I thought of what Reverend Somers had said about hell. What I saw of the storm looked like the mouth of hell.

Large and small objects began hitting the combine. I put my hands over my ears and shrieked to relieve the dreadful pressure. Suddenly, the combine wasn't there at all and the sucking stopped.

We three laid together afraid to move, but once the roaring was less we got up, fearful and stiff. The Baldwin combine was the first thing we saw. It was lying over on its side fifty feet away with the big platform sticking straight up in the air. The Allis Chalmers tractor was upended, too, and the gas was running out of the tank. All the wheat we could see was ruined and lay flat, or else there was just no wheat at all, the stems skinned completely clean.

Ray glanced around, like he wasn't seeing anything, really, and then we all started running for the truck, still intact. The twister was still roaring off in the distance. We got into the truck and headed toward the house. It had started to rain hard, but through the rain we could see that Ray's house and barn weren't damaged very much. The shingles were ripped off one side of the barn roof, that was about all.

Ray's wife and kids came running down the road to meet us. She grabbed Ray and pulled him out of the truck, crying and kissing him, and the two children whimpered and shivered up to them. Ray broke away and said that there'd be a lot of people needing help, and we had better go. Vera said we should go to Mrs. Settles' place first. The storm was heading in her direction and though they didn't say it, I sure knew that both Ray and Vera were thinking that the Lord's retribution had possibly struck.

I turned the truck around, and we headed up the muddy road. I was awed by the storm's mighty force. Quinn, too, sat quiet in the middle of the truck seat as if he couldn't believe what he was seeing. As we drove we saw telephone and electric lines down everywhere, and all the fields were stripped of wheat. A horse stood in a ditch with its shoulder torn out, a white bone sticking through the shreds of flesh. Lots of cattle lay in the open in crazy, twisted postures. As we continued the storm seemed to have increased in violence.

"She'll be dead," Ray said. I was also fearful of that, the way Mrs. Settles didn't hold with the ways of God.

And then, suddenly, we saw wheat shocks that I had made standing unharmed, dripping water from the rain. All intact. As we came within sight of Mrs. Settles' house, we could see that her buildings were untouched and that the horses and cattle were grazing easy in the pasture.

Ray told me to stop the truck. We sat silent at the entrance to the lane for a long while. It was plain enough that the twister had lifted before it reached Mrs. Settles' place. No damage had been done to her wheat. "I can't understand it," Ray muttered. "Everybody's wheat ruined but hers." I couldn't help but feel glad and happy; I was sorry for the folks who had lost their wheat, but I was sure glad it hadn't been Mrs. Settles'. I told Ray I would stay here tonight and see if I could help her. He and Quinn drove away. Ray was really confused by the strange ways of God, as he said.

I had an idea where Mrs. Settles was and trotted down the big pasture toward the wooden windmill. If God was going to destroy her, he would probably take the windmill first; it was what she really believed in, that windmill/temple her husband had made to have something to set against the wind and small-thinking folks. I kept on running, and when I came in sight of the windmill I saw her all right; she had climbed up on the platform and was standing there, looking off across the cyclone-swept country. maybe she was thinking the same as I was—that I would sure like to hear what Reverend Somers would have to say next Sunday. Because, according to him, Mrs. Settles ought to have been destroyed, not the good church people. I got an idea for the first time that it was really rough, like Ray said, to figure out the ways of God.

And there was something else. I began to have faint thoughts that the affairs of people were somehow played out on a huge stage which included the land, and the people working it, and the violences of nature. Mrs. Settles was like some character in a play that was too large for any theatre made by mere human beings. She was like a character on a stage made by God and nature. And maybe Dad was meant to be part of a play like that, with his love of the way things were; and even my own leaving home seemed as though it was part of a kind of play. I couldn't articulate what I felt, but there *was* a kind of plot and story that demanded that I move on to the next act. I only wondered what the next act would be. . . .

Women of No Importance?

Where are the Mrs. Settles of today? Of yesterday? While old men and women now in nursing homes tell me of family life in the ethnic household, the large families, perhaps five to twelve children, or more, each child working on the home place, and the older ones, especially, stopping school at about the third or fifth grade to help in the fields, it is nevertheless the women who were the backbone of so many families, so many stories. One wonderful woman of German descent told me what had happened to her, a girl of eleven—how she had worked beside her father in field and barn until she was eighteen; then she married a local farmer and herself embarked on the bearing of fourteen children. She said that she never forgot the great hunger she had as a child for reading, and she made a vow that she would educate each one of her children, so that *that* hunger at least would never be felt by them. Left a widow, she did, through great hardships, educate them all. All of her children finished high school, and she encouraged each one to attend college. Seven graduated with college degrees.

I have been extremely interested in following through on these stories and others about women, both since they are obviously material for many fine books (no writer can ever escape being impressed by what Wisconsin's women have done) and also because of the important legacy of women in Wisconsin.

My investigation of country cemeteries in districts where early settlement entailed hard farm labor has led me to believe that the women of the pioneers had a most difficult time. Beautifully contoured land, spacious barns, many silos, herds of purebred cattle and the like are visible symbols of the pioneers; and above such symbols stands the beautiful ideal of the pioneer mother. But actually, the vision of the ideal, strong woman came a bit later. Day by day in the pioneer crucible it was little but work for women from earliest dawn until well after nightfall; and tragedy, too.

Many of the women, the mothers, were used to heavy labor for they had been well prepared in other parts of the United States or in Europe. Some were of a gentler, softer variety, from city locations, but whatever their origins it isn't likely that the ambitions of the pioneer woman included martyrdom; yet a kind of martyrdom was what apparently happened. I have to believe what I see in those country graveyards: Mary, age 24, wife of Karl. Priscilla, age 41, wife of Johan. Betsy, age 28, wife of Thomas. Greta, age 37, wife of Hendrick . . . the women, a lot of them, died awfully young, and probably many died and had no tombstone at all. Certainly no obituary.

In a word, although I do not wish to seem to destroy the myth of the pioneer woman willingly giving all for family and land, the women did endure, apparently, a kind of martyrdom. It took a strong woman to work in the fields, to care for animals, to provide for a large family, to bear a child most years, to make the psychological adjustments necessary, to be the nurse to the ill, to be the cheering element when there was male discouragement, when crops failed, when storms destroyed, or when there was death, to wash and dress the body, and when neighbors needed help, to go, without question. And there was childbirth, sometimes easy but many times not, with a doctor not easily available, and the woman alone save for a neighbor perhaps, or an older daughter if there was one, or the husband himself helping. That was part of it. There was also loneliness, uncertainty, homesickness. There were no alternatives. It was "go on, bear it," overcome, or it was the cemetery.

The successes of such women are among the most inspiring tales we have produced. From a tombstone in Mayville I copied the following tribute . . . and what is written there could be said of many heroic women, I suppose: *"Caroline Buchen Klieforth. Her history: If she had had the benefit of education, such as was available to her children, she would have reached fame, however, she did not despair, she transferred her own ambition to her nine children. Each of them had the same chance. She gave them ambition and opportunity.*

"Mothers who had great wealth accomplished no more than she accomplished. She not only brought up her family of nine children, but worked to provide them with food, clothes and health as well as education.

"The nine children had mothers, each one of the children was her favorite child. She was endowed with a tremendous physical vitality and mental energy. She sacrificed her life for her children. She died as the result of fifty years of sacrifice and overwork.

"Her last conscious thought was concerned with the education of her youngest son, her last-born. When the end approached she asked no favors for herself. She worried about her early death only because her life's work—that is the education of her children—was not complete. She is a living tribute to the benefits of education acquired the American way, without the benefit of wealth. She died a martyr to the cause of Christian education."

In furtherance of what happened to some women who pioneered in Wisconsin, there's the story of Sarah Pratt, a young easterner who set forth from York State on lake boats for the journey to Milwaukee. She was faring forth in search of her sister, Jane, who had married a young man caught up in the Western migration fever. Word from the sister had been so meager that the family was greatly worried about her. Sarah decided to find her. Her journey to Wisconsin was carefully recorded in a diary which she kept until almost the time of her death by malaria, prevalent on the Wisconsin frontier. Well Sarah finally found her sister. She went to the primitive cabin very timidly and knocked at the door of the dwelling which neighbors said was that of her sister's husband. A woman answered her knock. For a moment Sarah did not recognize her sister, so changed was she by work and hardship. She had, though young in years (only 24), become an old woman, now gray and frail.

At times, I have often tried to memorialize the pioneer woman. I recall that Clarence Shaler, the Waupun manufacturer who invented the cold patch for automobile inner-tubes, had a major interest in becoming a sculptor. He made a number of statues, among them the large, bronze figure of a pioneer woman, an idealized strong mother, the salt of the earth, and the strength of the Wisconsin land. After Shaler's death the figure lay for years in a University warehouse; then when the College of Agriculture moved most of its experimental farm operations to Arlington, north of Madison, it seemed fitting to place the statue of the strong, agricultural woman, high on an eminence at the Arlington place. I wrote the text for the dedication ceremony, and it was performed on a gray, rainy day in May 1965. Despite the weather the statue signified the hope of the College, that the strength of pioneers, both men and women, would prevail. Her long gaze across the lands that were once known as the Arlington Prairie, give meaning to what the land has become.

But today the tendency is to use the past to interpret the present. Many women can recall hard times as did Minna Breitsmann, retired homemaker. "I had a little doll, one of those with a china head, you know, and pink cheeks. Well, that was my Christmas present in 1900. And the next year mother'd go and put a new dress on it and just keep on handing it down to the next girl in line. There were fourteen children in our farm family. We had wonderful times—on just nothin'."

Or Elizabeth McCoy, whom I've revered, who believed that the trees planted by the early settlers symbolized much about the past:

"At one time the whole frontage of the farm was a line of elms and maples, planted alternately. The Dutch elm disease began in the area about four years ago, and it took the elms along the road one right after the other. At the same time they said that the silver maples were about through, and were about to fall across the highway. They took them all out then. I have a few elms and maples in the yard, but the great line of trees is all gone. In the beginning there were some Douglas firs that the early settlers had planted. They were along the drive as you came up to the house. There is a unique thing on the place, white lilacs, and the white lilacs have a very interesting history. Over near the fish hatchery, on the hill, the Lakeland family had their first log cabin. They later built their house down on the crossroads. But up on the hill there is one white lilac bush. Still doing well. The white lilac I have was transferred from that in 1874. The Lacy family came in territorial days, before 1848. The lilac is still blooming. And other cuttings have been placed around. At the front of the house there is a hedge of lilacs. Probably the first bush was planted because the pioneer wife wanted some flowers." Like that lilac, Elizabeth McCoy's legacy still blooms.

In the memories of their beloved elder relatives, women find the values of an earlier generation. Bess Bartlett told me about her husband's mother who devoted her whole life to hard work: "When she and grandpa got old they moved into town. But she wasn't ever very happy. There just wasn't enough for her to do. It got to working on her mind, I guess, and she just had to get back out on the land, so she and grandpa came back to the farm and lived with us. Grandma worked hard till the day she died. She was happy that way."

The women hark back to personal landmark events that set the course of their future: "I was a fifteen-year-old farmgirl when I had my first date. I had met this young man for the first time at a dance at the crossroads dance hall, and he said, 'Can I come to see you Saturday evening?' And I said yes. And when he came he drove up to the house with a beautiful open carriage and a snow-white and a coal-black pony. It was the most beautiful team! I was just flabbergasted. I thought he'd come with an old farmhorse. And here he come with that beautiful team . . . and I'm married to that man now. Fifty-four years!"

Marriage, hard work, pregnancy, labor, child bearing, child raising, cooking, cleaning, supporting, teaching, smiling, enduring. This was (and is) the reality for so many of our Wisconsin women. The names and faces so easily forgotten. Let us not forget that if it were not for them, the courageous survivors, then our past and our present would be significantly diminished.

KANSAS CITY

Now, as I look backward from my Academy cave I realize it was pretty tough, my deciding to go on from Pratt to Kansas City. I guess I left because around home I had always heard so much about that big town. Kansas City was *the* place everybody wanted to go. I hadn't ever been there, but a lot of my friends had gone, and they always told whopping stories about what happened to them. I got to thinking that if Kansas City was really a place where most anything could happen to you, then maybe I could get some information there on what it was Dad had sent me to look for. If you looked at it one way, though, I had already seen and felt a good bit since I left home: I had been in a squabble with a couple of bootleggers; been robbed; been through a cyclone; seen how God did what He wanted, regardless of who asked. But most of all I remembered Mrs. Settles and how she had showed me you didn't need to go around believing something just because everybody else believed it. Even Dad had never built a wooden windmill out on the open prairie. All Dad had was about one acre of prairie grass left over from the great prairie days. Yes, I never would forget how Mrs. Settles stood up like a tall, old-wooden windmill, skeletoned against the wind.

I was getting to enjoy wondering what was going to happen to me next. It caused me to feel excited—nerved up—and ready for most anything. I felt that way for a few days after the cyclone, and then I decided to say goodbye to Mrs. Settles and to Ray's family. I was really fond of them, but then I didn't want to stay any longer, and most of the remaining wheat was torn up anyway. Ray paid me some money, all he could afford, and Mrs. Settles gave me some, too. When I left I had more than fifty dollars. It was really big money, more than I ever had before.

Once you get to thinking about things that really get inside you, like Mrs. Settles did me, and you get to thinking that maybe they are like a big tree standing firm against the strong prairie winds, and that you probably won't ever meet anybody else quite the same, well it does things to you. It made me feel that I had to keep on moving, to try to find another person who had something really special, the way Dad had the wild grass in him or the way Mrs. Settles had her whole life tied to her freedom. I kept thinking about the wooden windmill in her field, and I wondered if I would recognize the next person I met who might be like the Stranger Dad said everybody had as a part of him. I suppose I wanted something deep and mysterious like that to happen which would give me a quick way of knowing that I had found what Dad had told me to go and look for.

Ray said that he knew a guy who was supposed to be the boss of a road building gang somewhere out on the south side of Kansas City, and if I was going to go that way I ought to see him. The guy's name was McBride, and Ray had known him in the World War. McBride had been top sergeant of the company that Ray was in, and he said that McBride was a guy you just never forgot. Ray had kept track of him through a buddy who was in that same company; McBride was really considerate, Ray said. If I could find McBride, he added, and tell him I'd been working for Ray, why, maybe McBride would give me a job on his road gang. McBride was a strange guy, but had a soft spot in his heart, Ray said.

Now I wanted more than ever to go to Kansas City and get a look at that Mr. McBride, because the way Ray described him, it was like McBride was a windmill-type himself, unbelievably strong and independent. I figured I would learn where I was going from people like that, and maybe that somebody would turn out to be the Stranger.

I said goodbye to Mrs. Settles—she shook my hand very hard and said she hoped I would find what I was looking for, and never to stop looking. I really wanted to see Kansas City, and I had in mind to go to the "Y" there and look up Charlie Gribble, the guy who had picked me up in his Dodge on the way west. He had said I should come to see him sometime. Charlie, though, wasn't a guy who would have gotten along very well with Mrs. Settles. She wouldn't have listened to him for very long because he had what Dad called "diarrhea of the mouth" but I figured I could get a room at the "Y" cheap and stay there a couple of days.

I got a ride with a truck driver outside Junction City, or maybe it was Cottonwood Falls, and he took me clear through. We went by way of Lawrence, crossed the Kaw River there (it sure looked low), it reminded me of our Neosho River down home when times were dry. The trucker, though, said he had seen the Kaw come clean up to the bridge, roaring like a tornado, and he said it could happen whenever there were heavy rains up along the rivers and creeks north and west.

We rolled into K. C. over the long viaduct between Kansas City, Kansas, and Missouri. I could see how the Kaw and the Missouri came together there, and I had heard Mom talk about seeing it herself when she was a girl and was on her way to the World's Fair at Chicago. She made it sound so beautiful, how those rivers joined, but I couldn't see anything beautiful. Down below, in the valley, was a mess of little buildings and warehouses, all setting there baking in about the hottest sun I had seen since I left home. It was so hot we could hear the truck tires sizzle. The trucker let me out in North Kansas City because he was going on north to Excelsior, Missouri.

After he let me out, I walked toward what the driver had said was the center of Kansas City. I wished I didn't have my old valise, because it sure drew attention to me. Without it I would have been just another hobo; with my valise I was different, a kind of tourist. But I didn't know what to do with it, and it held everything I owned. Still, I was thankful that those guys who had taken my money had left the old valise.

I thought maybe I would walk to the Missouri River, first, before I went into center town, to see how the big river looked from along its bank. All my life I had heard about the Missouri and how important it was in the way the West was opened up. There was a girl back in my class at school, when I was a kid, who claimed her folks were related to the Clark who went up the Missouri in the real early days with Lewis. Dad claimed that there were a lot of steamboats on the Missouri when he came west, and here at Kansas City you could believe there might have been because the river was so big. I walked down there, toward a place along the bank where it was kind of open, and the bank was low. I wanted to get on top of the water; because a river is an important thing to a

Kansas boy, especially one that doesn't dry up. It seems somehow mysterious and unreal. I dipped my hands in the Missouri to wash them there on the bank and I felt different, as though I had done something worthwhile. I didn't know why I felt that way except maybe Dad would have felt the same if he had washed his hands in the Missouri. Only he would probably have talked about it and said a lot about the way it was in the early days.

To my right I noticed an old fellow fishing, and I decided I'd go and speak to him and find out how the fishing was, because I loved to fish. Even on the Neosho River back home you could set out trot lines and catch some big cats in the night. I did that a lot of times, camp on the river bank with a frying pan, some potatoes, some bacon or ham, and some of Mom's homemade bread . . . just stay there all night and go out every once in a while in a boat to see if there were any fish on the trot lines I'd have put in before dark.

Seeing this old guy fishing sure gave me the urge, all right. I went over there and found he was a nice old guy about seventy-five or eighty, maybe, and he had a long bamboo pole stuck into the river bank. He was just sitting there taking it easy, smoking his pipe. He didn't have on a shirt, just an old yellow-looking undershirt, and he had found about the only shade there was along there, alongside a couple of big bushes and an old outhouse. He wasn't catching much, but I guess he really didn't care. He just set there calm and easy, puffing on a pipe, easy to talk with. He said that along where we were was one of several places where the covered wagons had come down to the river to get ferried across, ready to roll out west. He said that his dad had been in the business of helping to outfit wagon trains and had told him many stories about the people and where they came from. He thought that Kansas City, or Westport as it was called, must have seemed more like a city then with all those wagons and people and the kids and animals running all over, than it did now with the place all built up, and everybody so hard up. He wished it had stayed the way it was, with the steamboats smoking up and down the Missouri, going down to St. Louis and up to Omaha. He said the whole river changed when the settlers began to plow up the country out further west, and that the Missouri used to have a lot more water in it.

The old man wasn't any poet like Dad, but what he said and the things he remembered stuck with me, and I got to thinking that Dad and the old fisherman must have been there when the big things happened. It made me feel kind of humble. I hated to leave him, we were getting along so good, but I had to keep going. He told me where I could catch a streetcar downtown, and I rode it down to what looked like the center. The streetcar driver yelled out that it was Main and 6th. I got off and a drunk who was on the platform got ahold of my valise and tried to get it away from me. I had to pull on it hard and broke the handle. I swiftly walked away only to be approached by a couple of panhandlers who asked me for dimes. I never gave them any, maybe I should have, but everything there was too different, too crowded.

I walked around a while in downtown Kansas City; everybody seemed to be after something. I was stopped twice by women, both of them looked like they could have been my mother, they were that old. And a guy came up alongside me and said something that sounded dirty. I passed the Muehlbach Hotel and a place called the Milwaukee Delicatessen. I was hungry and bought a steak sandwich and a cold bottle of grape pop that sure tasted good. I asked where the YMCA was, hot-footed over there and got a room for the night for fifty cents. My impression of downtown Kansas City was that it wasn't so great. When you're used to the open, to hearing the birds and feeling the wind across the fields, being where you can see the whole sky and when you have just come from a wide open land with yellow wheat as far as you can look; and when you have seen big winds come and rip everything up, well, it makes a big city look kind of tame. I had found that out fast.

I'm not sure what it is about the way things just somehow work out as if all of life was put together in a big circle. Like you heard about something one day, and then that exact same thing would crop up again, and it would eventually change something for you.

It was that way with Charlie Gribble, the guy from the YMCA who had given me a ride to western Kansas. I never paid much attention to all he said that day, but I remembered that he asked me to come and see him at the K. C. "Y". Yet I never figured he was anybody special, or had any influence or anything. But you never know.

I stayed two days at the "Y". I asked for Charlie and learned he had a small office at the back of the building. He seemed very glad to see me, and showed me around the "Y" and warned me to stay away from all temptation. He also got me to go and see that fellow who could look at your handwriting and tell a lot about you, and maybe help you find the work you were the best at doing. This expert said that by looking at my handwriting he figured I was going to be a poet or something like that, but he was afraid that wasn't going to do me much good at getting a job. I had an uneasy feeling about what he said. Sometimes, when I'd be listening to Dad, I'd get a strange notion that I could talk like he did if I wanted to, and a few times I'd even tried writing things down. I was awful excited when I did that. There were times when I'd be out walking around the farm and I would almost try to say how I was feeling about things. Thus, I was excited by what the handwriting expert told me.

Soon something definite happened. I asked Charlie if he could help me find out where the Forbes Construction Company was working . . . the road building gang that Ray's friend, Mr. McBride was the boss of.

"Did you say Forbes Construction Company?"

"Sure."

"Where in the world did you hear about them?"

I told Charlie about my wheat-farming friend having known McBride, the boss, in the War, and he said that I should ask him to give me a job.

"Jobs are awful tight here."

"Yeah. I know that."

"Well, you got to have influence to get a job now. Buddies in the War is okay, but you aren't going to make it without more help."

"I figured I'd try, if I can find out where they're working."

"If I help you, you got to keep shut up about it."

"I'd sure do that."

He told me that to wait in the lobby because he was going to make a phone call. I thought he was going to ask somebody about where the construction company was working. I sat down and started to read a *Kansas City Star* newspaper that was lying around. The headline was about some murders that happened in an old hotel on the south side of town. The *Star* said the murders were part of a gang plan to take over the beverage business in the city. They said some guys pretty high up in the city were running things in a gang war, but they didn't say really who they were. Charlie came back.

"They are working in the Blue River bottoms out

south of town. They're building a road out there, a new concrete highway. You still want a job with them?"

"Yeah. I got to work."

"Well, if I can help you, you won't tell who did it. You promise."

"I promise. I sure do."

He went away again. I put the paper down and started to think about Charlie, and I couldn't see why he should do much to help me. I didn't know him hardly, but he had been really nice to me. Dad used to say that if somebody did you a favor he would be your friend for life, and maybe it was like that with Charlie. He gave me that long ride and everything. I couldn't see what he was doing around the "Y" either. He seemed to be a kind of an arranger and knew most everybody. He was certainly religious, and he almost overdid it sometimes. But I couldn't figure how he could help me get a job on a Kansas City construction company or even how he found out so fast where they were. But after awhile he came back and sat down again.

"Maybe I got something for you. I had to use some influence to do it. You wouldn't get anywhere on your own. You know that, don't you?"

"I sure do."

"Well, I never figured you'd really come to Kansas City, but I told you to come and you did. That's where you were smart. We have to have a lot of good guys like you to make the world run better. Now here's what you do. You go out there—take a Holmes Avenue car and ride it as far as it goes. Then you got to hitchhike south on the Blue River road, down about eight miles, clear down to the river bottoms. They're working down there. You might have to ask. And when you get there, see the boss, McBride, and tell him that Mr. O'Neil sent you, and that he won't take no for an answer. Don't mention my name. I don't know what they'll do. It's a tough outfit; they might lead you astray. You got to watch out. Hear me . . . You watch out what you do."

"I will."

"You have any trouble, don't phone me. You're on your own."

I said thanks and we shook hands. I never did see him again, but I never forgot him. I still don't know what kind of a job he had at the "Y" that he could help me so quickly over the telephone in such hard times. But Charlie knew his way around—he must have had influence. In fact, I guess he had a lot, but why he really took such a shine to me I suppose I'll never know.

University and State

That other river, the river of Wisconsin, will flow for awhile here and again, to make it plain, as I talk with people at the Academy or practically anywhere, that it has been vital to all I have tried to do, that the State and University are of one being. The Wisconsin I know and to which I came home, could only, through its unique nature, have created the University I know. The University of Wisconsin is attached to almost all aspects of state tradition, personality and life. For example, in Dane County in Primrose Township, there is the birthplace farm of Robert M. LaFollette Sr.—Fighting Bob—certainly the most famous son of the state, and doubtless its greatest public speaker. He learned the art of oratory at the University. In his early days of political barnstorming he used to speak from the back of a wagon; sometimes the crowds numbered upwards of 5,000, yet no one ever said that Bob LaFollette could not be clearly heard. He had the gift of projection, just as Abe Lincoln did when he spoke on a windy and dusty 1859 day in Milwaukee to 30,000, and was, apparently, understood by everyone. The noted speakers of that generation like LaFollette—Robert Ingersoll, Stephen A. Douglas, Edward Everett—did not swallow their words. They spoke deep down, from the abdomen, casting words from the front of the palate, throat and mouth relaxed and moist, spitting it out to the furthest edge of the audience. They never dreamed of amplification.

I have strong feelings about LaFollette. From his earliest boyhood he had an inclination to self-expression. When one of his teachers requested that Bob address the little country school, LaFollette, unwilling to do anything so usual as stand in front of the class, climbed to the top of the belfrey and spoke to them from there. He had a natural gift for language, and particularly loved the words of Shakespeare. It was not an accident that he chose the subject of Iago for his most famous collegiate oration. He chose it because he understood that there was a gulf between good and evil that required exposition. He learned, from his early oratorical experiments, a method of swaying audiences which he was able to use throughout his life. He wanted at one point to be an actor, but from humble beginnings became a symbol of a richer life for all.

His neighbors in Primrose Township were Yankees from Ohio and Indiana, along with Norwegians, Swiss, and some Germans. In 1856, in February, Bob's father, Josiah LaFollette, passed away, killed by diabetes and pneumonia. The services for him were very simple ... just a prayer by Deacon Thomas and some hymns. He was buried on Green's Prairie near Postville. Young Bob was scarcely ten years old when his father died.

LaFollette never did get over the loss of his father. When his mother died in 1894, LaFollette, Dr. C. A. Harper, and his brother William drove to Postville, taking with them a coffin half-filled with cotton batting. LaFollette himself then went into his father's opened grave and collected what remained. Somehow, the father remained an ideal with him and symbolized the strong ethical values which Robert LaFollette later came to represent. There was no doubt that the LaFollette Progressive Movement had within it the seeds of a Wisconsin and a new American view of culture.

LaFollette first learned to speak and project at the University from Professor Frankenburger, the most heralded speech teacher and master of rhetoric Wisconsin has ever had on its faculty. After his most glorious oratorical triumph, the Middle Western Oratorical Championship at Iowa City in 1879, LaFollette returned to Madison and was met at the Northwestern depot by a hoard of students, stirred in those simpler days by an oratorical championship. It was a great day for Bob and for Wisconsin because soon thereafter he cast his lot with those attempting to create a better society.

Out of the crucible of the University as it was in those days came LaFollette, well grounded in ethics and moral point-of-view by no other than the mighty University president, John Bascom, who personally taught ethics to every senior. Bascom was slightly unhappy with LaFollette because the country boy from Primrose had been entertaining some very liberal religious views. On the day Bob returned from Iowa City, Bascom, out of displeasure over an essay Bob had written that seemed to doubt the power of faith, did not attend the arrival of the young conqueror at the station. Reluctantly, he later allowed Bob to graduate. Bascom believed that man should extend his mental threshold far into the realm of faith. But LaFollette was, apparently, somewhat more practical. In any case, after his entrance into the practices of law and politics, LaFollette developed deep social concerns. No doubt these were results of his observation of the needs of farmers and farmer's wives, and of the whole mood of reform in government, economics, and culture. He developed basic ideas which led finally to the creation of the magnificent "Wisconsin Idea," so all-powerful through the early years of this century in setting the thread and temper of the University and its relationship to the State.

As I grew more interested in the State and learned more about LaFollette and his personal life, I developed a strange sympathy for him, and a personal bond that, I suppose, must have come partly from his father-son relationship. LaFollette's father did die when Bob was a very young lad, a baby, and as he grew up, through the stories his mother told and the antagonistic comments of his step-father, his concern about his real father, long dead, became a vital force. From the illusory life he built around a dead parent grew strong idealisms that eventually made LaFollette a state leader in political and economic reform. I even believe that the illusion of his father had something to do with the concept of the "Wisconsin Idea," as LaFollette developed it.

The "Wisconsin Idea" was a term coined by Dr. Charles McCarthy, Professor of Political Science and head of the Legislative Reference Library in the Legislature, to describe the socio-political ferment in Wisconsin in the early 1900's. Wisconsin was, at that time, extending political democracy by passing and administering laws, such as workmen's compensation, that eventually were accepted throughout the country. But the "Wisconsin Idea" was complex: it meant the drafting of experts—such as Dr. McCarthy—in framing and administering legislation for the benefit of the people. The University, naturally, played an important role in the innovations. In education, the "Wisconsin Idea" meant extending the educational and cultural opportunities of the University to all the people of the state. It meant, according to the pronouncements of University President Van Hise, a classmate of LaFollette, "service to the state" by the University. Dr. McCarthy was one of a small band of enlightened men who worked for the development of University Extension. In 1907, the Legislature approved a budget which greatly expanded Extension—which actually had been started as early as 1885—and brought Extension within Van Hise's definition of service to the state.

Charles R. Van Hise will long be remembered for the part he played in bringing the University of Wisconsin to the people. He was famed for his knowledge of rocks and minerals; he had acquired a national reputation as an authority on political economy; he was high in the counsels of the nation in matters of national and international importance. But it was in the field of educational democracy that he will be best remembered by the people of this country.

During the fourteen years of President Van Hise's administration of the University, Wisconsin blazed the way in smashing American university traditions. Wisconsin led the way in the idea of a new university dedicated to the principle of service. Insofar as the University of Wisconsin could be made an instrument for the advancement of the welfare of the people, to that extent would it meet the ideals and principles which were being formulated by those leading it. The University went out into the state. The University of Wisconsin no longer was a thing of mortar and stone, of books and courses of study, of declensions and formulas centered around a campus.

The University of Wisconsin went out into the fields and made two ears of corn grow where one grew before; it went into the barns of the state and made cleaner and healthier livestock; it went into the crossroads school houses and put fire and ambition into the young people of the state; it went into the communities and brought better sanitation, better ventilation, better municipal government, purer water, set up preventives for sickness and disease; it brought about cleaner milk, better cheese, kept hogs healthy; it elevated the people into higher regard for educational values, and responsible citizenship.

I also believe that the entire state is interlinked through its traditions with the University (now the interlinked and merged University of 27 campuses which may be the great climax of the idea) in a very real and perhaps even a mystical way. It could be that the ancient Indian gods had something to do with the creation of this original university on the hill above Lake Mendota; for if the old Indian shamans conducted councils and ceremonies seated around the effigy mounds on these heights, how logical that the wisdom which has since derived from College Hill in the humanities, arts and the sciences should follow the track of the ancient wise men. The entire spirit of this place may well have drawn to it, through the very magic of a mysterious past, a range of personalities including LaFollette and Van Hise who have pressed the reputation of the University far beyond the shores of Lake Mendota.

There is a great Burr Oak tree that still stands on the University of Wisconsin campus at Observatory Hill, not far from the old astronomer's house. This dwelling, now the home of the Department of Social Work, was formerly the residence of the president of the University; in the 1890's they moved the president to the lower campus to an old Victorian dwelling.

But before all that happened, the president's house was there on top of the hill, and the old oak tree nearby became known as the "President's Tree." It has been there for at least 400 years, my friends in botany tell me, and it was there when some of the Indian mounds were created. The tree has seen a fearsome number of events and persons come and go. A few years back President E. B. Fred had the old tree cabled together, fearful that a heavy wind might destroy it. He left clear instructions that if anything ever happened to the tree that it was to be taken down and carefully examined.

Events the tree has witnessed in its interesting life include: its use as a target by the sharp shooters at Camp Randall, then the state induction camp for Civil War soldiers (supposedly the tree once had a great hole in its trunk where a cannonball had struck—the hole apparently healed, and whether there is a cannonball inside no one knows for certain); Blackhawk, the Sauk chief, retreating in 1832 with his band, crossed the UW campus near the old tree; likewise, there is a story that Abe Lincoln, who got as far as Fort Atkinson with the Illinois militia, supposedly arrived at the future University setting and climbed "College Hill." Whether true or not, the stories and myths are fascinating.

The land on which the University of Wisconsin-Madison now stands was once owned by a fascinating half-French, half-Indian, named Pierre Pacquette. He is one of my favorite Wisconsin characters, a big man who could lift huge objects with great ease, variously heaving to his shoulders a live horse, a keg of lead weighing upwards of 800 pounds, and it is said, once lifted an iron object weighing 2,000 pounds. Perhaps the tales are exaggerated, but Pacquette was apparently an extremely strong man, one of the giants of pioneer times, capable of drawing his fair share with a full-grown ox.

For the most part Pacquette was a gentle soul, very trusted by the Winnebago Indians. He may have been the victim of one of the first "contract murderers" in pioneer Wisconsin. He was shot in the breast by Man-zi-mon-ika (Iron Walker), an Indian who, Pacquette's great grandson Joe Kerwin told me, was sent up from southwest Wisconsin to murder the strong man. Reason? Pacquette was too influential with the Winnebago, and thus many good land deals might be side-tracked. It certainly is true, as I've mentioned, that folks were after Indian lands in those days, and Pacquette well may have been an obstacle. His feeling of sympathy for the Indians was great. All of Pacquette's land, and other possessions, vanished in the settlement of his estate.

To illustrate how curiously the University is interlinked in all these matters: about one hundred and thirty years after Pacquette's death, in the early 1960's, when the great University had spread unbelievably over the whole hill and surroundings, I heard Pacquette's story from his great grandson, a retired Madison fireman. I conceived then the notion that Pacquette should be the leading character in a massive regional drama which would celebrate many of the historical and mythical happenings at Portage. I had plans, with the City of Portage, to build a "revolving amphitheatre" on a huge turntable and produce the drama around the circumference turning the whole audience to the stages: the various scenes of settlement, of Indian war, perhaps even exploration, certainly the military presence of Fort Winnebago. Pacquette was to be a leading figure; so was Zachary Taylor and Jefferson Davis, once soldiers at the Fort; so was Juliette Kinzie, wife of the Indian agent, a cultivated, lively and deeply sympathetic woman from Connecticut who brought a flavor of civilization to the frontier.

I wanted very much to see the project come to reality.

How thrilling to the thousands of Wisconsin citizens to have seen the great events of the Portage unfold, scene by scene. But the theatre was never built nor was there ever any play. An anti-trust suit filed by the United States against a large corporation which was on the point of funding the project, killed it.

But the University is and was a catalyst, and can bring interrelationships into play, cause ideas to be born, dreams to float, and surprisingly often something does really happen.

Anyway, I am virtually certain that at some time, Pacquette stood on the land that was later to become the UW campus beneath the "President's Tree." I would have liked to see them together, a mighty man and a mighty oak tree.

Yes, there are many ways in which the University is attached to Wisconsin's most colorful personalities. The John Muir story is yet another example. Muir, a Scotch lad, came with his family to Wisconsin, to the little lake called Fountain Lake, where he learned his early ecology; I have never forgotten the story of how the raw farm boy set forth from the homestead when he was about nineteen, laden with his inventions, including a couple of curious home-made wooden clocks. He exhibited his ingenious treasures at the Wisconsin State Fair then held in Madison, and eventually found his way to the University seeking knowledge, thirsty for it, and the University admitted him, though he had no academic background. His room at the northeast corner of North Hall was filled with laboratory apparatus, books, and clocks.

Muir got his first lesson in botany under the "Muir Locust," a black locust tree that stood on the slope above Lake Mendota (Muir Knoll, now), and there Muir and a kindly fellow student, Griswold, talked about the locust blossoms. The old locust tree died in 1953; some of the wood was made into paper knives and gavels by Walter Rowlands, a noted agricultural specialist, and President Edwin Fred presented these objects to many friends of the University.

Part of my affinity for the State certainly comes from the spirit of the University which offers help to any citizen desiring it. I believe this is the source of our greatest strength as an institution; that the faculty of the University of Wisconsin has been willing to share knowledge and to help people. In the folklore of the University this is the great truth that emerges again and again. Example: the development of dicumarol, the miracle drug developed from sweet clover, important in the prevention of blood clots. . . .

A farmer from upstate, whose cows had been dying, simply put some blood from one of the dead cows into a milk can and set out for Madison. It didn't matter that it was Christmas morning. He came anyway, and by chance, found one of the research scientists of the University at work in his biochemistry lab. Karl Paul Link heard the farmer's story and recognized his difficulty as "the sweet clover disease." Cows that had been eating spoiled sweet clover hay had developed hematoma, a blood leakage under the skin that caused them to become weak. Eventually they died.

The farmer's visit started Link on a lengthy research problem which finally lead him to dicumarol, and then to Warfarin, not only the greatest rat killer ever known, but one even more successful than dicumarol in treating and preventing blood clots.

But then Wisconsin folks have always been enterprising and have always risen to challenges, possibly following the example set by a noted state citizen, Hercules Dousman of Prairie du Chien. In order to repay Dousman for some valuable services which he performed in the early days, the Federal government told him that he could have title to all the land he could ride around in a single day. I suppose they pictured Hercules leisurely riding around a few acres in a buggy. Not so. Dousman stationed a swift horse every five miles and did a solid day of Pony Express-type riding. He covered so much land that the Government backed off a little, but he eventually owned a large chunk of southwest Wisconsin . . . according to the folktales.

In a sense it is this delightful type of enterprising spirit that makes Wisconsin so attractive to me. I come down the Wisconsin River canoeing, these days, and remember the great rafts of sawn lumber with steering oars fifty feet long, and the strong raftsmen who brought them through the narrows at the Dells and around the "Devil's Elbow." And although the rafts have vanished and the mighty timber has long been cut, I still think of the bard of the lumber camps, Emery DeNoyer, and the songs he often sang.

And I think of all the folklore that has made up our

early industry, and the people who sang and told stories that reflected their work and needs ... thinking about the way the timber was cut and what happened then; and the new necessities that arose in agriculture and science as the patterns of life inevitably changed.

It isn't hard to recall how naturally the University responded to the change-over from timber to agriculture in the north, and how the University suggested new methods that helped folks on the farms overcome the stubborn cutover, to farm in new ways, and to look ahead to an overwhelming tourist industry.

Or when I am traveling around the state and see the big barns and fine herds, I can't help thinking of Professor Stephen Babcock and how, without his milk test, dairying might never have attained the stature it did. Babcock lived in a yellow house on Lake Street in Madison. I didn't know him, of course, but I knew the house well, and the Hollyhock garden behind it. Most fittingly, seed from the Babcock Hollyhocks has been given out and scattered over the entire state by 4H Club kids.

I like that: throughout the State the springs of lore nourish something or somebody at the University; and the University brings back to the State some expansion of a stimulus or idea and spreads it for the good of all. If the State has its own kind of lore and heritage, so does the University, and one is related and often made out of the other. It's a fine feeling to have been a part of the Wisconsin tradition, and of the University where all of my work has been done. I suppose none of it could have been undertaken, though, had it not been for that germinal summar, and memories of that time force me back again and again to re-identify my trace.

Working for Mr. McBride

It was a long way out south of Kansas City to where the Forbes gang was working. I rode the streetcar as far as it went, like Charlie Gribble said, beyond the suburbs to the south, and got off at the end of the line and started walking. It seemed as if the city just went on and on forever—it was so big and spread out. Two or three times I had to ask directions and twice I simply got off the road and sat under the trees, wishing that I didn't have to do anything but sit back out of sight, and feel how good it was just to be lazy. I'd worked awful hard in the wheat fields, and a little rest felt good.

I must have walked five or six miles, and I caught a ride for a couple of miles, too. It started to rain before I got to the road construction and I got pretty wet, but I kept right on going because I wanted to see Mr. McBride that afternoon. It rained harder and harder. After I arrived at the new road grade and walked along it for a ways, I could see that the construction work had stopped for the day. None of the machinery was operating, and nobody was working. I passed a big tool box with "Forbes Construction Co." lettered on it. A guy wearing an old raincoat told me that work had knocked off for the day, but that a bunch of the workers were resting down the grade under a bridge. I asked for Mr. McBride, and he said that maybe he was down there, too, but he wasn't sure. I slogged down the grade hoping to find him but not caring much, either. If he wasn't there with the others I probably could find someplace to stay that night, then I'd try to find Mr. McBride in the morning.

I heard yelling before I got to the bridge. Underneath, the workers were in a close circle, some squatting, some standing and leaning in, and one was shaking dice and getting ready to make a throw. I had only seen this in cow barns down home on rainy afternoons when some of the neighbor guys were there, and once or twice in a garage uptown at Iola, when I would be coming home from school. I hadn't ever done it—shooting craps—myself. Mom didn't hold with gambling of any kind and wouldn't even let a pack of playing cards in the house. She said that gambling was a main station on the railroad to hell, and that nothing would set a man to wandering and be fiddlefooted and restless as much as gambling. Even if I did remember what Mom had said, I went under the bridge and stood there watching.

They were a rough-looking gang of guys. Nobody paid any attention to me at all, so I listened to them talking to the dice and hollering—about "little joe" and "box cars" and "eight-a-macada;" and about "little joe pickin' cotton" and "fever in the bunkhouse" and "shootin' for nine kaline the monkey's mine." As I got interested in the game and pushed in closer, I didn't see the big man come up at all.

The gang saw him though, and the gambling stopped for a moment. I turned around, and he was standing a little ways from me—one of the biggest guys I ever saw. He was a lot taller than I was and very husky, not fat at all. He had a big head and was wearing an old derby hat. His shirt was faded, an old dress shirt I guessed, with no collar. He was weather-burned deep brown, and there was something very unusual about his eyes. They were hard eyes, but they weren't squinted up exactly; rather they were tight, making him look stern and hard. The gamblers acted scared of him, and very respectful, too. There wasn't anymore dice throwing, until the big man said, "Go ahead and throw. Don't let me stop you. Just don't say that I done it, when your women come after you for the money."

The guy who was holding the dice shot and made his point. The big boss-guy started to leave, and I nervously eased up beside him. I still had my valise and I felt awkward. It made me look like I was leaving, or coming maybe. Not right, anyhow. It's hard to ask about a job with a valise in your hand.

"Mister McBride, Ray Ellefson sent me to see you."
"Who?"
"Ray Ellefson, he was with you in the War."
"I don't know any Ray Ellefson."
"He said you were his top sergeant and that he and

you and another guy were all that were left of a company."

"Don't know anything about it."

"And Mister O'Neil said you were to put me to work on the steel truck. I wasn't to take no for an answer."

It sure sounded funny saying it like that, but it was what Charlie Gribble had said to do. It wasn't the way I wanted to say it, but I was simply following what I'd been told.

For a second, I thought he was going to hit me. I got ready to jump back, since I didn't want any trouble with him. I don't know why the name of O'Neil upset him so much, but it really did. He stared at me, and his eyes grew tighter. I saw his large hands clench like they had hold of somebody they hated.

"Who are you, kid? Who's your connection?"

"I don't have any connection."

"You know you do. They wouldn't send out a kid like you unless there was a good reason. And I had a phone call about you, too." He grabbed hold of my arm. His grip felt like a heavy iron hook. "Who sent you out here?"

I've never been as scared. I couldn't say anything, besides Charlie had told me to keep my mouth shut. I didn't know what part he had in this anyway, but suddenly I realized that I never in the world could have the slightest chance at a job unless there was pressure and influence somewhere. The name of Roy Ellefson, who was supposed to be McBride's friend, hadn't had any effect at all. But the name of O'Neil stirred up a storm. I wanted to break loose and get out of there, because suddenly there was something very scary about the whole thing.

"I can't tell you who sent me."

"They told you not to, did they? Damn them to hell, trying to run my end of the business. They can build their own stinking road; make their own dirty money."

He turned me loose and started to stride off down the grade. After a few steps he wheeled back. "I don't hold with having laborers shoved onto me. I don't give a damn who they are. They shouldn't do it. But they've sent you out here, so I'll have to take you on. I had to lay off my own nephew last week. You ain't going to enjoy the work. Be here at six tomorrow."

The crap shooters sure weren't shooting craps. They were all staring at me as if I had committed a big crime or something. And I felt as if I had. I didn't know what it was, but I guessed I had done a bad thing. I started to move away from there and heard somebody say, "I wouldn't want to be that kid. He's got it comin'."

"Someday he'll really bust loose," someone else said. "I wouldn't want to be that kid."

I walked back the way I had come, not knowing what I was going to do. I had a job, sort of, but I had never figured a job would be like walking into a lion's den. That was the way I felt about Mr. McBride—he didn't like me and I had forced myself in, or somebody had forced me in, and now I was caught in a kind of box. I thought about leaving, except that I didn't want to get Charlie into any trouble, and I was afraid that if I didn't stay, it might get him in hot water. I sure would have liked to know what he had told Mr. McBride about me. And I wanted to know what Charlie's connection was. I never found out.

I walked back up the grade. It had stopped raining, and the sun was about to break through. There were woods on both sides, and I wanted to go in there and hide or something . . . get away from whatever it was I was trying to do. The trouble was, I didn't know whether I was doing it for myself, or for Dad, or whom, I was really confused. But I kept on walking and finally arrived back near Kansas City. I passed an old house with a sign out in front advertising rooms for rent. Although I wasn't too anxious to rent anything, or to go into a strange room in a private house, I really didn't have any other choice. I rented a room at the top of the house. It was boiling hot, plus, it wasn't much of a room, and the landlady was old and scroogey looking. Before she rented it to me she asked me for two-weeks rent in advance. I told her that I was going to work on the road gang, and she said she'd give me breakfast and make me up a lunch every day for an extra dollar. I guess it was all pretty expensive, but it was the best that I could do.

I started in to work the next morning but I still felt like a thief, stealing somebody's job; and Mr. McBride had made me feel like I was a piece of worthless and unwanted garbage. I suppose I should have faded out of the picture, but being inexperienced and not knowing what to do, I stayed.

My first job was on the steel truck, a really old International with a flat body and racks on both sides. The racks had to be loaded with steel bars thirty feet long and more than an inch in diameter. Then the bars had to be distributed along the sides of the road grade so they could be used as reinforcement for the new concrete.

The temperature was over 110° in the river bottoms where the steel piles lay. The truck driver, a thin young guy with a small patch of black moustache stuck to his lip, looked unbelievably clean, as if he never touched anything dirty at all. His name was Clyde. When we stopped beside the steel, Clyde got out of the truck, stretched and yawned.

"Well, kid, get going."

"What am I supposed to do?

"Get the damn steel loaded on."

"How do I do it?"

"You grab 'em and heave 'em on. I'd help, but a truck driver's not supposed to do a damn thing but drive." He sat down in the shade of a bush.

The bars were twisted and snarled together like a thousand hot snakes. I pulled them this way and that and eventually got thirty bars loaded on each rack. Then I had to walk along behind the truck and pull off each bar as Clyde drove down the grade so as to space the bars out for the concrete layers. But I hadn't loaded the bars well and some of them were wrapped around each other. The truck would move and I would pull. Sometimes a bar would slide off the rack, but more often I'd simply be pulled along by the truck, holding onto the bar and taking a terrible beating. My hands were badly torn and my belly muscles ached.

We hauled three loads of steel by about mid-afternoon. Clyde said that I should go under a tree and rest for a couple of minutes. But I told him no, that I felt fine, even if I didn't. I didn't want him or anybody else to think I was beaten. All the time I was rolling the steel and loading it, Clyde was loafing under a bush. He would doze awhile with his hat down over his eyes, or he would sit there slapping at the flies with his gloves. Sometimes he would take a little pair of clippers out of his pocket and work on his fingernails. Every once in awhile he would yell for me to hurry. When he did this I really wanted to whip one of the long pieces of steel at him, or try to jam the hot steel up against his neck. It was a terrible way to feel. I'm sure that Mom would say that I should love my brother, but I didn't love Clyde. I wanted to kill him.

As I toiled, I kept thinking about the old wheat fields and they sure seemed awful good. Even the cyclone was better than this. I never hated anybody like I hated Clyde—I've always been like that with somebody who isn't doing his fair share of the job. When we got all the steel hauled, Clyde said that I had better grab a spade and start digging for the steel forms that had to be set in level at the sides of the road grade. He said that Mr. McBride had ordered him to watch me sharp all day and make sure that I never stopped working hard. He said that Mr. McBride was just itching to fire me and that any excuse would be all right.

I also worked hard at the digging, because I felt it would be a disgrace to Charlie and Dad and Mom if I got fired. In the terrible heat the water boy never seemed to come around my way. I realized by now, though, that Mr. McBride was trying to get me killed off so I would quit. I had seen that done in the hay fields down home when they didn't want a new guy around, so they would put him in the hardest, hottest job. Once we had a Polish guy working for us and the other men didn't like him, so they sent him back in the mow to keep the hay pitched back. It was terribly hot and dark up there, and he fell down an open hole into the cow barn on top of the cows that were standing in there. When he crashed down on top of them they started bellering and pushing and they got him down in the loft. It sure was a mess.

I began to dig out for three forms in the rock formation but the rock just shattered away to pieces at the end of my bar when I jammed it into a crack. I was so mad. Pretty soon an old black guy limped over to where I was working.

"Workin' too hard, son."

The old man sat down on the ledge of rock and lit his pipe. He must have been about sixty-five, stooped, and he spoke in a real soft kind of voice. "The rock'll all be there tomorrow."

I jammed the bar into a crack and pried.

"Rock'll still be there. Always be more rock. Nobody's bigger'n the rocks and nobody can fight the rocks. The rock'll always win, the rocks'll be there forever."

"To hell with you."

"Name's Jim. You didn't mean to cuss me. You're just mad."

"I'll do the whole job by myself. That's what they want."

"Nobody'll do the whole job by himself. You need a lot of other folks to help you. You're killin' yourself off."

"I'll bust this crowbar right in half."

Old Jim shook his head and turned away from me. He walked off and came back in a while with the water bucket. I guess the water boy had gone to sleep someplace and had left the bucket sitting by the grade. The water in it was almost hot. I drank from the dipper, then splashed a little of the hot water in my eyes.

"Thanks."

"Welcome. You take it easy, son."

"I will."

Yet I went ahead working as hard as I could. Sometimes when you're crazy angry and hot and thinking a lot of mean things you just tear into it. The sun, slanting down just above a hill in the west, now seemed hotter than ever. Clyde came around, finally, and said that I might as well go on back to Kansas City. Mr. McBride didn't want me hanging around on the job, and it was going to be tougher and tougher. It would get tougher every day. McBride didn't like being made to take anybody onto his gang.

"Mac said that them characters downtown can take you and stick you, kid. That's what Mac said. He said you get back to K. C. and tell 'em he ain't gonna stand nothin' more like this. He says he can get workers better'n you by the thousands."

Clyde might have just gone on and on talking that way, but nobody had ever talked to me like that before. Something broke loose inside. I thought of Zill and the robbery and the Depression and the heat and the rocks and everything all at once. It seemed like everybody was trying to throw dirt on me. I grabbed a spade and chased Clyde down the grade about a hundred yards. I was gaining on him, but he jumped on the back of a dump truck and got away. When I returned to my digging I was so winded that I could hardly catch my breath. There was so much sweat coming out of my hair and forehead that I couldn't even see.

After that I got chilly and started to shake, but I kept right on working. Dad once said that hard work would solve anything. With him, and a lot of other old timers, work was a kind of religion. Some of the guys on the gang had stopped what they were doing to watch me. When quitting time came I had dug out about seven forms, about as many as had ever been done in that much time by one guy in the rock, at that's what somebody said later. My hands were totally blistered, and my lips were cracked wide open. I staggered over under a tree and blacked out . . . just keeled over, that's all.

When I came to, Mr. McBride was bending over me. I tried to get up, but the boss pushed me down.

"I won't work for you," I said. My voice sounded faint and far off.

Mr. McBride grinned. He sure looked different when he grinned. "My nephew shot craps for sixty dollars last week. A guy like him don't need to work. I'm puttin' you permanent in his place. You get out here at six-thirty tomorrow. I won't stand no late time."

Why he did it I don't know. Maybe he felt like Dad about hard work. I got up and staggered away. But I was on the job bright and early the next morning. I still don't know how I made it, but I was there even a couple of minutes early. I knew that by looking at the watch Mr. McBride had in his hand when I stumbled past him.

INFORMAL LORE

I love the informality of the Wisconsin people, and their willingness to just come in and gab about things. In fact, my Academy office (or cave) had become an important assembly-point for a great deal of indigenous folklore. I heard, for example, about the way crops are (or were) planted; for the old farmers had their planting lore and spoke it to the moon. But in an age of much larger farms, and now, less total family participation in agriculture, the old customs brought from New England and New York by the early farmers aren't followed much. Yet sometimes I do hear farmers of old American descent swear by the moon as a guide in planting, reaping and harvesting.

"My family," said a southern Wisconsin dirt farmer whose folks came from New York State, "has followed Wisconsin farm folklore for many years and has always planted with the moon." The following are excerpts from a recent calendar and are characteristic of the practice of those of us who find wisdom in the ancient traditions:

First Quarter—During the first quarter of the moon plant the following: Asparagus, Broccoli, Brussels Sprouts, Barley, Cabbage, Cauliflower, Celery, Cucumbers, Corn, Cress, Endive, Kohlrabi, Lettuce, Leek, Oats, Parsley, Onions, Spinach and seeds of flowering plants.

Avoid the first day of New Moon for planting, also the days on which it changes quarters.

Second Quarter —During the second quarter plant: Beans, Eggplant, Muskmelon, Peas, Pepper, Pumpkin, Squash, Tomatoes, Watermelon.

When possible plant seeds while moon is in the fruitful signs of Cancer, Scorpio, or Pisces. The next best signs are Taurus and Capricorn.

Third Quarter—During the third quarter plant: Artichoke, Beets, Carrots, Chicory, Parsnips, Potatoes, Radish, Rutabaga, Turnip and all bulbous flowering plants.

Fourth Quarter—During the fourth or last quarter of the moon turn sod, pull weeds and destroy noxious growths, especially when moon is in the barren signs, Gemini, Leo or Virgo.

—Planting is best done in the signs of Scorpio, Pisces, Taurus, or Cancer—all fruitful signs. In addition, astrologers aver it is best to plant all things which yield above ground in the increase of the moon, and all things which yield below ground when the moon is decreasing.

—Never plant anything in the barren signs, as they are only good for grubbing, trimming, deadening and destroying noxious growths.

—For grafting, cut your grafts from good bearing trees at any time while the trees are dormant, usually from December to March. Keep them cool in a dark place, although not too dry nor too damp, until time to use them. Do the grafting just before the sap starts to flow, while the moon is from new to full (first and second quarters), and while it is passing through the fruitful watery signs of Cancer, Scorpio, Pisces or the earthy, productive sign, Capricorn.

—Planting or grafting done on Sunday will probably not succeed, as this day is ruled by the sun, and therefore considered a dry and barren day.

—Pick apples and pears in the old of the moon and the bruised spots will dry up, where if they are picked in a new moon the spots will rot.

—Harvest all crops when the moon is growing old—they keep better and longer.

—Dig root crops for seed in the third quarter of the moon; they will keep longer and are usually drier and better.

—Grain intended for future use or seed should be harvested at the increase of the moon.

—Timber cut in the old of the moon will not become worm eaten or snap in burning; and fence posts set in the old of the moon will not "heave" out.

—Fruits and vegetables gathered just before Full Moon in the second quarter will usually stand shipment better than others.

A simple but practical demonstration of planetary influence is to plant some seed when the moon is in a fruitful sign such as Cancer (the most fruitful of all) and then a day or two afterwards, when the moon is in the barren sign Leo, plant more of the same lot of seed. There will be significant differences.

My good friend and colleague, Professor Walker Wyman of the University of Wisconsin at River Falls, presented in his pamphlet "Wisconsin Folklore" a few more bits of homely wisdom:

—When the bees stay close to the hive, rain is close by.

—If corn husks are thick, there may be a cold winter ahead. (Possibly true because the thick husks have developed during a warm wet summer, and a cold dry winter may follow.)

—When a dog eats grass, it is a sign of rain. (Possibly true, since low air pressure and high humidity may cause internal pain to a dog and he wants to purge himself. More likely, the dog has worms.)

—Flies bite more before a rain. (Heat causes sweating and releases more body odors, which attract flies, and heat and humidity presage rain.)

—Crickets are accurate thermometers. (Count the chirps for 14 seconds, add 40, and you have the temperature.)

—When the leaves show their backs, it will rain. (Leaves lie with the prevailing winds, which come from the northwest, but storms may come from other directions and ruffle the leaves the wrong way.)

—Northern lights bring cold weather. (Possibly true, but this is debatable.)

—Rainbow in the morning, shepherd takes warning; rainbow toward night, shepherd's delight. (True since storms move from the west, and when a rainbow appears in the west, the storm has passed.)

—When smoke descends, good weather ends. (Storms bring high pressure, causing smoke to stay close to the earth.)

—When joints ache and corns hurt, stormy weather is ahead. (Possibly true because increased humidity may affect them in some unknown way.)

Generally, on the farms where they still speak of the old planting and harvesting lore, there is more time for telling generally of the old heroes of countryside tradition.

In a darkened barn on an afternoon of rain, in from

the hayfield, resting, with the smell of the rain beating the dust I have heard old timers tell of Ben Hooper, the Green County pioneer who brought his favorite yoke of oxen with him to Wisconsin when he came from Ohio. Old Josh and Jehosophat. They plowed his sod, and tromped out his grain, round and around they walked, tied to a pole, and the yellow wheat laid out on the ground. They trod the grain out. But one day Ben tied them to the extending branch of a hickory tree. They went around and around and twisted the tree right out of the ground. So old Ben turned them and they twisted the roots right back into place. Ben got twisted hickory nuts off that tree for twenty years. . . .

And once, cried Charley Henderson, who knew some Ben Hooper tales himself, once I seen old Ben (he didn't, Ben was dead a good fifty or a hundred years before) fire his old muzzleloader right into a flock of pigeons. Split the limb, the ball did, and the pigeons got their toes caught in the crack. Old Ben had him a pot-full of pigeon that day, I tell you!

"Comb your hair arter dark
Comb sorrow to yer heart"
said old Grandma Gandy.
"An if you sing in bed,
The Devil'll dance on yer head!"

That's the way the old Wisconsin pioneer women advised their daughters. When Grandma Gandy's daughter, Betty, was to get married, Grandma gave her this advice. "Now, Betty, sees you don't git up and build the fire the first mornin'. If you do you'l git an old house over yer head." What Grandma meant was that Betty better not start something she didn't want to keep on doing for the rest of her days. Informal people, informal lore.

The old world German-Dutch custom of "shooting the bird" (Schutz) is, so far as I know, followed only in Brown County, since shooting is no longer so much a part of the daily lives of Wisconsin families. But in the neighborhoods of Springfield Corners, Ashton, and Pine Bluff, there are memories of this custom which included the making of a great wooden bird out of hardwoods, carved into it as a large creature with spread wings and upthrust head. This bird was then fastened to the top of a wooden pole fifty-feet high. Most early Wisconsin communities had a "liberty pole" made and decorated in honor of the principle of human freedom.

Sometimes the bird was attached to the top of the liberty pole. When the bird was placed, and the festivities ready, the shooters, each with his favorite weapon, gathered for the contest. The idea was to clip off the wings, the head, and finally to bring down the body. Prizes were awarded for the shooting down of each piece. There were hundreds of watchers, many shooters, and the festival after the shooting lasted into the night. There would always be a dance, and plenty of good German beer.

There are so many images like these upon the Wisconsin land. But above all else the ancient wisdom and lore of the Wisconsin Indians casts a ligering spell. Andrew Beechtree of the Oneidas has said that many, many years ago, when the morals of the Oneidas were of high degree, there lived an elderly widowed Oneida woman. With her lived her maidenly daughter. One winter morning the old woman awoke and found an infant lying on the mat of her supposedly virgin daughter. On the impulse of the moment, she seized the infant, carried it outside, and threw it into the bushes, thinking to leave it there until it froze. She returned to the house and mumblingly resumed her duties. Suddenly, her attention was again attracted to the mat where she saw yet another baby. Again she seized the infant and carried it outside. This time she shucked the infant into a hole in the creek ice, and the child was immediately drawn under the ice by the swift current. Again the woman re-entered her home and to her amazement, there lay the infant again. It was then that her entire body thrilled as a new intelligence dawned upon her. She realized that this happening was of extraordinary import. She then went and gently lifted the child to her, kissed him, and said to him, "I love you and will care for you as my own child."

Time passed, and under the care and guidance of this foster grandmother the infant grew into manhood. As a man he became an educator. He taught the people to love one another; he promoted the communal life so that the swift hunter might share his kill with the aged and sick and the crippled; and he removed the emotion of covetousness or greed. He taught them to kill only enough game animals to meet their needs. He taught them to use beaded wampum to record their agreements. He showed them the folly of destroying each other while engaged in war between their several clans or tribes. He helped them form a government, leaguing together their several tribes, to which their differences might be submitted and settled to the benefit of all concerned. He provided them with implements of war and taught them how to fight when it became necessary for their self-defense. At last, his policies seemed to be well-grounded among the people, so one afternoon he built a great campfire. People from miles around gathered to hear and see what was to take place at this "special council". At the customary time the great man arose and made a speech, thanking them for their cooperation and telling them of his appreciation for their adoption of his policies. At the conclusion he said: "We have relatives across the lake. Tomorrow I shall go to see them."

On the morrow the great man departed with the rising of the sun. He went forth to the east, walking upon the waters. As he advanced into the sun the rays created a halo about him. Time passed, and many years later he made his reappearance among his people. His features showed much suffering. As the people gathered about him he showed them the punctured marks on his hands and feet and sadly said, "These are the marks of what our other people did to me. For that they must suffer much before they can return to their spiritual kingdom. As for you, you have listened to me and adopted my teachings; your obligation shall be to remember me once a year."

With the conclusion of this instruction there departed the Oneida Saviour, Sago yehwata, "The Awakener." (Hiawatha to us.)

So now every New Year's morning Oneida women are prepared to welcome with food, drink and warmth and adopt (in pretense) the children who come to the doors of the Oneida homes, saying as they enter "Hoyan, Hoyan" (and now another time).

There is a timeless quality about regional art, and local folklore, the subject-matter of local life lived and observed. When I view these and other examples I find myself coming back to the mystery of memory. I can't get the notion out of my head that the people who have created this country and given it its character—the old Indians, the French, the early settlers—are really gone. The land they created in spirit is still here, altered and shaped by generations, while I recreate the mystic memory sights and sounds. If you can imagine that the sounds of an older day do haunt the land, the woods, the sky, then what an adventure it is to travel, to see, and to mix your own reality with fantasy.

For me it is always as though I am lingering on a spiritual doorstep, and can hear and sense the whole thing. I often, in fancy, hear the sounds and voices of the early ones: sounds of laughing teamsters; rumbling of heavy wagons; wheels turning, sucking in mud; crack of the bull whips, hammering of pioneers building, building of logs, then sawn timber. I hear the sound of a sod-breaking plow, tearing roots; cries of thousands of birds in the furrow; flights of ducks, of sandhill cranes; of women's voices sometimes sharp with fear and pain. I hear the rattle of military gear, of early settlers singing.

The voices are somehow never stilled by time or the distance of memory . . . if the possibility of nostalgic memory does exist in you. The voices that have broken and transformed the earth remain and linger forever, and wheels, both old and new, turn and turn restlessly as though the book were never opened.

The Speakeasy

During that long summer of my odyssey, Clyde, the steel truck-driver, and I got to be good friends. Sometimes after we finished the day's work, Clyde would drive the big old truck along the Blue River to a place where the water was deeper and we'd go swimming. Even though the water was brown and the bottom was always sucky mud, the wetness felt like heaven on our parched skins, and we didn't mind the marks the dirty water left on us after we got out.

Sometimes there'd be six or more guys from the work crew swimming too. Often they would josh me, since I was probably the youngest and all, but I never minded it. Everyone was friendly and warm. What I did mind though, was someone trying to do harm or to be mean, but most of the guys weren't that way. I was really enjoying being a part of the work gang.

But there was one guy, named Joe Malone, who would occasionally talk nastily about Black people. Malone seemed to have Black folks on his mind all the time; he was always talking dirty about how much he would enjoy raping a Black girl, or how much he would love to castrate a Black guy with the sharp knife that he always carried. None of the gang ever took him very seriously. They even teased him about his knife. But he was big alright—heavy-set and strong, with a long scar on his neck that ran down his chest. I wondered whether some Black guy had given him that scar. Maybe that was why he hated Blacks so much.

Things were sure a lot different in the early 1930s; black people and white people were really divided, and only because they were a different color. Around Kansas City there were always bad feelings and scary talk that race riots were going to happen. Down home, as far as I could see, it just never made any difference at all, at least not with my folks. Mom wouldn't stand any racist talk like that, and she said that God and Abraham Lincoln both said that folks were made equal, and that was all there was to it.

One noon hour Clyde and I were sitting on the truck running board eating lunch when Mr. McBride came driving along in his Model-A Ford Coupe. He stopped beside our truck and stuck his head out the window. He never took off his derby hat, least not that I ever saw, except that it was off the last time I ever saw him.

"How's the kid workin'?"

"He's workin'," Clyde said.

"He better. You shag your tail every day, kid."

"I work hard."

"Dam' if you don't. Get in my car, kid. You deserve a coolin' off. We'll be back, Clyde, before they need the steel. You wait here, case anybody comes. You guys that really work ought to have some fun. How I love a hard worker. This kid's one, all right. I'd hire the Devil himself, if he put out the labor."

It was a real honor to be asked to ride in the boss's car. Clyde had been to places with Mr. McBride, but not many of the common laborers had, and Mr. McBride was taking me along. He was the kind of boss who didn't have many close friends. Usually the ones he took along with him, when he would leave the job for an hour or so, were those who were having problems of some kind and needed straightening out. Everyone said that McBride always helped the men who were hard workers and were really independent. Anyway, by this time I had terrific admiration for the boss, sort of almost a hero worship, because I marveled how he managed the gang with a great deal of justice. I never did know who his own, higher-up bosses were—they never showed themselves or anything. And the thousands of stories the guys told about Mr. McBride made him even more of a hero to me. So far, he was the third person I had ever met who really impressed me. He was like a big tree that stands out by itself; he and Mrs. Settles, and my Dad.

Mr. McBride wheeled the Ford around and headed down the grade. I started to think about the way I had left Iola that June morning (which now seemed a million years away), sitting between Zill and Harry. Now I was sitting beside Mr. McBride, and I sure felt different. We went a couple of miles and turned south on a crossroad. Soon we turned into a farm driveway and stopped in front of an old house, weathered gray, with the eaves falling down at the corners of the roof. Tall weeds were growing in the yard. There didn't seem to be anybody around the place, and it looked as if it hadn't been lived in for years.

Mr. McBride got out of the Ford and I followed him. He went around a corner of the house and lifted up a slanting, dilapidated, cellar door like all the old farm houses used to have, the type of door that our root cellars and cyclone cellars down home had.

Inside, solid cement steps led down into a deep basement. As we went down Mr. McBride pulled the cellar door shut behind us, so we felt our way through the dark. We were still blind from the hot, bright sun. We entered a large, very cool room. A light bulb was hanging down, a sort of glimmer, not much more, and I could see then that the floor was hard-packed dirt. There was also a strong smell . . . of like river mud, earthy, moist and mucky. There were several tables and chairs and some benches. Mr. McBride pulled out one of the benches and sat down. He kept his hat on all the time. I sat down, too.

A small, sandy-haired guy came out of an adjoining room. He was sort of sneaking in as if he was afraid of something. He was wearing bib overalls, and his face looked a lot whiter than if he was a working man.

"What'll it be, Mr. McBride?"

"Brew, Sandy."

"Some eggs?"

"Some salt, too."

"O.K. Mr. McBride."

Sandy hurried away, back out of a door. I could see several doorways leading out of the big room. Sandy returned right away with a couple bottles of home brew. I'd seen stuff like it a lot down home, being passed around in barns, or else around where some country guys were talking beside the river. But I had never tasted it before. Mr. McBride picked up a bottle of home brew.

"Green?"

"No. Oh, no. Mr. McBride," replied Sandy.

"Not much older'n a day, is it?"

"Some."

Mr. McBride made a doubtful noise. Sandy opened up the brew, and it spurted out over the top. It looked like a geyser spouting up, it was so powerful. Mr. McBride grabbed the bottle quickly and ran the neck into his mouth, gulping down the foam. It ran down over his chin and into the neck of his shirt. I looked at Mr. McBride, and he indicated that I could try it. Well, the stuff was very yeasty and had a sharp bite on the tongue, but I'd have to admit that it was one of the best drinks I ever had. After working in that river-bottom heat, the home brew was absolutely cool and delicious.

"Green as weeds," Mr. McBride said. "Well, bring me a glass, Sandy."

"O.K. Mr. McBride."

Sandy brought a big water glass, and Mr. McBride poured the home brew in it. Then he broke a raw egg into the brew and drank down the whole thing. Sandy hurried out and brought in more home brew, and Mr. McBride drank all that, plus another egg. I just sat there and watched him. He seemed even bigger to me, larger than any man I had ever seen. Mr. McBride then downed another bottle of home brew and had another egg.

Sandy came back. "Them guys was here again the other day."

"Those with the black truck?"

"Yeah."

"Crooks."

"They come here and they told me what I got to do."

"What'd you tell 'em?"

"Told 'em nothin'."

"Good. They ain't having their own way much longer. They can drive people only so much." Sandy moved off.

"You got a girl?" Mr. McBride suddenly asked me.

"No."

"Well, I had two wives. They was fine women, but I couldn't live with either one. They wanted too much. They wanted me all the time. I would be with them sometimes, but mostly I wouldn't. I live for the roads and the tools, and the hot and cold, and my workmen. Left both of my women."

I was proud to be in the company of Mr. McBride. It was the greatest thing that ever happened to me, greater, even, than seeing Mrs. Settles stand up on the windmill. Being alone in the cellar with him made me feel more important than I had ever felt, except maybe for a time or two when Dad and I had gone fishing together. Right then I didn't want to leave the road gang. Not ever. And I wondered whether Dad had ever known a man like Mr. McBride, or if the Stranger Dad had met in the grass was like him.

"When the job here is done, can I go with you to the next one?" I asked.

Mr. McBride just sat for a while. He never answered the question, just kept right on drinking. All the brew didn't seem to bother him at all.

Sandy came back. This time he was running.

"They're back again."

"Ones in the black truck?"

"Two of 'em. Same guys."

I heard the outside cellar door squeak as it was pulled open. A couple of guys came into the place, blinded as we had been by the dark. They just stood there, not able to see us, I guess, until their eyes got used to us. They wore fresh, clean white coveralls with the sleeves rolled up, and they had identical hats, white straw with a ridge down the top of the crown and the front of the brims turned down. They were wearing white shoes, too. I had always wanted a pair of white shoes, but Mom said that black was more pleasing to the Lord.

They just stood in the cellar at the foot of the stairs, sort of glaring. One of the men who was heavier than the other, finally took some steps toward the table. I could see him glance sideways at Mr. McBride, like he knew he was there. Sandy started to shake and back away. When he talked, I could hardly hear what he said.

"What do you guys want now?"

The heavy one's eyes moved to Mr. McBride, but he talked to Sandy.

"Made up your mind?"

"I told you."

"You didn't tell me anything."

"This here ain't your territory."

"Whole country's our territory, bud."

The slender one came up, and he took a little nickel-plated gun out of his pocket. He was looking at Mr. McBride, too, but he kept moving up on Sandy. Sandy was about to have a fit, he was shaking so hard. I didn't know what to do. I didn't figure that what they were after involved Mr. McBride and me, our being just customers, but the way the guy held the gun made me plenty nervous. A guy down home used to hold a handgun careless like that and get off a fast, dead-straight shot. If this guy here could do the same, and if there was to be trouble, somebody was going to end up dead or something. Now the guy had turned and was facing Mr. McBride. But he was just setting there, staring at the brew bottles on the table in front of him. He didn't seem to be looking at the guys or even noticing them at all. I decided then that probably he was drunk.

But something made me look closer at the bottles. Mr. McBride had drunk four bottles, I had counted every one, and I was sure there had been four bottles on the table. Now, though, there were only three in front of him. Just then something brown flashed out from under the table. The brown thing struck the slender guy in the stomach with a loud, hollow smack, like hitting an empty barrel with a ball bat. Mr. McBride then followed in a great leap, spilling over the table and chairs. He mashed the slender guy up against the cellar wall and hollered for Sandy and me to pin down the heavy one.

Only Sandy wasn't around. I guess he hadn't liked the gun very much. He had jumped through one of the doors and was long gone. I was plenty scared, too, but I had such a feeling about Mr. McBride that'd I'd have done anything he told me to. So I jumped at the heavy guy. He swung his fist at me and hit me on the upper chest. It really hurt, but I was coming on him fast. Being as work-hard as I was, I eventually bowled him over. I grabbed him, using an old wrestling hold I had learned down home, and clamped down on his neck and shoulder. He really squealed, and we fell down in the dirt. He screamed something in a foreign language that I didn't understand. I twisted his head around so his face was down in the dirt, and as he kept cussing and threshing, I tried to push his head down harder.

The slender guy was groaning bad, too. Mr. McBride had him under his arm and dragged him over to where I was scrambling around with the heavy guy. Mr. McBride put his foot in the middle of the heavy guy's back.

"Let the bastard get up."

"Maybe he's got a gun, too."

"He'll only try once to use it."

I let the guy loose. For just a moment I flashed on fighting in the road with Zill. The heavy guy slowly began to get up, his clean white coveralls a mess and his mouth and lips full of dirt. As he raised up, Mr. McBride put his foot on his neck and pushed him down hard. He also was holding onto the slender guy—neither of them had a chance with Mr. McBride. They might as well have been in a steel vise.

Mr. McBride took the heavy guy by the collar of his coveralls and jerked him up like he weighed nothing. He held onto them both, and they swore and said they were going to get him. He let them cuss and talk for a while and then he said, in a low voice that silenced them, "Why do you curse?"

They didn't answer. I guess they were surprised that he would ask it. "Once a tough bird thought he didn't like me," McBride continued, "made the mistake of coming around my gang of workmen. Going to get me. Going to fill my belly with lead. Listen to this both of you. He's under a new slab road in Kansas where about a thousand cars every day roll over him. And we're laying slab around here. Get out now. And don't let me hear about you bothering this bootlegger again."

Mr. McBride dragged them to the outside cellar door just as Sandy poked his head out of one of the inner doors. Sandy just stood there in the doorway, like a pointer dog, ready to run. Mr. McBride roughed those guys up a little more, then he kicked them upstairs. He didn't need any help from me, that was sure. They stumbled out, and I heard their motor start up and roar away.

We left and were greeted by a hot, blinding sun. I stumbled and Mr. McBride put a hand on my shoulder. It was as if I'd been touched by a king. I felt so good. We climbed into his Ford.

"I should of killed them. They'll be comin' after me. If they do, they'll die. You'll have to watch for 'em, too, Bob, maybe you'd ought to leave."

What he said made me feel awful nervous, but he didn't say anything else while we returned to the steel truck. I wondered whether violent action was going to be a regular part of my life. Dad sure hadn't said anything about that. I hadn' t sought it, but violent things had come anyhow, like the force of the wind in the cyclone. I sure didn't think that the rough stuff was what I was supposed to be looking for, but Dad did say once that the name of God was mixed up in a lot of violent things. I don't know whether Dad believed in God or not, but he used His name once in a while anyhow. He said that when violent things happened, why, maybe God wanted it that way. I wasn't too worried about that, but I sure was worried when Mr. McBride said maybe I ought to leave. He let me out beside Clyde's truck.

I told Clyde all about what happened. He later tried to tell me that those guys we had fought with would try to get back at us, but I wasn't really scared about that. I should have been, but I wasn't, because I figured, I guess, that Mr. McBride and I could just about lick the whole world.

I was lying in my bed and it was very, very hot. It must have been about two o'clock. I had been asleep because most nights I was so tired I just went to sleep right after supper since I had to get up at four-thirty to catch the truck out to the job. But this morning I awoke early, so I heard the truck come up in front. Then somebody was out there calling my name. I got up and went to the window and looked out. There was enough light from the truck's headlamps to show somebody standing there. I answered, but not too loud, because I didn't want to wake people up.

"It's Clyde. Come on down."

I grabbed my overalls and shirt and shoes and went down. He was waiting for me in the front yard.

"We gotta go. Fast."

"Where?"

"To look for Mac. He's missing."

"For gosh sake, he'll come back won't he?"

"I don't know. Those guys have been after him."

"Those guys we met at that beer place?"

"Yeah. Those and maybe some others. He ain't gonna run from them, you know that."

He got the truck going.

"What is it? What is the matter?"

"It's tough. This is a dirty town. Half the concrete and stuff that goes into roads ain't any good. Somebody's getting rich. The damn politicians. Mac hates them. They'd have murdered him long ago, but he's got something on them. I ain't sure what."

"He'll be all right, won't he?"

"I heard they was after him tonight. We got to find him. I got a couple of steel bars, just in case."

I could feel the short bars down under my feet. I was really upset, partly because I wanted to find and help Mr. McBride, and partly because I felt that somehow I might be responsible for the trouble he was in. I didn't know how, though. I think I would have tried to kill somebody if they hurt Mr. McBride. I had never respected a man so much. It was kind of strange too, that at the same time I started thinking of the night when I had gone looking for Dad.

We looked for Mr. McBride the rest of the night. We never found him. We went around to all the places Clyde knew on the southside where he might have gone . . . all the speakeasies, and the farm houses where there was a farmer selling home brew. We visited them all; most were locked up tight, but once in a while we found one open, and we went in, each with a two-foot steel bar down our pant's leg. I didn't know what I would do, but I sure was stirred up and mad. If there was somebody who had hurt my friend, I would have probably gone crazy. We looked everywhere, and we didn't find him or anybody who had seen him even. So when it was getting light, we had to go back to the job.

I figured that I would never again see a man like Mr. McBride. More and more he had become a giant to me. He was there along the grade, or driving by in the dust with the uproar of heavy machinery and shouting, and braying mules, and swearing. That was where he belonged. He was just naturally part of the life of working men; of building, of getting it done. I bet that Dad would have thought he was a great man, too.

Sometimes I would watch him when he was around and every time he moved it seemed important to me and to all of the working men. When he came close to them, they always said something respectful. He didn't make anybody do it, it was just something about him. I figured that if anybody in the whole world knew what was going to happen, and could make it happen, it was Mr. McBride. I wanted to stay around just to see what he did.

But there was also something kind of sad in Mr. McBride, too, like he had a big problem and didn't know what to do about it. I wished he would tell me about whatever it was, but I knew that he wouldn't. He wouldn't tell me anything, but I sure felt like I was kin to him. And I would have liked to see him and Mrs. Settles and Dad together. I would have just liked to be there and listened to them talk. But the whole thing crashed, and I mean it really did crash. It just ended all at once.

Clyde and I were loading steel that afternoon about three o'clock when a dump truck roared up. The driver leaned over to yell at us. "Hey, you guys know Mac's been shot?"

Just like that. That was it.

Clyde had hold of one end of a steel bar. I had the

other. Clyde let his end drop. I just stood there holding onto mine.

"Shot?"

"Yeah. At the Jipson place."

"No."

The way Clyde cried it out was about the saddest and angriest thing I ever heard.

"About half an hour ago they found him. They shot him through the head. Everybody's going over there."

Clyde ran to the truck and began to tear the bars of steel off the side holders. I helped him, and we had it off in a hurry. He jumped for the wheel when we had the last bar off. I just made the seat as he had it in gear and was off down the grade. The roar of the old truck engine was so loud that we couldn't talk, but I guess we wouldn't have said anything anyhow. The only thing Clyde said was, "Jipson place was only one we missed last night."

There were a lot of people standing around outside an old farm house which must've been the Jipson place. It was quite a distance, I guess that's why Clyde and I hadn't looked there. Clyde got out of the truck and pushed right in. There were a few fellows from the work gang and a guy in uniform, I guess he was from the sheriff's office, at the door. I would have stayed out in the yard, but Clyde pulled me along. He went right up to the door and the sheriff guy put out a hand to stop him. But Clyde said we were part of Mr. McBride's family, and he got us in someway. Inside there were about twenty or more people in a large, hot room which was back of a living room at the front. Clyde pushed us through, and I was tall enough to see over most of the crowd. There were some old wooden chairs and three or four tables and a counter along the back. Flies were buzzing around pretty loud, and there wasn't any air moving at all. I felt hotter than I had ever been in a cornfield, or in the wheat harvest; but I couldn't sweat either. I just felt kind of dead and sick.

And then I saw Mr. McBride lying down in front of the counter. I just stared at him and couldn't believe it. He was lying on his back, with a bullet hole between his eyes, and flies were buzzing around and lighting on him. I could see it easy from where I was standing, and his derby was lying over at one side. He was all sprawled out. All I could think of was how Mrs. Settles' windmill might have looked if it had fallen over and busted and collapsed when it hit the ground. By Mr.

McBride's side, behind his head, was a revolver, nickel-plated. I knew that I had seen that same gun before, or one just like it. I started to say something to Clyde, but he turned around and pulled on my arm. He kept swearing low and angry as we walked back to the truck.

I grabbed Clyde's arm, figuring we could help Mr. McBride by finding out who shot him and get them.

"I saw that gun, or one just like it. Over where we were. . . ."

He shoved me into the truck and started up the engine. He put his head over close to me.

"You want to stay alive? Shut up."

We went back to the grade on the job and he let me off. There wasn't a bit of work going on. I don't know where Clyde went, but I walked away to be by myself.

Grassroots Art

In connection with my work in regional literature in Wisconsin I have often tried to identify the great literary themes of our part of the United States, and I believe they would include loneliness, pride, hard work, sheer ability to survive, sacrifice, a consciousness of family, suffering of many kinds, strength and pride in strength, will to overcome, and a deep sense of homeland. Conditions were definitely tougher in Wisconsin than the European settlers, at least, had been led to expect. Climate was more severe, and mere survival during the first Wisconsin winter with hardly any shelter, poor bedding, and inadequate clothing, must have been difficult. The values of strength and will were called upon in full measure. I presume that many settlers simply didn't make it. But many did, and what they had was better than in the old country.

During the late 1940s I offered a University of Wisconsin course called "regional writing." In the course I encouraged the students to write about subjects and scenes very personally associated with their own experiences, particularly their ethnic background. One of the most interesting students was a retired school teacher of nearly seventy who wrote excellent stories associated with her family who lived in the small city of Wisconsin Dells.

My seventy-year-old student had the rather intriguing name of Fidelia Van Antwerp. She was a tall and regal lady with a great crown of beautiful white hair. She and I became very good friends, and I told her about my concern for the rural women who wanted to write. She accepted the challenging situation and instantly insisted that I use all her time and talents. We were able to establish her as head of the Wisconsin Rural Writers Association.

Of the many organizations, institutions, and programs that I have had a hand in starting in Wisconsin, the writers' movement is one I am very proud of. The movement reflects the writing surge that now occupies the spare time, or in some instances the full-time, of a large number of Wisconsin people, young and old, giving them a reason for living and furnishing their lives with rich overtones. The writing program is slowly developing a native Wisconsin literature, and as I was on the spot when the idea first sprang to reality in 1948, I am still here today, 1981, at the University of Wisconsin, struggling as I did when I first came in 1945 with the complex and exciting problem of grassroots American culture.

For a long while I had wanted to open up the creative writing idea, expand it beyond just playwriting (for the theatre was my primary art). I realized that there were several considerations one must make in developing such a literary movement. My aim was not only to awaken people to the creative factor in their lives but also to stimulate them to the ultimate production of literary art forms. I recognized the values of a self-expression program on a broad sociological level in keeping with the general principles of the "Wisconsin Idea," but I also envisioned actual fine books, plays, poetry and stories arising out of the broad movement through a relatively few particular talents. The third notion inherent in the idea of a popular literary movement was, of course, that of area interpretation. I hoped for poetic or deeply sensitive writing about home themes, places, ethnic scenes and characters, events that people knew intimately.

I thought that my first effort had to focus on the rural areas. I had a hunch that quite a few folks would respond to the Rural Writers idea. I was really quite alarmed, however, to find my mailbox loaded each morning with manuscripts. To the horror of an already overburdened small staff, over two thousand poems were sent to us in a few days' time. There were short stories, too, articles, and a few plays. The curious thing was that the material for the most part seemed above average. There was some bad verse, but most of it had at least an honest ring. For a while, until I could get special help, we were all reading innumerable manuscripts every day—at lunch, at dinner, at night—and all of us would usually be walking from this to that task with several rural-life poems or stories or plays stuck in our pockets.

In attempting to make sense of the apparently

phenomenal popularity of this movement I arrived at a number of contributing factors. Writing is an art that can occupy the mind while the hands are busy with other tasks. It can engage the subconscious while the conscious mind is intent on other things, thus offering an opportunity to slip away from the routine task even while busying oneself with it. It is an art that does not require an outlay of money for its enjoyment—a pencil and paper are really all that are required. It concerns itself with the substances of everyday life; newly fallen snow, a stony field, the harvest, humor, economic matters, a neighborhood rumor, a church supper—any of these may be the germinal idea for a poem, a story, or a play. Receptivity has been made easier, too, by ventures in other arts stemming from University Extension—the Rural Art project, rural music, and correspondence courses, and by the encouragement and the whole prestige of sponsorship by the state University. There is, of course, one final main reason for the popularity of the Writers' movement: the itch to write, which is apparently universal.

In a very short while Fidelia Van Antwerp became the leader of a highly individual organization of about a thousand Wisconsin rural citizens who placed creative writing very high on their list of favorite things. She started an amazing series of "round robin" letters which circulated from writer to writer and gathered an accumulation of personal problems, hopes, despairs, and much valuable literary criticism. For some, the written works of each member of the "round robin" usually accompanied the massive letter. Soon the various writers were in correspondence with one another, and many life-long friendships grew out of the "round robins."

Fidelia Van Antwerp was the fountainhead of the rural writers and she sped to many parts of the state offering advice, criticism, and sympathy. Once in a while the Extension Dean helped her out a little with expenses, but mostly she did it all herself. The rural writers repaid her, not with money, but with almost fanatic love. She received no public notice for her work, and the University of Wisconsin did nothing to recognize her. But when the University fell upon tough budgetary times in the early 1950s (much in the same way it has today) and was threatened by an unsympathetic governor and legislature with many financial cuts, Fidelia rose to lend the University her influence from every corner of the state. She mustered her rural writers and caused an onslaught of letter-writing to the legislature that has never been equalled in Wisconsin. Against this great "woman of no importance" the governor had no chance. Fidelia in her own way had decreed that her University should not be injured. The governor eventually called off his campaign, the University went about its business, and Fidelia and her rural colleagues went on writing.

Upon the Wisconsin land are many remnants, which I never tire of searching out. The singers, the workers! What nailers and spike-drivers these earlier heroes who forced new rails through forests and along rivers; who drew locomotives when necessary by ox team over plank roads to a new railhead. They all have their own story. What lumberjacks! What diggers the Irishmen who cut the Portage canal, pick and shovel in those days, spade among roots, pickaxe, grubbing hoe—the Irishman's bulldozer; cutting the channel seven foot deep for the larger boats. Still upon the Wisconsin land I find the descendants: of those who turned the first spadeful of earth for a canal, or for a railroad. Workers from Europe, spitting upon their hands, fifteen hours they labored. No union. Pride that they were there. For a few cents a day, they stayed and placed their indelible mark. And they went into the woods, and the white pine roared to earth. Skid the logs to the streams! First log seven foot at base . . . the rivers jammed with the logs and the river pigs and the raftsmen dying . . . buried on the bank with a name carved into a tree. Such was the fabric of real drama and literature, of honest-to-goodness grassroots art.
Similarly, I have felt constantly the influence of Zona Gale who has established the idea of neighborliness in the small town as a living part of Wisconsin countryside life. One morning I attended a tiny country church and heard a prayer given by the young minister. He said: "Dear God, we have celebrated here today one hundred years of our community life. Our heritage is good. We come of a stout stock. But, God, don't let us turn our eyes too much backwards. Let us remember, and let us use our memory to live more fully in the present and in the future. God, we are beset with problems our ancestors never dreamt. We are beset and alarmed, for the world is troubled. But, God, we have one thing that will see us through. We are neighbors, Lord. And as neighbors let us live."
In all of my sifting, each region of the state and its culture emerge. I have treasured the quiet well-being of

Walworth and Rock Counties in the south, settled by New York State people in the 1840s and 50s, who brought that feeling of New York State to southern Wisconsin. And in contrast I have savored the central Wisconsin sand country where agriculture was difficult but where the places are warm, often, with the folk dances and wines of the Polish people. I have an intimate feeling for Taliesin, the low-roofed home at Spring Green of the famous architect Frank Lloyd Wright who believed that beauty should be a part of the everyday experience of everybody. And I have the same sort of intellectual intimacy with "The Clearing," the home of the great landscape architect, Jens Jensen, in Door County, who believed that creative man could express himself best in terms of a deep and intimate association with nature.

So many of my efforts are, in part, only a prelude to the very special and unusual encounters that occasionally take place. I remember one fall-time journey which carried me into the woods north and east of Hayward, a country of deep swamps and timber where coarse grasses rasp together slowly in the filtering breezes. It is country where a flick of movement sensed far away through and among the splashed shadows might mean an alerted deer, a country where the moss-covered stumps and the dim trails recall the days when the forest was a setting for crawling, endless motion and echoing sound of the great lumberjack days. I had heard of a man in this woodland who was delicately attuned to all the sights and sounds of the forest and whose pencil, crayon, and brush had given life to the essence of the forest itself. I wished to meet him, for the image of woodland artist living in solitude and sketching and painting with sensitive, intimate passion for the forest reality stimulated my curiosity.

I found his cabin, finally, and stood for a moment looking at it. It was a shack of unpainted boards with one tiny window and a low, plank door. The dooryard was a bramble patch with a path to the outhouse. Among the brambles were the skeletons of old machines, bleak, unidentifiable. The whole scene was interlaced with loneliness, and the ugly vestiges of human habitation filled me with uneasiness. I walked around a skimpy woodpile and approached the door.

As I came to the door I could hear a soft, yet rough, sound from within the shack and I paused a moment trying to define it. It rose and fell and fell and rose and was somehow echoed by the broken flow of the wind in the tops of the pines away from the clearing. I knocked at the door.

Instantly the sound stopped and a tremendous barking began. A voice said, "Quiet! Quiet, damn ye!" and the barking stopped instantly. There was motion beyond the door and suddenly it was pulled open violently. The smell came first, even before I could focus on the man who stood in the open door, a smell that instantly flooded my mind with memories of other bachelor shacks I had visited in Kansas and New York and Alberta, especially Alberta, where bachelor living was defined on prairie and on mountain by rigid rules of filth and convenience. As I peered at the man and the cluttered interior I could see that he was short, that his hair was intensely black and uncombed, that he wore no trousers at all—only dirt-streaked drawers that ended in huge, thick-soled shoes. I could see at the far edge of the room his bunk, out of which he had quite obviously just crawled. It was occupied now by two huge hounds who looked at me steadily from the depth of human-warmed blankets.

There is a delicacy about situations such as this. Doors close so easily. Perhaps intuitively my eyes stayed on the dogs and I said, with the memory within me of dark-tan hounds in an eastern Kansas woodland on a frosty October night, "Those are fine dogs."

He moved slightly. "They are."

"They trail?"

He said, "They are good."

To break the conversational ice I told him I had lived near a river, the Neosho, in Kansas, a great coon river, where there were mussels to be had in plenty, where there were ravines and tall cottonwood timber, where in the fall a good dog's voice could be heard near two miles, and where, when the dogs would call, we would hurry through the woodlands and over the frost-stiff grass with a lantern throwing crazy shadows around us as we ran.

He moved away from the door and I went in. We fenced, jockeyed, and eventually I admitted that I was from the University, that I had heard he was an artist, and that I had a sincere desire to view his work. He quite properly denied this for a time, but eventually he reached under the bunk and pulled out a bundle wrapped in old canvas. He grabbed the hounds by the necks and jerked them off the bunk. He laid his bundle carefully on the bunk and unrolled it. Here were some cheap crayons in boxes, a couple of dime store watercolor trays, some pencils and brushes and tubes of oil. There was also a roll of what looked like common, white shelf paper. He lifted the roll and smoothed it out. One by one he lifted sheets of paper and spread them on the bunk. The wildlife of the northwoods was there, suddenly, in the filthy shack, reproduced in breathtaking originality against delicate backgrounds of swamp and grasses and the dead rubble of decaying forest. I stood for a long while gazing at the pictures. After a time I said, "I've got to be going. Thanks for one of the great experiences of my life."

"Come back anytime," he said, and he began to gather his pictures, tenderly rolling them again for the bundle. He retied the bundle and thrust it under the bunk. As I went to the door the hounds jumped on the bed again and snuggled into the blankets.

Two Decisions

Mr. McBride had been shot. Was it true? Had it really happened? I could say the words but I still couldn't believe it. For several days my life was a mere blur—I was lonely and depressed and lost. They hired a new boss and the construction work went on, but it wasn't the same.

Nobody ever did much to try and find out who murdered Mr. McBride. I once thought about going to the authorities and telling what I knew, but Clyde stopped me. He said the last thing Mr. McBride would want was for me to go and do that; he wouldn't want anybody doing anything for him. Even though Mr. McBride was now six feet under the ground, Clyde was right. So, I never went and told anyone.

The entire gang was depressed too. Like me, they seemed unable to get over his death. Mr. McBride had been holding up the gang's whole world, and now that world had busted apart. I never saw things so upset. Tools were disappearing from the toolboxes, and a spirit of meanness and vengeance was settling around; there was even a lot of talk about going to downtown Kansas City and taking it out on some guys down there, but I guess it was just talk since nothing ever came of it. But the entire mood had changed—I could feel it. There'd even been a number of fights—a guy named Carl Morgan was in the hospital with a fractured skull where a Black boy about my age had smacked him with a shovel. Carl had been talking ugly about Black people, telling what he'd done to a Black girl, when the kid just up and smacked him. The shovel cut through the top of Carl's ear and broke his skull. He laid there in the dust below the grade while everyone stood around, shocked and scared. The Black boy started crying and ran away into the bushes. Afterwhile Joe Malone got whispering around, and some of the gang started to beat through the weeds. Joe would call for the kid in a coaxing voice, telling him not to be afraid and to come on out. They looked for a long time, but they didn't find him. Someone said that he would probably be hiding out in the Black section of Kansas City, and that they should go down there some night. They would fix him. Joe Malone told everybody what he wanted to do to him with his knife.

There was this kind of sickness over the whole job. If Mr. McBride had lived I might have gone on working forever with a spade or shovel, or stringing the long, hot bars of steel along road grades. But now the boss was gone and I didn't want to stay around the road gang any longer. If there was a meaning to it all, to the violent things that guys did to each other, or that the elements, the wind and the rain, did to the guys; or of struggling for grub; or of the smells of people and the stinking river bottom; of heat and loneliness; if there was, I hadn't found it.

I thought of going home and asking Dad if I had searched enough for the tall grasses, and whether I could now come home and lie under the silver maple in the yard where the leaves were turning over and rustling and not worry if there was any reason for the things that men and women did, or whether there was a real God, or a wide, free swell of virgin grass. I wondered whether Dad knew himself. Maybe he knew there wasn't any other meaning in the adventures or experiences one person had except just having them, and maybe Dad had sent me off from home because he was just longing to relive the experiences he had when he was young.

One Sunday morning during work I walked down toward the river bottoms where the weeds were taller than a man's head. It wasn't much like the grass in the prairie acre at home, but in the heat and sweat and fertile stinks of bottom earth and muddy water I sat down in a clump of the tallest weeds, and wondered if Dad was also out there in the grass that morning. Close to where I was sitting a couple of the gang were taking a "bath" at the edge of the turgid, thick water. Through the weeds I could see them splashing the brown wet on their upper bodies as they stood knee-deep in the ooze at the edge. One of the men was Kel Brown, a dump-truck driver. I couldn't tell who his partner was.

In the slow rustling of the weeds above me I believed even more that I was hearing the voices of the grasses in the prairie acre back home, because whenever there was any kind of a breeze the tall grasses had a voice. They talked about Dad's wild prairie, and they seemed to know that the reason the prairies were wild and free was reason enough for everything a man did. The grasses also knew that the notion of freedom was reason enough for dreaming, and even for everything that happened in anger and killing. The wild grasses gave a fellow his dreams. Maybe that's what Dad had been saying. Dreams were sure important to Dad, and once they had been important to Mr. McBride, too. I suddenly wondered whether my part in all this might be to tell about what I had seen and done, and about what it all meant. I had tried writing down a little bit about the storm and Mrs. Settles—it hadn't been too hard but I didn't have the least knowledge of how to write or what to do.

All of a sudden, Kel Brown and his partner started talking louder and making a lot of splashing noise. They were joshing each other about a girl in Kansas City that they both knew. She was a big girl with long legs who worked in a restaurant in the Country Club District. Kel's partner dipped up a double handful of water and swished it into Kel's face. When the water hit him, Kel lost his balance in the deep mud where he was standing and flopped over backwards into the crick. He landed on his backside, made a big, dirty swash, and churned around, trying to find something to hold onto in the ooze and slime of the deeper water. He finally got his feet under him and sucked on towards the bank, splashing and yelling that he was going to toss his partner's butt out into the middle of the river. I sat up in the weeds, figuring that it would be fun to see what Kel's partner was going to do.

Kel's partner, though, was standing on the bank with his mouth open, with the water that Kel was splashing up at him running out of his mouth. As I watched, the guy's face turned kind of green and sick, and just as Kel approached him, the guy lifted a shakey hand and pointed past Kel and hollered, "Look, look!"

Back behind Kel I saw a black thing rising up out of the dark water. There was a bubbling noise, and mud was swirling around it. As the black thing rose up a bit more, I could see a black arm and a hand. I got to my feet and shoved back the weeds. The workmen who were sitting up and above on the high bank also came slowly down, sliding in the soft black earth. They held their eyes steady on the water.

They all lined up along the creek and Kel said, "It's the boy, ain't it? One that busted Carl?"

"Somebody got him," said Joe Malone. I noticed a crazy look twisting up on his face. "Somebody got him good. Bet it was Carl's cousin. One runs the grader. Wisht it'd been me."

"Let's get him out," Kel said.

"Hell, let him stay in the crick."

"We gotta tell somebody."

"Don't. The cops'll be out here."

"Not them cops."

"Wisht I'd done it." A little saliva oozed out of Joe's mouth. Old black Jim came sliding down the bank and took a long look at the boy's body in the water. His whole body quaked as he cried, "Lawd! Lawd!" and he started to walk further down the crick bank.

"Where are you goin'?" Joe asked him.

"Going to get somebody to take care of him!" the old man said.

"You're not goin'."

This tension was followed by a seemingly endless silence. I was reminded of the story we learned back home about John Brown. People used to say that when John Brown came out to Kansas in 1856 and killed some of those Missouri slave-state men he came on south and hid out from the pursuing Missourians in a cave. So sometimes when a bunch of us neighbor kids all got together we would play a game called John Brown and the Missourians. One night I asked Mom, "What were they after John Brown for that they had to kill him?" She told me that he was a friend of the colored people who was eventually hung because he helped the Blacks. I remember saying to her that "I wouldn't want to get hung for being a friend to colored folks." Maybe this would be my John Brown moment.

Joe hollered at black Jim, "You're a nigger ain't you?"

"I'm a Black man."

"You stand right still."

Joe took out his knife and brandished it. He ran his left thumb along the blade, testing it good. He just stood there and wet his thumb and tested it again, all the while looking at Jim.

"Let's cut him."

The gang stood silent. There were some round pieces of gravel near where I was standing on the crick bank. I really don't know why I did it; I guess it was all the sadness and confusion I felt, because I'm never one to take the lead. I reached down and set a round stone between my right thumb and forefinger. I curled my forefinger around the smooth, flat, oily-feeling rock. It was a natural thing for me to do, because down home I was always throwing rocks around, and could throw a long ways. The rock fitted perfectly in the round place.

Joe started to walk towards the old man, and I called to him, "Hey Joe." I don't know if he heard me or not, because I didn't speak up very loud. Joe looked kind of sideways at me as I threw the rock. I had never set out to intentionally hurt anybody before, and I don't know why I threw the rock right then, either. Something about Joe Malone and the way that he talked made me feel different. The hunk of rock busted him just above where the wet sweat-mark under his left arm came to an end. It hit with a really strange thud. To me it sounded like that beer bottle when Mr. McBride hit that guy in the speakeasy, sounding like "ka-bunk." Joe dropped his knife and cried, "Jesus, Jesus," and put his hands on the place where the rock hit him. He started to stagger around on the bank. He tore his shirt halfway off, and there was a large round, red spot on his left ribs. The mark looked really ugly, and I was stunned at having done it to him. He gasped and grunted and groaned for the longest time.

The other guys just stood there acting surprised. The body of the black boy kind of floated in the muddy water. I didn't know what would happen next. I knew what I had done and that I couldn't take it back. I might even have said, "I'm sorry," to Joe except he started coming after me. He was looking around for his knife, too, but it had flown off into the mud. Joe said to the guys on the bank, "Give me a knife," but nobody did.

Joe started to edge toward me. I was standing a little way above him, and we were both close to the edge of the crick. I let Joe come and I didn't back off. I couldn't. I didn't want any more to do with Joe but I knew it was too late and I had to do something. I said, "Joe, go away," but Joe just kept coming. I doubled-up my knees as I jumped and grabbed hold of Joe's ears and hair. I felt my knees strike Joe in the stomach and we both tumbled over backwards, me on top, and hit the mud at the edge and slid right in. I held Joe's head under water, his hands were tearing and sliding. He lashed and splashed and the mud was really flying. I kept ahold of Joe's ears and afterwhile his hands weren't tearing at me at all. I didn't know when he quit. It was like I was paralyzed or something. Finally somebody yanked us out of the crick, and I overheard someone say that he thought Joe was really dead.

I wiped off my face. Kel and his partner were placing a stick under Joe, lifting him up and down and smacking him on the back. Some slimy water was coming out of Joe's mouth. Nobody said a word to me as I walked up the crick bank. I thought maybe I heard Joe cough as I went. I sure hoped so because I was feeling like I didn't need a murder on my hands.

I walked along the road back towards the city, heading to my room to pick up my things and get my valise. The bushes and parks along the road sure tempted me; I just wanted to leave the road and crawl into them and think things over. Not that I was ashamed of what I had done, but it sure made me feel uneasy. Somehow, I always had this feeling that I was to blame for something, even if I wasn't, and sometimes it made me act scared. But in truth I am more afraid of doing something "wrong" than I am of the thing itself. Some folks thought I was a coward at times, but they never really understood. I just didn't want to do a bad thing.

Well, I knew for sure that I hadn't fought with Joe Malone because Jim was a Black man. I just liked old Jim because he was a human being and a good, hard worker and he had been nice to me. And I liked that Black kid because he was a hard worker, too, a sight better worker than Joe who was always goofing off. I wasn't any John Brown either, I knew that, and I didn't want to go to jail. Dad said that no Gard had ever been in jail; Mom wasn't so sure about the Gards but she said none of *her* family ever had been. So I wasn't anxious to be the first Gard to go. My folks wouldn't have approved, and Dad would probably say that I wouldn't find the wild prairie grass behind bars.

I heard a truck coming up behind me, and it turned out to be Clyde driving the old steel wagon.

"Get in."

"Where you going?" I asked.

"I'll take you home."

"In this?"

"Sure."

"You're liable to get into trouble. The police'll be coming after me."

"What for? Joe ain't dead. He don't feel very good, and he's got him a bellyful of crick water. But he ain't dead. He sure wants to kill you, though."

I felt a lot better, Joe not being dead, but I was nervous about his wanting to kill me. I got into the truck.

"Will Joe come after me?"

"I guess. But you sure tamed him good. Maybe he's scared."

"Not as scared as me. Did they take out that black kid?"

"Yeah."

"Who killed him?"

"Who knows. They'll never know. Just like Mac. They'll never know. They don't care enough."

The big flat truck roared along.

"I'm leaving." The way I announced it even startled me.

"Stick around. The gang likes you. I don't really think that Joe will bother you no more."

"It's not the same without Mr. McBride."

"Mac was a good guy. One hell of a boss."

There was a silence between us for a time.

"Slow down, Clyde. The house's the next one."

Clyde slowed the truck. "You thought Mac was quite a guy, didn't you?"

I couldn't ever say aloud how I thought about Mr. McBride. Like a windmill, only bigger. A giant.

"Mac was all right," Clyde said. "Hard to figure though. He was fixin' to fire you, did you know that?"

I stared at Clyde. "Me?"

"Yeah. Day before he got it. Mac told me he was going to fire you. Surprised me. You and him was getting on good."

"This is the house," I interrupted.

The big truck stopped. I didn't have anything more to say. "Thanks, Clyde."

"Okay, kid."

"I'll be moving."

"Goodbye. Glad you ain't going to jail."

The old engine turned over and the truck jerked away. I waved a hand to Clyde, but I felt really sick inside. I'd tried to be a good worker, and Mr. McBride was going to fire me. I believed Clyde—his word was good and Mr. McBride confided in him. But why would he want to get rid of me?

I went into the sagging, yellow house where I had that hot, rumpled room. The torn window shades were pulled down and the room was half dark. A big fly was buzzing between the screen and the window. As usual, there stood the unmade bed with one dirty sheet beside a writing table with a missing drawer. I laid down on the bed. I reckoned that Dad wouldn't think much about what I'd done at the crick. Once when I was twelve Dad had tried to tell me something about justice. He said that no man had a right all by himself to figure out what justice was for any other guy. And I guess I was guilty for applying my sense of justice to Joe.

Whenever I thought about Dad now, I suddenly realized I was thinking deep. Dad, and home, and all his experiences were twisted up with the prairie grass where Dad liked to sit. The prairie acre was a landmark to me now, and when I thought about that tall patch of old grass I liked to believe that it provided some kind of deep comfort to Dad.

As I continued to reflect I also sensed that in all the tall grasses across the country—graveyards, old fence corners, along old railroad lines—there would be relics, forgotten furrows of old trails you could hardly see anymore but that were once deep ruts with heavy, grunting oxen, mules, horses and heavy wagons pulling along people who were searching out, hoping to find their dreams. And I knew too that there were a lot of relics in musty rooms, barns, and attics across the whole continent that could tell stories through their rust and jagged edges: an old piece of wheel; a rusty old pistol or an old knife blade, stone arrowheads, a woman's dress with old stains on it; or maybe a cradle of whittled wood. Things like that had never meant very much to me before, but now, the wild, tall grasses of the prairie and the old relics made the whole past come alive. I guess I had been dwelling on thoughts like that for a long time, without really knowing it.

I still hadn't any idea where I'd go next. I only knew that I had to search on and on for what Dad had sent me to find. And now it all seemed to grow more urgent. There were so many men driven by the hard times, men who weren't drawn by the lure of any tall prairie, but by the fear of being poor. A whole generation of men just wandering around the streets of

America. Who could say what they were searching for? Or running from?

I had to admit that at the heart of it was the growing idea that I wanted to, and could, write. More, I had a flash of the realization of material from which writing is created. Could I write about Dad and the Stranger? Could I ever tell what it all meant in terms of the land, of the violences of nature and of people, and the growth I already sensed in myself? Could I write about Mrs. Settles and Mr. McBride, and especially about the search that had sent me forth from home, and that was leading me . . . where I could not guess? I felt a thrill when I thought about writing like that, as if, just maybe, I had discovered in my inarticulated expression, my own tall grass.

I went to the closet and tossed whatever clothes I owned into my valise, plus an old notebook that I had been carrying around. I changed into a clean pair of blue overalls and a clean shirt, dug my savings out of the lining of my valise, and counted it. I had more than a hundred dollars. It seemed impossible, but I had saved almost every penny beyond rent and food expenses. I still had all my harvest money, plus what I'd saved from the road gang. I felt rich.

I sure did want to go home. There was an acre of homesickness in me. I could see the Neosho River and the hills below the rapids that lay under a big bluff. The fishing would be pretty good there this time of year (late August) with the channel catfish striking savagely at hunks of liver we'd float down on long lines. There was one old Sycamore tree on top of the bluff that had great roots, partly exposed, and I sat often among the exposed roots, looking out on the river and up at the wide Kansas sky. Yep, I sure did want to go home.

Under the excitement of this reverie, and my newly discovered flair for writing, I sat down, pulled out the tattered notebook, and began writing a poem. As if I was in a trance, the poem wrote itself, causing me to realize how much of what Dad had told me was deep inside.

> *There was one who knew, when he was old,*
> *that the innocence of the primitive had ended;*
> *that he had despoiled what there was of the*
> *wilderness he cherished. What, he wondered,*
> *would then become of his son? What bequest*
> *had he to leave of the wild prairie, and the*
> *memory of the way it was?*

As he knew, finally, what it was that had been
left for him, the son spoke:

My father sang the song of pioneers
And broke the sod; he made the prairie bloom.
But I who came to manhood in a different way,
Found little left of grass and less of way.
My father dreamt of victory over roots;
Saw cities limned against a prairie sky;
Saw derricks pumping wealth and homesteads rife,
Saw every man a king: a god of life.
But I—what was there left for me?
When pioneers had sapped the soil of its juice
And given all the glory of their strength
To occupations that to them alone had use.

For I, yes I, a singer also bold and free
Was eager for to pit my strength against the earth,
To sense my destiny and girth,
And set my course against a prairie sea.
One morning when I'd turned just twenty years
My father led me through a field of tasseled corn,
"There yonder lies one acre of the virgin sod," he said,
"It will never be turned; wild grass must stand
Tall to the shoulder, hiding beast and man."
Strong roots in fertile soil to the breast
Of earth and season pressed and pressed.

For this to him the symbol of the past
More real than hungers of my restless heart
To know what lay for me beyond an acre's edge,
And of a mystery where no broken earth had part.
"I walked out from Illinois, boy, was seventeen
More sense,
More will, and drive, ambition.
Something keen,
A wringing knowledge that I must succeed.
And look, of all that was, this acre only left.
I conquered all.
I am what I set out to be.
All this, our hope, our will.
We conquered fear.
We won.

And you—
What, boy, of you?"

Yes, what of me, poor singer with no song,
No song of wild grass to tell my dream;
And where to go and what to seem.
You had all the grass, father.
What indeed, of me?

He said:
"We own a nation open, wide and free.
Walk out as I did. Seek the prairie sea;
Find the new prairie and come home to me."

The answer, father, when the grass is sped,
The cities builded and the spirit dead . . .
No great wide sky, no wagons rolling slow,
No yoke of oxen, no stalwart man with hoe?
No clear, pure stream that man has not defiled,
No unpolluted air, no unsuspected star,
No moon, unthreatened, to hang above a glade?
You've left me only doubt, and I'm afraid.

Away from the acre walking as he walked,
I searched the west; and
Set my face for prairie rain
But tasted gall and sensed a nation's pain.
I heard the warplanes in the skies
Read the tall headlines blazing blood;
I saw the streets filled with a violent mob
And heard that man had murdered God.
Is this the heritage you left: despair and fear,
For which to struggle and to sing our song?
To find our own black soil deep and strong
Discover words we dare to hear?
Oh, father, father, I came home to you,
To tell and ask and seek what you might say.
I found the acre but a broken gash
And one lone crooked tombstone under which you lay.

I honestly didn't know why I ended it that way. Dad
wasn't dead, I knew that—but ending it like that seemed to
make the search I was on possible to continue.

Again, I wasn't sure where I was exactly headed, but I was on the move once more, maybe to find my Stranger in the tall prairie grasses, or beneath the lone, crooked tombstone.

Dooryard Trees

Such is the quality of thought and memory. When I was at the Academy it was as though I was a kind of receiving set for thoughts and memories sent out from everywhere. I seemed to have no way of knowing what was going to stimulate me next . . . whether it was away back there in a boyhood past, or something near at hand.

Elizabeth McCoy used to always talk about the dooryard trees that the pioneers planted . . . her white lilacs and elms and maples, and the bushes around her place, were very important to her. Down in Kansas, as a youngster I remembered best the Osage orange hedges, thick, thorn trees that the pioneers used to make quick fence lines or to mark out section lines. But in Wisconsin it was more likely to be dooryard trees, or windbreaks. Near the front door of our home in Madison we had one of the largest elms in the area. Maryo purchased the house and property in 1955 because of that great tree. Often she said, "If that tree ever goes, I go, too." We had the wonderful tree for 20 years; then, though we struggled to save it with many scientific treatments, it withered and died. My lady wept when the men came to cut it down.

Something soon happened to our environment. A ground cover died the next summer; ivy began to cover the front of our house. The whole front looked different, inadequate. But Maryo didn't go, she stayed; and we planted another tree, a gingko. She said it would probably last for 500 years. I didn't want another tree. I felt the change. As a writer, the loss of the old elm desensitized me for awhile, until I began to ponder the death of elms across the breadth of the land.

Yes, most of the great elms are gone—victims of

rampant Dutch elm disease. The streets the elms once adorned are now blank, empty. The feeling of grace, of an almost ageless tradition, ended with the disappearance of their tall arch. With their passing, an atmosphere has vanished; the whole air of permanence, of a corridor through time, has passed. Correspondingly, we have witnessed a generation of turmoil and unrest.

When I was a lad, I heard of the arch of the elms of New England, and I was told how Kansas pioneers, many of whom came from the East, first planted elms in the town square and lined the new streets with the sturdy trees, almost before they built houses. The stability of America itself somehow was symbolized by the elms.

Lately I visited my old hometown of Iola in Kansas. Once there were tall elms in the courthouse park and green wooden benches placed beneath them. At one side stood an old horse watering trough, an image I associate with the morning I departed on my personal journey. But when I visited last summer, the trees were all gone—so was the trough; so, indeed, was the old red-brick courthouse. A low structure of yellow brick, entirely unshaded, sat uneasily in the middle of the park.

I cannot believe that the death of the elms has had no effect upon us as a people. The tradition of a leisurely college life, enhanced by the presence of great trees above a quadrangle, or along a student walkway, appears to have departed. Perhaps students are more restless than they were a generation ago. Could it be that the great trees that spoke of quietness, a timeless tradition, and a deep feeling of place, had their effect upon the young?

There is a bleakness now in the atmosphere of colleges. Two or three generations hence, when the new trees have grown, the old, quiet atmosphere may return. But what in the meantime? Colleges are not necessarily known for the beauty and uniformity of their architecture. Without the trees, the buildings oftentimes look stark, and their windows empty and lonely.

A 1978 visit to Cornell distressed both of us because all of the great elms that once shaded the Arts Quadrangle are gone. However, the Plant Pathology Department at the College of Agriculture and Life Sciences at Wisconsin has developed a disease-free elm, and Maryo and I, as soon as we returned to Madison, arranged for three of the Wisconsin trees to be planted at Cornell, in memory of our old friend and teacher Alexander Drummond. Perhaps there will again be permanent elms at Cornell to provide shade once more. . . .

I have noticed also, as the trees have disappeared, that the traditions of the colleges themselves have grown less important—indeed, the traditions seem often forgotten. I recently found the Senior Class Calumet—the peace pipe smoked in friendship by each senior class at the University of where the Redlegs and the Jayhawkers were struggling for slavery or freedom, and old John Brown was trying to help the University, has disappeared. Nobody knows where. It was the wagon that students drew with ropes, hauling the victorious team from railroad station to campus.

And the tradition of great professors of magnificent bearing and influence . . . where are they? In a time of great elms great professors likewise flourished. Bennie Snow, noted professor of physics, who received a "skyrocket" before each class; "Wild Bill" Kiekhoffer, great economics professor with a deep love of students; Carl Russell Fish, historian and lecturer par excellence who was literally followed by groups of students wherever he walked under the elms . . . these great professors have vanished with the trees. With them, of course, have gone the cherished stories. . . .

Ah, for the great trees again.

I have many older friends these days, especially since I myself have qualified for the golden years. Once the elderly sat peacefully beneath the elms. The tales they told there carried on an oral tradition for generations. A bench now, set on a bare corner or in a treeless park, seems forlorn, though it may be occupied by two or three old cronies. Their daily meeting, the passing talk, seems to lack the benediction of the elms and often my older friends comment on the feeling of loneliness and uneasiness.

"Elm shade," one said, "was once the essence of friendship. Most of our elms are gone in this town. We moved in from the farm, my wife and I, to be under the elms . . . that's what my wife said. She liked this town because of the trees. She said the elm was a woman's tree, a woman's friend. This town will never be the same to us since the elms have gone. It's harder now to make new friends."

Our national values, our national character, may be affected by the loss of the trees. There are many, many reasons why our whole system of ethical and moral behavior is changing. The elms certainly are not to blame; yet the changes have occurred simultaneously with the death of these trees. The elms have always symbolized home and its values; the lure and pull of a homestead, of waiting friends and parents when one returns. Once, the trees planted at the doorstep to commemorate family events furnished shade and comfort in times of joy and grief. Now the trunks, dead and gray, stand sometimes in the yard beside the door. Or else there is simply a blank space—or a stump remains where grandfather planted the elm sapling when the first baby died in the fall of 1861. . . .

We are certainly a nation which has developed its character through the associations of family life. Family life relied on the elms. The effect of their going may be subconscious upon us; but a phase of American life—the serene elm phase—will probably never come again.

THE STRANGER

Before I ever got home that summer that was so deeply important to me I did considerable more wandering. I worked for brief spells here and there, and finally, by coincidence beyond belief, I found a version of the Stranger.

I had turned home, finally, in the fall, and north of Iowa I hit the really bad weather. Rain and more rain. The 1930s weren't all dustbowl—in some northern reaches they were also a time of great floods.

All the way south I had heard snatches of talk from the people I rode with about floods in the prairies in northern Kansas. It had been a very wet fall in the higher western lands, and the big plains rivers were rampaging. A salesman I rode with between Des Moines and Leavenworth said we would be lucky if we got across the river at all, and sure enough when we got to Leavenworth the Missouri was roaring high. But we got across all right, and from there I hitched in short jumps between Leavenworth and Lawrence, Kansas.

Along the way there was water in the ditches along the roads, and the sloughs were pouring full. A truck driver brought me into north Lawrence, and he told me that the town was getting ready for an awful flood. The Kaw River, he said, was higher than it had been in years. As we crossed the Kaw bridge between north Lawrence and the main part of town, I could see what he meant.

The great brown rolling river that rushed out of the prairie lands was almost to the top of the bridge arches, and down below the bridge the water was spreading out over the flats. A few people were out on the bridge watching the water.

I remembered the folks down home when the Neosho

river was in flood, and I imagined how the people of north Lawrence looked often toward the Kaw with dark, shadowed eyes fearing the brown floods that swept the valley—boiling sweeps of water that Dad said were fed by the Republican with its creek system pouring waters from the Prairie Dog, the Sappa Creeks, the Beaver, the Arikaree, and the Lodgepole. Waters poured in from the Big Blue sweeping down near Manhattan to join the Kaw. They rushed down from the Little Blue, from the Smoky Hill as it joined the Solomon, from the Solomon flowing southeast from the plains of northwestern Kansas.

The people in north Lawrence, I imagined, had all moved their furniture to upper floors. The women stood along the river bank watching the water creep upward along the measuring pole at the bridge.

The truck driver said that there was heavy rain in the north and west but that on the plains of the South and the Southwest there was trouble of another kind: in Texas, Oklahoma, and western Kansas, the whirling winds were picking up the dust that had once been crop-growing soil, and were carrying it upward in dark, stinging, gasping clouds.

The truck driver let me out on Massachusetts Street in Lawrence, just across the bridge. Dad had often told us that Lawrence was the proudest town in all of Kansas. He said that it was more like New England than any other Midwest town because so many New England folks had come west in the early days before the Civil War after the Kansas-Nebraska Bill to try and vote Kansas in as a free state. "Lawrence was the freestater's capital," as Dad liked to phrase it.

In the truck on the way into Lawrence I had seen the University buildings spread out high on a hill. After eating a thirty-cent dinner in a Lawrence restaurant, I walked along a quiet, beautiful street, with a lot of great elm trees arching high, toward the University buildings.

I walked until I came to the beginning of the hill slope where the University was spread. Dad said they'd named the hill Mount Oread in the early days of "Bloody Kansas" when the Redlegs and the Jayhawkers were struggling for slavery or freedom, and old John Brown was trying to help the "Free state" cause, murdering quite a few in the process. Mount Oread was a high lookout point over the whole Waukarusa Valley to the south. Dad said that a branch of the Oregon Trail cut across the southern and western edges of Mount Oread, and that it was fitting for the great State

University of Kansas to stand high above the camping ground of those pioneers. It gave the University blood and fire, he said, things that came also from the little pioneer cemetery where the folks that had been murdered in a Civil War raid lay buried. They too had died for freedom and education, Dad said, and they died for what Kansas men and women sought for most—the keys to progress. Dad was real big on progress especially when he was talking about the past.

I decided to take a look at this pioneer cemetery and I learned from a guy I met on Tennessee street how to get there. He added that it was quite a piece and maybe I had ought to find a ride. But I set out to walk there just the same, travelling across the University campus.

As I walked I got to thinking that what I had been doing this entire summer was like a story Mom read to me when I was little, one about a knight on a quest after the Holy Cup that Jesus had drunk out of at the Last Supper. Occasionally in those old stories, the White Knight would find the Holy Grail, but usually he found it in pretty unlikely places. Now I was thinking how I was after a Grail of sorts myself, something which was mixed up with the tall grass and the Stranger in it. Somehow I knew it would be the Stranger who would reveal my secret to me. While sometimes in those old stories the person who was searching for the Holy Grail would find it inside himself, I really couldn't see how it could be like that with me. Still, when I looked back over what had happened, it did seem as if there was a hand or something guiding me to so many unforgettable experiences.

The grass of the Grail-search that Dad had sent me out on was now an obsession with me. I had never thought of myself as any White Knight, but the way things had happened, it seemed uncanny that I was always there when something unusual occurred and opened up some kind of a door. And for somebody like me, who didn't know much, it seemed to be the way his whole life could be changed.

But I didn't think any of this had anything at all to do with why I was going to see the old pioneer cemetery at Lawrence. There wasn't any reason except that Dad had seen it, and I felt kind of homesick. It goes to show that you never do know when one of those guiding hands will come to move you along.

The old cemetery where the pioneers were buried that Quantrill (the marauding Confederate guerilla) had murdered sat back aways, high up on a hill. The tiny spot was off by itself . . . a little field of secluded, tall prairie grass. There were quite a few old tombstones among the grass, reminding me of the grassy acre down home that Dad loved so much. I stood there for a little while beside an old gate that was sagging on its hinges, thinking about Dad and home. It was getting to be late in the afternoon, and I could see the University buildings on Mount Oread, and the flood waters covering the country off to the south.

Beside the creaky gate was a stone with writing on it, telling about the people who were buried in the cemetery. There were a lot of them because Quantrill rode unexpectedly into Lawrence, in the early morning of August 21, 1863, and he and his men shot and killed practically everybody. They simply rode into town and started killing. It was an awful thing—Bloody Bill Anderson and Cole Younger and Frank James and George Todd were supposedly there with Quantrill and shared in the killing. Eyewitnesses said that young Jesse James wasn't with Quantrill that day, but Dad claims he knew somebody who was sure that Jesse James was there and got his start in killing at Lawrence.

Some of that was written on the stone. I stood quite awhile, thinking. Maybe if old John Brown hadn't been dead he could have done something, because he was a fighter and didn't believe in just sitting and being meek when there was a lot of violence. Some Kansas men seemed to think that it was a good thing to just sit and wait for people to get tired-out killing you. It sure did cost many Lawrence folks their lives, though, because they just weren't prepared for everything. But Dad disagreed. He said the Gards never had been like that, and never would.

Standing there and thinking about all those different things gave me a feeling similar to that I had in the old pioneer graveyard at home; like there were a lot of ghosts, and somehow I was making them move around and talk, and act scared and be heroes as if I was a part of it.

While I was gazing at the cemetery and dreaming, a guy driving an old Durand car pulled up to the gate. He got out of the car, came over near where I was, and started examining some of the stones. He was a short man, about forty or fifty I guessed, with curly brown hair. He was wearing a pair of khaki pants and a white shirt with the sleeves rolled up; and he was smoking a cigar, with the smoke curling up over him a little bit. I kept watching him, and wondering why he was staring at the old stones, and if he knew about the Quantrill story. I almost asked him what he knew about the place, but he went to the other side. I had a funny feeling as I watched him, that there was something strange about him. Maybe it was that just then I was remembering what Dad had said about my meeting a Stranger; and I was wondering whether I was ever going to meet any Stranger who would be more important to me than the ones I had met already. That was why I was always watching people when I found them in places like the long grass.

With evening coming on and the sun going down and my standing all alone—except for a stranger—in the middle of tall prairie, it was easy to think like that. I guess I thought that the short guy would say something important to me, and I began to wonder just what it might be and how he would say it. But he just walked around for awhile, making some notes on a pad of paper. Then he got back into his Durand car and drove away. I didn't hang around long either, and pretty soon I picked up my valise and headed back to Lawrence.

I walked back up to the campus. The sun, obscured all day, came out for a moment, and there was a last wavering of brilliant light over the valley. A flag on the largest, and what seemed the oldest building (a sign said it was Fraser Hall) hung down around its shaft. The windows were sheened with a departing light that touched me like distilled loneliness. I walked to the far edge of Mount Oread and sat on a stone bench looking south down the steep slope.

As I sat there the valley before me changed, and a deeper, golden tone came over it. There were some little hills far out across the plain, and I could see the vast spread of flood water over the floor of the Wakarusa, a creek that cut through south of Lawrence. I sat for a while, then walked down the hill.

I walked down toward the Kaw river and came to a park with nice old trees. I was strolling through the park when I bumped into a little shingled building where campers could wash up. I went in and was splashing the dirt off my face when a tall, gawky guy with long, blond hair came in and started washing in the next bowl. He was a really friendly type.

He splashed water on his face, wiped on a paper towel, and started combing his long hair.

"Ain't this a hell of a country?" He asked no one in particular.

"Wet enough." I grunted.

"Ain't that the truth. You ain't a student?"

"Nope."

"Just passing through?"

"Yeah."

"Well, wish I was getting out of this wet hole. We had nothin' but water here for a month. My name's Kip. University student. What's your name?"

"Bob."

"Real nice to make your acquaintance."

"Any cheap hotel or rooming house around here Kip?"

"Sure, but I wouldn't go into any of 'em. Come along. Show you where *I* bunk."

I followed him out of the shingled building, and we walked a ways in the park. Pretty soon, in one of the parking areas, we came on to an old Model-T Ford sedan. Kip stopped.

"This is my place."

"This Ford?"

"Sure. Look."

The guy had a little oil stove in the Ford. He had taken the seats out and had made the floor level. He had a tiny folding table and a bed that came down in a kind of semi-circle. He lived in the Ford, he said, the entire school year, doing a little furnace tending for the grub he needed. When school was out in the spring he folded up the bed, tied a suitcase on top of the Ford, sat down on an old, broken kitchen chair behind the steering wheel, and drove back to his folks' western Kansas farm.

It was sure an interesting set-up, and I wasn't through looking at it when Kip took me by the arm.

"Where in hell is everybody hurrying off to?"

He pointed toward the distant street, and we saw a number of people hurrying toward the river.

"I don't know."

"Well," Kip said, "let's git along and see."

I left my valise behind in the Ford. Now there was a strange lightness in the whole sky and a deep red glow on the clouds low-down in the west. We walked over to the bridge and joined a crowd, mostly men, who were hurrying across. There wasn't much talk. Just the sound of hurrying feet on the cement.

The Kaw River was pretty high, up to the tops of the bridge arches now. Maybe, I thought, a bit higher than when I had crossed earlier. We stood at the rail for awhile looking down at the water, watching it suck down under the arches and send the driftwood (chunks of barns and houses) bumping against the bridge.

The whole bridge was vibrating. Over against the railing, across from where we stood, a small group of folks had stopped to watch something in the water. Kip and I walked over, and in the fading light saw a white chicken, perching as well as it could on top of a small outhouse. The house was bobbing and whirling around, and the chicken was shifting and balancing with the movements of the building. The outhouse spun for a minute before the suction began to take it, turning it over on its side. The exhausted chicken gave a little jump off the shingled roof onto one side of the house just as the other side began to go under the bridge. The sucking continued to pull it down, and first, as it went, slowly, the chicken could climb to the higher part, but as the house revolved faster and faster, and the white chicken dug its toes desperately against the side, there eventually was nothing for it to hold onto. The last edge of the house went under, and the chicken clung to it until the water covered its feet and legs. Then it spread its wet wings and opened its bill. It lay on the water a second before the sucking took it.

Kip and I walked on down the bridge, following a bunch of people off the north end to where there were a lot of county trucks lined up. It was quite dark now and lots of mosquitoes hummed around. The men stood beside the trucks. There wasn't much talking.

After a while one fellow lighted a lantern and set it on the platform of one of the trucks. He got up on the platform and started talking. He said that the dikes along the side of the river north of Lawrence were weakening from the big force of the waters, and he said they would have to be strengthened or the water would probably smash through the whole north side. He asked for as many workers as he could get on the trucks. Most everybody jammed onto the truck platforms; the truck motors started, and the vehicles bumped off.

We were driven along the edge of the river where the banks were high, then the drivers cut across the outskirts where the banks were lower and some dikes had been scraped up. Kip and I were pushed together at the rear of one of the trucks.

"Ain't a flood a hell of a thing?" Kip said.

"It's really horrible! I seen some floods, too."

"But it ain't as bad as a drought. Christ, there ain't enough ground left on our farm to grow a blade of grass."

"A flood is worst," a guy behind us said.

"Like hell," somebody else chimed in.

"Everytime."

"You ever lived in the real dry country, mister?"

"Hell, no. I lived around Lawrence all my life."

"Well, Christ, you don't know a damn thing. Our country is flying off to hell in a basket. Got so, out our way, when a guy faints, you got to throw a bucket of dust on him to bring him to."

"I still say a flood is the worst thing."

"You want to make something out of it?"

"I don't want to fight."

"Then shut up, mister. A drought is a lot worse than a flood."

Things were quiet for a moment.

"A twister is the worse thing I ever saw," I said.

"A twister is bad all right," Kip agreed.

"It ain't as bad as a flood," argued another guy.

"Like hell it ain't."

"A flood'll tear up all along a watercourse," the guy said, "and away beyond the course of that river, too, the cricks'll be raisin' hell, and beyond the cricks the sloughs'll be tearin' up, and beyond the sloughs there'll be the ditches cutting through the fields in a time of bad rain. A flood'll tear hell out of the whole country. A twister now, ain't so bad."

"A twister is hell," Kip said, "but it ain't as bad as them little whirlwinds that'll come across a field one right after another, seems like, sweeping the ground till it's slick enough and hard enough to be the floor of a Kansas City whorehouse. It's them little winds that're the bad ones."

"A flood is the worst thing," the guy said.

We were all quiet for awhile. The trucks bumped and churned on gravel and spun in mud, the hot motors sending up gasses through the floorboards. All the men clung to one another and coughed and cursed. We swung up to the dikes across a chunky gravel stretch of road, stopped, piled off the truck, and went to the river.

There was only a little light left in the clouded skies. We could see the waters dimly and could hear the veiled churn of the flooded Kaw. The edges of the river were at our feet along the dikes, and there was wetness spreading through in a few places. Above, there was lightning in the skies, and the booming thunder rolls echoed faintly down the valley until their volume increased as they rolled nearer and nearer. Grasses and reeds clung against me, and the whole place was filled with unreal sounds and half-seen objects. I was thinking about a lot of unrelated things: tall grass in a strong wind; cyclone-splintered cottonwoods; white human faces lifted up to skies opened by strange lightnings; smashing rains that have mashed corn to the earth, and cries of fear . . . things that Dad would of thought I guess, and that seemed kind of right.

The thunder rolls echoed out on top of the great flood like mighty wheels set loose on the rock floor of a vast, echoing cave. The men stepped back from the edge of the flood until somebody placed a few lighted lanterns on the platforms of the trucks.

Someone jumped up on one of the trucks, shouting and waving his arms.

"Spread out along the dike, men! We're going to sandbag her. The sand trucks'll stand about here, and we'll sandbag down river about three hundred yards. This here is the weak spot where the river curves in."

This guy yelled for us to space out all along the dike, so that we were close together and could easily pass the sandbags as they came down the line. Kip and I were pushed clean down to the end of the line. It was very lonely and frightening. I had never been so close to flood water, to the really wild force of it. Kip was on one side of me, and there was another guy, the last on the line, on the other side. I couldn't really see him. A smell arose from the flood: of earth in churned-up solution, of boiling sand.

Up at the head of the line the shovelers filled sand bags as fast as a whole line could carry them. There were a lot of guys filling bags, and others wired the tops. Then the bags were passed down the line. They came in a heaving, grunting stream, and slowly the dike's top had a line of sandbags, then a second row behind that one.

We had worked for a long time, and along about eleven o'clock on as dark and scary a night as I ever remember, a whisper floated down the line. I didn't stop to figure out why everybody was whispering but it seemed fitting. The guy working next to Kip whispered to him that the crest was expected about midnight.

"What'll happen if this here dike busts?" Kip asked.

"I reckon we swim home."

"Hell, I can't swim."

"You better shag ass for home now then."

"Not me. I'll find somethin' to ride on when the time comes."

Somebody came along the dike with a lantern, one of the engineer guys who was supervising the sandbagging. He paused to hunker down and inspect the bags at our end. He held his lantern low, and in the pale yellow light I could see the arms and legs of the men working on either side of me. As he rose up again, and said we were doing it all right, I could faintly see the fellow at the end of the line. I couldn't tell much about him except that he was small. He cussed as I lifted a sack to him and asked if I could use a drink.

"A drink would go great about now."

I felt a bottle jammed against my hand. I took it, uncorked, and poured some liquor down. I wasn't used to strong liquor. It tasted of cherry and had a wicked burn. I handed the bottle to Kip and he said, "Two of these drinks, and I'd jump in for a swim."

The bottle went back and forth a few times, and before long it was empty. Kip asked the guy what his name was. He said his name was Crafton and that he was a professor at the University.

We kept on working. The bags seemed to come down faster and faster. The trucks roared and backfired. The drivers hauled the sand from town as fast as they could. Somebody set a lantern down at our end of the line, and every so often someone would take up the light to examine the water level. It was coming up all the time, and just before midnight there was a big, sudden rise. One minute the water was safely below the sandbags, then it was up with a rush around the lower bags, and coming through and across.

Guys up the line began to yell and holler, and I felt water squish under my feet. The bags seemed to come even faster. The lightning flashed every once in a while, and the human shapes would be lit up in a wild pattern of action. Then the dark after the flash was always blacker, and there was only the feel of grasping arms and heaving bodies.

Yelling grew down at the far end of the line, and a cry began to spread. "Everybody out! Everybody out!"

Some of the guys near me began to fall back from

the dike and to move towards the head of the line. For me the crest of the flood was nothing new; I was too tired to care.

"Shall we go?" I asked someone.

"Better. Hell yes."

"I'm gone!"

We stepped off the dike into water that was already beginning to swirl and have a really strong pull to it. The water was way over the tops of our shoes. The guys ahead of us began to run, and a panic seemed to take ahold. There was an unholy terror in the night now, and in the terrible force of the river. My tiredness was suddenly gone. In my imagination flood fingers were busting through here and there, all over, to catch me, to cut me off, to drown me. The water was a living, crawling monster, a real thing with long, sucky arms reaching out and out. I thought of the white chicken and of me in the middle of the flood with my arms spread out and my mouth open.

I ran like the dickens. But it was hard going in the water in the dark with the rough ground under it. A guy ahead of me fell down and I stumbled over him. He grabbed hold of me by the foot and we struggled. A couple of other runners smashed into us, and we all laid there in the rising water, thrashing around. I got up, finally, cussing, and ran away.

The trucks were waiting—their motors running and their headlamps on. Everybody piled aboard. I couldn't find Kip nor the professor guy. Everybody was yelling to hurry up. The bunch I was with tried to pile onto one truck that was already too full. They shoved us newcomers away. We tried other trucks and they were full too. The water was coming up around the truck wheels when we finally got pulled on the last truck heading toward Lawrence.

We sloshed our way back, passing small houses and families scurrying for protection. We came to the Kaw River Bridge where there was a large bunch of people heading for the main part of Lawrence. In the faint bridge light, those folks looked sad and silent. A few carried household goods. Some of the women had kids in their arms. I got off the truck and walked across the bridge, feeling the jar of heavy pieces of drift striking it.

I stood around at the end of the bridge under a lamp and pretty soon Kip and the professor came trudging along. Never had anything hit me quite so hard as seeing him. I hadn't known it down there on the sandbag line, but I could see now that the professor was the same guy who had driven up to the old pioneer cemetery in the Durand car. I had been thinking so much about all the things that had happened, trying to figure them out, and here now was something else, one more thing, that was put there for me to wonder about . . . meeting a guy I had never seen before in a cemetery in the afternoon, then, at night, being placed right next to him in a crowd of maybe two or three hundred. For a guy like me who was looking for something and who was constantly under some kind of a pressure, and putting himself in places where strange things could happen, it was almost too much to take.

"Figured you was drowned," said Kip.

"He won't drown if he can swim like he can run," said the professor, "and by God I wasn't far behind." He didn't let on that he had ever seen me before.

"I never was so scared."

"Damn frightening."

"Damn if I don't believe a flood is worst than a drought."

We stood at the bridge for a while and watched the people sludge by in the half-dark. They were coming across slow, and when they almost got across they all turned back and looked. The professor guy stood there smoking a cigar. He didn't look too impressive, nothing like a mysterious Stranger, just wet and dirty and bedraggled. I didn't know what would come next.

God but we were all done in—exhausted and covered with mud. We had lost to the Kaw River, its water was already in north Lawrence, and there was nothing much anybody could do. The professor said that the houses in the low places would be full of water in the morning, and there'd be a time of waiting for the water to go down. People'd stream back across the bridge then, and poke around in the mud on the floors of their houses, or look at their ruined gardens and lawns and fields. The mud'd dry slowly and the earth would begin to stink. It would dry out in the hot sun, and the cracks would come in the top, and the kids would try to pry up the crazy shapes of the cracking earth just like they were fashioned, or to build mud houses or just throw it at each other.

Pretty soon Kip suggested that we go over to his Ford and have some grub. He said he had a quarter's worth of hamburger and some bread and a jug of elderberry wine from his folks' farm. Kip and I waited for the professor to say something. I guessed that he probably wouldn't eat poor, student grub cooked in an old Ford sedan. But he said, "Let's go," and we walked over to the park where Kip had his Ford. Kip crawled inside and set his stove to burning while the professor and I sat outside on the running board. Kip passed out the jug of elderberry wine and we each took a long swig of it.

"Pa says wine don't need age," Kip said, sticking his head out the window. "Pa drinks it soon as he can. But I hid a couple of jugs on him. This wine is real old. Made last summer."

We took another pull at the jug and settled back. I was completely tired out. There was still lightning, but further off now, and a light in the park swung back and forth in a voiceless breeze. The professor laid there smoking, real silent, his body caked with mud. Inside the Ford the hamburger began to pop. I laid back on the fender and felt tired and easy.

Kip stuck his head out of a window. "Say, prof, whatta you teach?"

"Dramatic art."

"The hell! Never expected to see a prof of dramatic art heavin' sandbags."

"Like excitement."

"Can anybody take those theatre courses of yours?"

"Practically."

"Damn if I ain't gonna take one."

Kip had the hamburgers done and he passed them out, seared hunks of meat between slices of bread. We all wolfed down the sandwiches and drank the jug of wine. We drank it dry.

There was something warm and easy about the professor. We talked about the folks over on the north side of Lawrence and how probably some would have to be taken off rooftops. We talked about the mess and confusion, and how the panic took hold out there in the dark.

"I ought to go home, my young friend," the prof said to me suddenly, "but damn if I leave without asking what you were doing over in the pioneer cemetery this afternoon. I recognized you on the bridge when we got across. One hell of a coincidence turnin' up next to you on the sandbaggin' gang. What *were* you doing up at the pioneer cemetery?"

I didn't know what to say, or how to explain. There was so much, and nobody could understand. I didn't really know why I was up there, but I sure felt that there was somebody back of me somewhere pulling the strings. Maybe somebody was pulling them for him, too.

"Well," I said finally, "there's an acre of uncut prairie grass over back of our house on the Neosho River. It's about all the old prairie that's left. And my dad goes in there and sits in the grass. I guess he's dreaming about everything still being the early days. One day last June he sent me off from home to find something as exciting as that tall grass was to him."

The professor didn't say anything for a long time. I thought he just wasn't interested. Then he said, "That's really exciting. It could be the start of an epic. What'd you find?"

"I guess not the stuff Dad meant: all that tall grass, all that new country, doesn't exist. There are just bums and hobos all over, drifting around; the Indians are all sort of starving and the past is pretty dead for them. I saw a lot of things this summer, but nothing like what the tall grass was for Dad. The grass isn't there."

"Maybe it is."

"I've looked like hell."

"Maybe in the wrong places."

"I've scouted a lot of country."

"You could find your tall grass anytime, anyplace," said the professor. "Maybe it's just chance that causes things to happen; but they do happen, and you can, if you choose, put your finger on a thing that happened any moment of your life, and give it its own realness. I do that in plays. Anything that happens isn't fixed there in time by itself. It's a part of you, and before you were born there is the whole universe of the past, and after you are dead there is the possibility of continuance that faith makes real. To me it's really in drama, make-believe if you will, that I can understand what happened. In the theatre I can put my finger on anything, any idea, and make it come to life. And if I'm misplaced in time, I can, if I wish, do things like captain an immigrant wagon train, organize it at Council Grove, and take it through to Oregon or California, or even set out to find the tall prairie grass if I want. Maybe the things that were so real in the past can only exist for us now in make-believe."

He didn't talk any more, and I lay there thinking about what he said. I never met a man who ever explained anything like that—that there was a whole world you could make up for yourself, if you wanted. I didn't quite understand how it could be done, but it was a new idea that really excited me.

"Sorry the wine's run out," Kip said. "Another jug and we might of had us a time."

"The wine was good," the prof said. He got up and shook hands with us and told me to look him up sometime. I reckoned inside myself that I would probably see him again, but I didn't tell him I would.

He went off into the dark and I laid back on the fender and closed my eyes. You never can tell when a puzzle or a search will fall into place or when things will clear up all of a sudden, the way a terrible hot spell is broken by a fast, hard summer shower or how a cool wind comes in quickly from dark clouds. It's just that way. My summer had been a journey filled with adventures, some dark and rather bleak, that had come out of nowhere. And the way they all finally fell into place, or seemed to, was only right for me, not for anybody else in the whole world. That's what made it so incredibly wonderful. It was mine.

Maybe it was something the professor said or the combination of mud, the lightning, the flood, and death. I don't know. But suddenly I got this flash! *THE STRANGER IN THE GRASS IS THE ONE WHO MOVES YOU FROM PLACE TO PLACE, AND MAKES THINGS HAPPEN THE WAY THEY DO.* I figured that there probably was only one Stranger for everyone, but there might be more, and we never really know who they are. The main thing was that everybody's life has the tall grasses and everybody owns their own acre of prairie where they can look for the answers to things. Everybody has their own dream.

Dad sure had his own dream, and that was where mine started. I knew that I couldn't bring home any great object or message for him or descriptions of a new and wide sea of grass, but what I did have was a feeling that what I had seen and done was all mine, and that in my memory I would always have it and be able to use it. Maybe, like Professor Crafton said, I'd only have it as make-believe, but it all belonged to me. I guess that wasn't exactly what Dad had wanted, but I knew now that it was the tall grasses of my search to know and to look for what it was that was mine, not Dad's. I had to go home and tell him that.

Fruition and Homecoming

My coming finally home to Wisconsin was a kind of miracle. It was the termination of a search, and the beginning of a mission, at least so it seemed to me. It included my summertime adventures, trying to follow the fantasies of my father who still had his eye on the frontier; the study of drama, as much as I could get at the University of Kansas, from Professor Allen Crafton, the professor of the sandbags. And it included the burgeoning of an idea in Kansas for which Crafton provided the impulse.

I enjoyed working with Crafton in those Depression years at least partly because of his deep love of Kansas people and places. For some reason he liked me and trusted me. I stayed on as his assistant for a couple of years, and we talked increasingly of a theater of the Kansas people based on the history and tradition that seemed to make Kansas unique. One morning after one of our talks I was working on the stage and a thick cloud of dust began to drift down from the heights of the stagehouse. I was building some theatrical flats, but I let them lie and climbed to the attic. I went to the windows, and as I looked westward out across the great valley, it seemed to me that the valley was curtained with thick, black velours. The richness of the prairie country was blowing away; the Dust Bowl had hit its maximum strides and the whole plains lay in a whirling, drifting dark torment. It was as though from the attic windows I could sense all America writhing and gasping as from a great wound.

My father had been a Kansas pioneer, but the frontier that he knew had ended. It would probably never return or be relived; the Depression with its floods and hungers was the end, perhaps, of a scene that began with the push west and ended in the spiritual and physical torment of the American people. If the power, the drive, the call that had sent my father forth from Clark County, Illinois, to Kansas was now somehow responsible for young and old wandering futilely through the Depression, then, indeed, I thought, we must seek a new, inward expansiveness that would enrich us, not so much in silver and gold but in our whole soul and feeling.

Crafton said many times that this inward growing must be of the art that was in us and of a recognition by all people of the goodness of the stuff of America re-created in terms of theater, so that theater might be an accepted part of our lives. In his own way, in his own theater, Crafton was making his belief live magnificently as well as finding his own salvation. But I wondered how his idea could be spread—how it could come to everybody.

As I stood at the attic windows alone with the great dust curtain curling around Old Fraser, it did not seem strange to me that, somehow, somewhere, I might become a tiny part of the spreading of such an idea. Afterwards, I began to wonder whether the people of America might be drawn closer together in tolerance and in joy in one another through their stories and songs, their presents and pasts, told and sung in a theater whose stages were everywhere and whose actors were the folks in the cities and on the farms, in the crossroad places and in the back places where the American past lay quiet and undisturbed. The problem of the cultural arts was really an understanding of the heritage of the people. This idea struck me like a thunderbolt, and I realized that this was the reason for my own personal mission. I thought about it a great deal and talked it over with Crafton.

One day Professor Crafton told me that if I were really interested in native American theater I should go to Cornell University at Ithaca, New York to do graduate study with Alexander M. Drummond, who had made huge strides toward a New York State theater. I applied for a scholarship to Cornell, received one, and so at length the day before I was to depart Lawrence, I was standing with Crafton on the side of Mount Oread. It was then 1937. At my request we walked together to the old cemetery where I had first seen him.

There was silence between us, and my thoughts were reaching out beyond the valley to encompass my experiences in American places. I had heard American voices. Somehow I knew that these voices and feelings must relate themselves to a theater and a literature I earnestly desired to help create but could not really define. As I left Crafton and Kansas behind, I hoped Cornell and Drummond would teach me what to do, where to go.

It was my graduate study at Cornell, in the central New York hill and lake country, with the great teacher of dramaturgy, Alexander M. Drummond, that finally proved to me how much the past and present are of a whole fabric. For instance, when I pass one of the grand old Greek revival-style houses in southern Wisconsin, I have to think of the great old mansions along the Hudson in New York State; and some of the lesser houses hidden back in the central New York State hills. Such thought is very appropriate, for a large number of York State settlers brought their style of living and their talents to pioneer Wisconsin. The York State farmers, their land worn out from wheat planting, gathered up tools and stock and families and moved. The houses they had built in the New York hills were soon vacant, perhaps inhabited again by people who also came and tried the land. Those who remained behind and heard back from the others who went west to Wisconsin heard golden tales indeed . . . especially after ways were found to get the grain to market. For Wisconsin was itself a fertile growing place for wheat. In Wisconsin the patterns of living were about as they had been in New York. And so the same style of house was built by the country carpenters, the same facade, the classic doorway, the white pillars across a narrow front porch. There are many of these fine old farmhouses in southern Wisconsin. But York State and New England farmers wore the Wisconsin land out, too, and many of them restlessly proceeded on west and west, to the California gold rush, to the filling Mississippi basin, to Oregon. And as in New York, many of the Wisconsin farm houses decayed and rotted away.

When I was a grad student in the late 1930's at Cornell I went on many rambles through the hills. It was still Depression time, and I noted here and there a family occupying a classic, once grand, hill mansion. I spoke with many of these people, and their stories were almost always the same. They were Dust Bowl farmers from Oklahoma, western Kansas, Texas, who had to leave their homes. Some progressed west in a Steinbeck-like migration, to the grape harvests of

California; to the beet harvests of Idaho. And others migrated east, for the opportunistic and rather unscrupulous real estate men told them about the fine York hill country, so cool with rains, and fine, great houses to be had cheap—large white ones, on beautiful hills where the Revolutionary War soldiers once lived. To people stifled by dust and drought and poverty, the setting was attractive. They loaded old trucks in about the same way that the Joads in *Grapes of Wrath* loaded up, and struck out east for York State; not west, for California.

They couldn't make the grade in New York, either. I saw and spoke with many who were nearly starving in 1938 and the children seemed forlorn, as they played about the decayed residences. I didn't know then that I would someday come myself to Wisconsin. But one of the most touching things I do nowadays is to travel through rural Wisconsin and study the houses. Who built them? Were they New York Staters? And sometimes, yes, very often, they were.

The play I wrote at Cornell for Professor Drummond and which impressed him, was about those Dust Bowl people who went to New York State. It was Federal Theatre times. Hallie Flanagan, once of the Vassar Experimental Theatre, a small, forceful woman completely devoted to her job as national director of the Federal Theatre, had a kind of pact with America. It involved bringing the theatre with beauty and power into many American places. She and her friend Franklin Roosevelt planned something like that. She came to Cornell one day in 1938, and I drove her back into the New York hills. We talked of the people in rural America and how they could be joined to what she saw then as a great national American Theatre. I hoped that her pact would include telling stories on stage about the wheat farmers and the Greek revival houses of York State and Wisconsin, both having an important illusory and dramatic significance in America's past.

My play about this subject was called "The Wild Hills." I carried it to Professor Drummond with great hope that he would like it, that something fine for me might come of it. But the longer he held the play the more depressed I became. Surely he must think it pretty thin stuff. I dropped spiritually lower and lower; I had never been able to gauge what he really thought of me and my writing. His opinion was essential. To his students he was like a Greek god, all powerful, and a word of approval was golden.

Suddenly, I was being offered choices of things to

do, so one morning in May I went to Professor Drummond's office and told him that I had received an offer to teach at Sweet Briar College in Virginia (a high-class women's college). I said I guessed I would accept it. There was silence for a while; then he said, "Who told you to go?"

"Nobody."

"Better think it over."

He obviously had more to say. I had learned to sit and wait. "Better think it over," he repeated. "I've been working very hard for the past two months to get you a fellowship with the Rockefeller Foundation. I want you to stay and help me start a new playwriting project in New York State. Maybe we can learn something about stories and people and theater that will help the whole idea of American theater along, and help us to dramatize some of the great American heritage."

I sat very still. The reversal was terrific. I felt like laughing; then I felt a great wave of affection for this big man who knew so exactly what to do.

He said: "I have just this morning received a wire from Dr. David Stevens in New York. He would like to have you come down to the Rockefeller Foundation and see him."

I stood up. "I would like to stay at Cornell if you really think I could help."

He shoved the play I was so proud of across his desk to me. "I was going to send you back your play this morning. I'm sorry I kept it so long."

I took the play and saw that he had written on the cover: "This play has a flavor of America that I like tremendously. Come and see me. I have some news for you."

That evening I dined with Professor Drummond at the old Ithaca Hotel. There was a legend about him there. If a student achieved anything like respect from Alexander Drummond he might be expected to pay. The check lay between us on the table for a long time. Finally I picked it up; I couldn't afford it, but I understood that I had graduated in his regard to something better than I had been. I paid, gladly, though I believe I had to borrow a bit of the money for the check from him. I thought I saw him smile as he dug it out.

Drummond said that I was to go to New York the next day to show Dr. Stevens the play, and, said Drummond, perhaps Stevens would do something to further my career. Drummond told me that the Rockefeller Foundation was located at 49 West 49th Street, the RCA Building.

Filled with many self-doubts, I borrowed $35 from Professor Drummond for the trip; and clutching the manuscript and my old valise—the same one I had carried away from my Kansas home so long before—I boarded the Lehigh Valley Black Diamond Express at Ithaca. It was a six-hour trip between Ithaca and New York in those days, 1938, and all the way down I rehearsed what I would say to Dr. Stevens. I had never before been exposed to New York City. The name of the Rockefeller Foundation terrified me, but I responded eagerly to the Foundation's slogan, printed on certain materials I had seen which said: "The Rockefeller Foundation founded 1913, In Behalf of All Mankind."

I had to inquire the whereabouts of the RCA Building when I arrived at Penn Station. A stranger pointed somewhat scornfully up 6th Avenue toward the largest, tallest building in sight. I walked toward it, carrying my valise, feeling it impossible that anyone in the huge city, so rapid, noisy, and such a contrast to the rural scenes with which my life had so far been mostly involved, could ever comprehend what it was that I was after; could ever know the sensations I felt about the American land, the promise of its people, the stories of settlement, of achievement, the joy, the sadness I saw in faces; the sense of foreboding, the sense of hope. How could anyone here know?

I finally discovered the express elevator to the 55th floor, where the Foundation offices were located in those days, and when I arrived there I was sure that my mission in New York would come to nothing, that I was out of place, a foreigner, an alien, with nothing to contribute to the city or it to me.

I had built up an unusual fantasy about Dr. Stevens. In my imagination he was certain to be towering, aloof, cold, extremely critical, unsympathetic. I pictured him seizing my play, devouring it, not liking it, and sending me away in disgust.

The shock when he finally appeared, emerging from an inner corridor, nearly overwhelmed me. He was rather short in stature, gentle, very firm-eyed, and gave me a warm smile, as though he had instantly understood my uneasiness. He took me on a little tour, pointing out several famous persons whose portraits hung in the outer office. He finally, still in the hallway, looked at me directly as though he knew everything about me, and said, "I want you first to go back to Kansas where your roots are. Go and visit your home, your mother. Take stock of your experiences. Then return. We will arrange your fellowship in playwriting. There is no problem about that. I rely on the judgment of men and women I trust. Professor Drummond said you were worthy. That's all there is to it. I'm happy to meet you. Goodbye.''

That was my first visit with David Stevens, another of my Strangers. He didn't ask about my play. In fact he never even saw it. But he had the Foundation pay my expenses out to Kansas where I visited my aging parents. Stevens was absolutely right to suggest that I go. I was able to think things through, see more clearly there, at my boyhood home which I had once left, that what I wanted to do was to work with people, help them realize their relationships to the land, to their heritage . . . to write, to act, to recreate the heritage of American places, to find a sensibility of art and poetry. I tried, excitedly, to try to explain all this to Dad one afternoon. But he seemed to grasp it only dimly. He was then too buried in the past. He was proud of me, I think, but I never knew whether he thought I had found the Grail, the mysterious Stranger, or what. I could not tell him that I had, perhaps, met several Strangers.

Many things then transpired. I returned to Cornell. Professor Drummond had in production a master interpretation of Chekhov's "Uncle Vanya". It was a 1938 summer production in the Willard Straight Theatre, and for some of the key roles outside performers had been obtained. Performing the sensitive, beautiful part of Sonya was a young woman from Battle Creek, Michigan, also once a Drummond student, named Maryo Kimball. My own part in the production was tiny, the role of a serf, and at one time I brought onstage some needed props and whistled for the dog. But my role didn't make any difference. I watched every performance of "Uncle Vanya" through from beginning to end. As the summer closed Maryo Kimball and I were engaged. We were married in June of 1939 at her family home in Battle Creek.

Meanwhile Professor Drummond and I had accomplished or stimulated the writing of many New York State Plays. I was thoroughly steeped by then in the lore and legend of central New York, and would have been perfectly happy to remain there the remainder of my life. But at just this time I received a letter from Dr. Stevens saying that travel money (he mentioned $400) was available for an exploratory journey throughout the United States. The idea, I am sure, was to enable me to discover where I wanted to work and to live permanently.

David Stevens had a sure knowledge of men and women. He seemed to be able to tell always what a person wanted, what his essential dreams were. I had never articulated mine to him. He simply knew. Maybe it was because he himself had been raised in the crucible of the Middle West, and had the life and lore of the people of Mid-America deep inside him. I don't know. But along in the spring of 1942, after I was deferred from Army service, I received a further letter from Dr. Stevens. "I am sure," he wrote, "that you have been giving some thought to where you are going finally to work. Things will straighten out. Right now the bottom has dropped out of the arts in America. But the war will end, and the arts will come back stronger than ever. We will have a new kind of federal support for the arts someday, mark my words. Where would you like to work?"

I really couldn't answer, but the question fascinated me. Sometimes I had thought about returning to Kansas where I had lived as a boy, where I had obtained my first impressions of art, became tuned to nature, knew that I had some inclinations to become a writer, and from whence I had set forth on my first odyssey. But then there was the element of not knowing how to return. I feared to return to Kansas for of all journeys the return is the hardest, and the complexities of boyhood seemed too immense. So where?

I traveled again to New York to see Dr. Stevens. He mentioned Wisconsin among other places, and he ordered the financial officer of the Foundation to issue me the check for $400 . . . a special travel grant. When I returned to Ithaca, Maryo and I packed our Pontiac car and, with saved wartime gasoline coupons, set forth. There was never a journey, I thought, that had so much of wanting, of need, and of the necessity of discovering an intuitive relationship of self to place. We went west and north and curved back through mid-country. Our money lasted remarkably. Each week I sent Dr. Stevens a letter describing what I had seen, and the potentials as I felt them in regions toward an acceptance of a people's art. I spoke with people when and where I could; formed no deep impressions that this or that place was where we belonged. We were looking for a spiritual home. Finally, of course, and almost last, we arrived at Madison, Wisconsin.

I am in Madison suddenly, in June, 1942. I have left Maryo and the car in Michigan at her home in Battle Creek. Everything is a wartime scene, the Northwestern train from Chicago is packed with service personnel and college students. I have never before visited Wisconsin. I can get no taxi from the station. I walk up through the city square, stare at the State Capitol, wander up State Street. At the moment I have no thought that Madison will be my home for the next forty years. I am struck by the sight of the main building of the University of Wisconsin, Bascom Hall, as it rests on College Hill, visible from State Street; and I turn and see behind me the State Capitol, also visible. At the moment the jointure of state and university has no meaning. Later the meaning becomes clear.

Stevens has suggested that I visit at Madison with the Dean of the Agricultural College. I do not understand why. Shouldn't I proceed first to the University Theatre? Or to the chairman of the Department of Art? If I am to work in the arts, why the College of Agriculture? But Stevens knows better.

At Agriculture Hall I am directed to the dean's office. The dean is in and will see me. I am ushered into a very large room with a huge desk at one end. At the desk is an immense figure who, I have been told, is Dean Chris Christensen. The huge man rises as I enter. He appears to tower to the ceiling. Behind him, on the wall, is a large oil painting of a farmer in the midst of a yellow field of wheat. The farmer figure also is monumental, much larger than life. I recognize the painting, and the artist as John Stuart Curry, also a Kansan, a leading American regional painter. Dean Chris invites me to sit down and then wastes no time. "Stevens wrote me you were coming. Perhaps someday you will want to work in Wisconsin." He pointed at the painting. "I brought Curry here to lead rural people in art. I want to do the same with literature and drama. I want poetry in Wisconsin to become as important to Wisconsin people as dairying. Come and join us at Wisconsin."

Golden words!

I spent most of that day listening while a rural sociologist, John Kolb, and Dean Christensen told me about the Wisconsin people: the downtrodden peoples from Europe who sought freedom; the down-east Yankees and the wheat farmers and tradesmen from New York State who sailed on the packet boats of the old Erie Canal and then came through the lakes to Milwaukee where they spread out across the woodlands and the prairies like a wave. They told me of the Indians who left their names, their effigy mounds, and the mystery of their legends across the face of the Wisconsin earth, and of the lumbermen who hewed down the mighty forests of the north. Dean Chris spoke of the hunger of the people for education, of how they had opened the University in 1849, the year after Wisconsin reached statehood, and of how, little by little, the University had broadened its services until the whole state was, in effect, the University.

On the walls of Dean Chris's office were also several rather primitive paintings of rural Wisconsin, and he told me that an art movement was springing up among the farm folks. Every year there was a big exhibit of rural art in Madison. And there was a theater tradition, too. The great days of living professional theater were gone in Wisconsin, of course, but the State had had the earliest little theater movement, a group called the Wisconsin Dramatic Society, which was dedicated to the writing and production of plays about Middle Western life. Personalities such as Tom Dickinson in dramatic literature; Zona Gale, the young Portage author; and Loura Sherry from Milwaukee, were members.

Unfortunately the Wisconsin Dramatic Society was no more, but University Extension had, for fifteen years, kept workers in the field of drama, encouraging playwriting and play production in the cities and in the country. True, no great original plays of the people had yet sprung to life, but the public attitude toward theater was healthy; even the great Wisconsin Dairyman's Association was deeply engaged in theatre.

That evening when I wrote to David Stevens I said that of all the places I had visited Wisconsin had seemingly done the most to establish a popular concept of drama and art. Somehow everything clicked. I knew that it was in Wisconsin where I wanted to live and work. There was an atmosphere upon the Wisconsin land that was different from other states—an atmosphere that seemed to proffer a deeper humanness; a distillation of a folk desire for a complete oneness of human struggle and earth.

During most of World War II we were living in the Province of Alberta, Canada where I had an appointment at the University of Alberta. But eventually in 1945, as though it were all preordained, I received an offer to join the faculty at the University of Wisconsin. Alexander Drummond and David Stevens said it was what I must do. Stevens had been born at Berlin, Wisconsin, the son of a Methodist minister, and I think he was especially delighted that Wisconsin would be our new home. Maryo and I packed up to move to Madison. We wanted roots, a home. Wisconsin might be a good place to search for these prized things. Zona Gale, the famous Wisconsin author who lived in Portage, had said that Wisconsin was a land of good neighbors and friendly communities where deep, intensely human values of community life existed. We earnestly desired a neighborhood life worth sharing.

And as we entered Wisconsin from the northwest and drove through the gentle greens and browns and soft slopes of Pierce County, we felt that home was very near. Here was a friendly land, surely, and I said wordlessly to Wisconsin in general: "There is nothing between us yet; I will try to understand you and to respect your moods and appreciate your places. If I win your regard, never send me away a stranger. I want to be a part of you, and I want to do the best for you."

Maryo drove the Pontiac and I looked at the names on the map: Brillion, Lake Winnebago, Forest Junction, Prairie du Sac, Black Earth, Mazomanie, Spring Valley, Maiden Rock; simple beautiful names, surely friendly names . . .

And so it turned out. At some point on that initial journey, I was able to scribble in a notebook:

> If I am lonely in Wisconsin
> It is never the fault of the people
> For my friends are in every town.
> I have journeyed through years
> Of restless movement
> To visit Wisconsin places,
> That I might assist the Arts
> To grow a little . . .

And so the years have passed. . . .

It is 1976 now, and nearly forty years after I first met David Stevens in New York, I have just published *A Time of Humanities*—the recollections of Stevens looking back upon the years when he was Director of Humanities for the Rockefeller Foundation. How circular life is! Little by little events begun in one phase of time complete themselves in another.

The Wisconsin Academy of Sciences, Arts and Letters, is the publisher of the Stevens book. To achieve it I have made three recording journeys to California, to the White Sands of LaJolla Retirement Home where Stevens resides. In 1974 the Foundation indicated that they would support my attempt to gather from Stevens the memories of his dynamic years. I undertook the project as a labor of love, for I could clearly remember my first trip to New York to visit him, and ever since that time his constant support, along with wise advice and much-needed money, of the many programs I struggled to launch. I haven't said too much about them but their track lies upon Wisconsin. Although David was often far away, I considered him a full partner in the Wisconsin work I was doing. When he retired from the Foundation in 1950 he came home to Wisconsin to live. He owned a large, one-floored, weather-grayed house above Eagle Bay at Ephraim. I saw him often and drove many trips through the years between Madison and Ephraim to talk with him about plans and ideas. More and more he became the synthesis of the Stranger. Surely not many human beings have been blessed with such a friend. He had on his Ephraim estate a small log cabin fitted with fireplace, desk and chair, and this was mine if I wanted, when I was writing and needed solitude. I wrote several books in that cabin.

At length, of course, when he was about ninety, he entered the LaJolla home, and it was there that I followed him, seeking, I suppose, to enlarge his life and mine by tape-recording his memories.

How did he become associated with the Foundation in the first place? David was an ideal person to be a foundation executive because of his human breadth and his intuitive sense of the sincerity and character of individuals. He was a combination of scholar and successful administrator; his talent for administration, indeed, was so great and so early recognized, that he became vice president of Northwestern, then assistant to the president of the University of Chicago. He had met, at Lawrence, a fellow student, Ruth Davis, a remarkable young woman who at one time, in her twenties, and in a day when it just wasn't done, had traveled alone across Russia and China. Like David, Ruth towered as a human being and treated me always as a treasured friend.

David was invited to work at the Rockefeller Foundation by Max Mason, a president of the University of Chicago who, in 1928, became president of the Rockefeller Foundation.

A curious coincidence enters here. Mason, outstanding mathematical physicist, who worked out the first anti-submarine detection device in the University swimming pool, had been a professor at the University of Wisconsin and had courted and finally married the wife of a professor in the medical school. The house that Maryo and I eventually bought in Madison was the medical professor's home.

The White Sands of LaJolla Retirement Home is low and long on the street side. Vines cling on walls above small balconies, and red bougainvillea is in bloom in late October. At the back the building meanders down the slope almost to the beach, where the Pacific surf runs in high, broken a half-mile out by a reef. To the reef lobster boats come each day, and on the terrace above the sea there are walks, gardens and benches where the residents of the White Sands often come to rest and talk.

Earlier this morning I have walked on the terrace with David. He is ninety-one; I younger but not really younger either. I feel that I can never match the vigor and optimism with which he views human affairs. We have watched children on the beach, a small dog chasing and fetching, a young couple walking very fast holding hands. During our saunter he has commented on many things, on adventures we have had together, and news of many people we both know. We talk about our homes in Wisconsin where we both reside officially, he at Ephraim, I at Madison. We speak of his wife, Ruth, who has died the year before, and then we return to his room, for we must begin another assignment we have undertaken together.

His room is small, quiet, comfortable: a few cherished family pictures; a painting of wild geese landing on a marsh. (His talented son-in-law, Dr. Lee Monroe, has painted that.) There is a large desk, an electric portable typewriter rests on the pull-out shelf; a long side-table with fruit which his daughter Barbara Monroe has brought the evening before also has many books on it; there are two chairs, a small end table between them; the "New York Times Book Review" is spread open on the desk. Everything is convenient, comfortable, easy.

He and I will converse today of men in search, of human needs, of Humanities programs in governments and institutions, of the shaping of human talent. He speaks clearly, with force still. As he speaks, his penetrating, yet warm, eyes brighten with remembered challenge, clash, parry, with kindled recollection of place and persons. We place the recorder on the end table between us. I think he is perhaps a little apprehensive, for our conversations of the past have never had such firm purpose of systematic recall . . . his talk is largely about the Rockefeller Foundation where so much of his life was spent. But at one point he suddenly looks at me and says, "Just what was it you set out to do in Wisconsin?" He knew, but he wanted me to say it, I guess.

What indeed, did I come to accomplish in Wisconsin? I return again to my early days at Madison. It is 1945, a hot afternoon in early September. I am in the catacombs of an old red brick building they call Science Hall. It is where a man I am to work with has his office. Leslie Brown is slim, gray, very alert, very friendly. Among other subjects, he is concerned with the importance of the arts in people's lives. He is a specialist in popular education, in adult education. We fence for a moment, estimating our purposes, backgrounds. Suddenly Brown grabs an old straw hat. "Let's go have a beer . . . where we can talk."

We walk silently to a nearby tavern on University Avenue. Brown said, as we sat down, "There used to be over a hundred brands of beer made in Wisconsin and if it hadn't been for the opposition of the German Saloonkeepers League, we'd have had Woman's Suffrage a long time before we voted it in 1919. Also, there are practically an infinite number of bars in Hurley, Wisconsin, a town of about a thousand. And Wisconsin stands fourth in the national per capita consumption of all liquor; and first in the nation in consumption of brandy."

"Really?"

He said, "All that information is purely incidental. Now tell me what are you going to do in Wisconsin? There is a lot of curiosity about you here. What are you going to do that hasn't already been done?"

I took a deep breath. This was it, really. Talk before had been cheap. Now I had to say it. I said, "Look, Brown, I've done a lot of things and seen a lot of places, but nothing I did or saw meant anything until I tied it all up with the Arts and with theatre. That was back in Kansas. Then I was in New York and got interested in the happenings the people remembered; the way they spoke, the dramatic countryside events; and all of that became a theatre for me, too. Later I was working up in Canada, with the memory of the frontier right there, close enough to touch, and that was exciting; a great epic sensation of the past and how the land was transformed.

"Everywhere I've been it's as though there's a person or an experience that has revealed to me a new part of the picture; a picture that I want to help develop, and that I hope will lead to an art in America more widely accepted than we've ever dreamed. In Kansas a professor named Allen Crafton opened the world of theatre for me. In New York at Cornell another professor, Alexander Drummond, taught me discipline and the wonderful, strange mystery of tales and legends that are a part of the light and shade of this picture of America's raw theatre and art, because perhaps America will only be as great as her myths and traditions. In Canada I could see what profound effect the frontier has had on us as an American people, and how the necessities of life have to be a part of our art thinking. And long before all that, when I was a very young man, I set out from my Kansas home and experienced the raw, cutting edge of life—the Depression, the drunks, the revolutionaries, the con-men, the workers, the farmers, the weak, and the strong. Now, God help me, in Wisconsin I've got to discover still another part of the picture, and hopefully that will be the final part."

Brown took a large swallow of the beer that made Milwaukee famous. I couldn't tell whether he had been listening or not. "What is this part of the picture you'll try to find in Wisconsin?"

I said, "It might be something like this: There are rumblings again about a more deeply American National Theatre. I get letters and hear this talk all the time, about fine American plays touring through the American countrysides again, maybe under a national subsidy, and theatre centers and art centers growing in the larger cities. That will be wonderful, and it will be a part of the American cultural idea, but it will not be the largest part and it will not be my part. My part is in the back country, away from the largest centers, where the hardest battle is being fought. My part and work is with the creative force that is in the people, and this creative power, developed slowly, in keeping with the life of the people, might finally swell the idea of the arts to a national spiritual crescendo."

"You talk damn big," Brown snarled.

"And I tell you something else. I believe we ought to try to open a creative life for everyone; in the schools, the communities, on the farms, in the cities . . . maybe even in the bars and taverns. The arts must now come into their own. It's the next great American thing we must do."

The tavern was empty except for ourselves. Brown suddenly stood up and started to pace around, holding his beer glass and making gestures. "I can see this thing growing, too. Everybody ought to be a part of it. The kids and the high schools, and the community groups and the farm folks, the older people, working together and getting closer together through a big idea: through a sensibility of the arts as necessary in life. Maybe soon the federal government will really get into the picture."

"You've got it right."

"I don't know much about the arts," Brown said. "But I'll help."

Brown was wrong. He had the most profound sense of art for he understood that everyone has to live a part of his life in art and in make-believe. During the time he remained in Wisconsin he was a brother to me, and constantly an inspiration.

I have tried sincerely to keep those ideas I expressed that afternoon so long ago, foremost. I have tried to help make Wisconsin a proud territory of the human spirit; of the sensitive approaches of man to homeplace, nature and to art. Through the arts, through so many cultural summations of Old World to New, I have tried, tried, tried; so many communities, so much teaching, travel, seeding. Success? Looking backward now, the State, as I conceived it, appears like a battlefield. The debris of conflict is everywhere; discarded dreams lie helter-skelter like thrown shields of ancient warriors; yet a sense of unique Middle West civilization is there, too, and above the plain, some monuments.

Looking further backward at the years of my Wisconsin experience, I am appalled and unbelieving as I observe the scope and number of projects, ideas, schemes, educational programs and organizations that have been launched largely, I suppose, out of the sense of mission that brought me to Wisconsin. I only hope that the great men and women who shared my beliefs know somehow that the arts in Wisconsin are alive and that they are thriving through the work of University Extension and the much more recent Wisconsin Arts Board. Sometimes I even think that Mr. McBride would know and approve. I have often comforted myself by thinking that he was going to fire me from the gang because he knew I ought to be doing different work.

I recently found documents in our archives relating to my establishment of the Rural Writers and the friendship of a great volunteer leader, Fidelia Van Antwerp; to the founding of the Wisconsin Idea Theatre Conference; the Wisconsin Regional Writers; the Council for Wisconsin Writers; the National Community Theatre Training Centers. I found abundant correspondence with the officers of the Rockefeller Foundation; with David Stevens; with Les Paffrath of the Johnson Foundation (always a backer of my programs); plans for Wisconsin Folk Drama tours that David Peterson, L.G. Sorden and I launched; the fine program in behalf of minorities, the handicapped and incarcerated "The Arts and Human Need;" the Upper Middle West Professional Playwright's Laboratory with Dale Wasserman; with the founding of the Rhinelander School of Arts; programs of cooperation with the countries of Finland and England; the forming of the Wisconsin Arts Council and Foundation; work with Native Americans; with rural communities; with the Wisconsin Academy of Sciences, Arts and Letters; with state folklore and folklife; work with the elderly; with the Wisconsin Bicentennial Commission; with book publishing and scores of letters to and from my good friends, Cap Pearce and Charlie Duell in New York at Duell, Sloan and Pearce; projects with Augie Derleth and other writers; with Allen Crafton and Alexander Drummond; with a hundred graduate students and assistants; with the Arts and the Small Community; the National Endowment for the Arts; with 4-H Clubs; with the National Theatre Conference; with national surveys of the American Theatre; with national and international organizations; conferences with thousands of writers eager to realize themselves . . . and the establishment of the Robert E. Gard Wisconsin Idea Foundation at Aldebaran Farm at Spring Green. All these things I have done, or caused to be done.

My life in Wisconsin has been a rich one; yet overall the whole experience of "coming home to Wisconsin" has taught me how necessary it is to probe deeply into the life and background of a region if the feeling of what has really transpired is to be important. It is something beyond the superficial, and even beyond the bitter necessities that a land imposes upon its settlers; it is more the spirit of a place and its distillation in human lives. That theory applied now makes me sure there must be even more great writing about the development of Wisconsin. I do not mean more history, already splendidly done. What I mean is a great and dramatic portrayal of the spirit of the people of Wisconsin . . . in terms of their epic arrival, struggle, the design of their nationalities. A magnificent canvas ought to be created. I am familiar with the scope of the Wisconsin land, and how the land beckoned to people. I know what happened when they converged upon Wisconsin, freedom seeking, land seeking, their families destitute for the most part, their women self-sacrificing and humble, but with terrible pride and courage. I have read the epic novels of Rolvag, the novels of Moberg; I have read the novels and the stories of Hamlin Garland, but in all of them something is lacking that is implicit in the Wisconsin story. It is a vision that was here; a great responsibility to self, to future, that ended, finally, in the concept of the "Wisconsin Idea." If a writer could catch that flicker of world greatness . . . buried in so many, many humble and seeking hearts . . . there it would be. It was, of course, this elusive thing, this heartrending idealism of simple people and also the terrible intellectual necessities that helped bring about free education and libraries; the gift, at least in part, of early free-thinking German intellectuals, who beginning in 1845 brought and maintained the search for a world betterment. It seemed to congeal, to focus, to become inevitably a part of Wisconsin, the soul, the spirit.

All of this, with the smell of manure on the spring air, the way the rivers look in April, the dark of forest tracks, the far flung University that spreads its influence into every home . . . the farm girls and boys with multitudes of hard-won fair ribbons, the great cattle herds . . . the brown of fall corn, the silos, the barns so large, the fields so many, seen from above, in the air. The green of summer, the contours, and the wish for the cold green of primitive eras . . . all of this . . . drew me, draws me, and makes the Wisconsin sensation real for me. It is a sensation that "comes home" to me everytime I realize this is my Wisconsin. I am at home here with all of this.

*R*obert E. Gard, elected an "outstanding Wisconsin author" by the Wisconsin Library Association, was born and raised in Kansas. However, virtually his entire adult life has been spent in the state of Wisconsin. In this fascinating book he tells about the trail he followed in arriving, finally, in Wisconsin, and how he developed his deep affection for the state.

*G*ard, recently retired after almost forty years as a University of Wisconsin professor, is perhaps best known for his written interpretations of the great upper middle western state he has called home for so many years. For Robert Gard, time both past and present is of a single fabric. To him the coincidences that have shaped his life and experiences are a result of the necessity he has felt to help people realize their own creativity and to understand the significance of the events that have transpired on their own doorsteps. Gard has been called the foremost "grassroots arts" developer in America, and through his work in Wisconsin he has influenced the shape of the arts in many American communities. *Coming Home to Wisconsin* is filled with many unforgettable experiences and best exemplifies Robert Gard's dedication and deep concern for a state and for a nation.